Religion and the Rise of Nationalism

RELIGION AND POLITICS
Michael Barkun, *Series Editor*

Religion *and the* Rise *of* Nationalism

A Profile of an East-Central European City

Robert E. Alvis

SYRACUSE UNIVERSITY PRESS

First Edition 2005
05   06   07   08   09   10   6   5   4   3   2   1

The paper used in this publication meets the minimum requirements
of American National Standard for Information Sciences—
Permanence of Paper for Printed Library Materials, ANSI
Z39.48–1984∞™

Library of Congress Cataloging-in-Publication Data

Alvis, Robert E.
Religion and the rise of nationalism : a profile of an East-Central
European city / Robert E. Alvis.— 1st ed.
p. cm. — (Religion and politics)
Includes bibliographical references (p.) and index.
ISBN 0-8156-3081-6 (hardcover (cloth) : alk. paper)
1. Poznan (Poland)—Religion—19th century. 2. Nationalism—
Religious aspects. 3. Nationalism—Poland—Poznan—History—
19th century. 4. Poznan (Poland)—History—19th century. I. Title.
II. Series.
BL980.P6A54 2005
322'.1'0943849—dc22   2005012095

Manufactured in the United States of America

082505 - 2901 H5

For Andrea

ROBERT E. ALVIS received his Ph.D. from the Divinity School of the University of Chicago. He is currently an assistant professor of church history at the St. Meinrad School of Theology. He is the author of several scholarly articles that explore the history of Christianity in Central and Eastern Europe.

Contents

Illustrations

Acknowledgments

I would like to express my sincere gratitude to the many individuals and institutions I have relied upon while researching and writing this book. Foremost among the scholars at the University of Chicago who have guided my progress is my *Doktorvater,* Martin E. Marty. His enthusiasm, intellectual curiosity, and historical insight long have proven both an inspiration and an important resource for me. Catherine Brekus and Katherine Taylor gave generously of their time and expertise in reviewing my work. The late Jerald Brauer offered a great deal of encouragement and practical advice. Peter Dembowski and Helena Lopata (Loyola University) graciously offered their assistance in opening doors for me in Poland.

A number of European scholars took the time to comment on my work, offer suggestions, and provide valuable references. They include Lech Trzeciakowski, Stefan Kowal, Witold Molik, and Przemysław Matusik at the Adam Mickiewicz University in Poznań and Adam Walaszek at the Jagiellonian University in Cracow. In Berlin Thomas Bremer and our colleagues in the Arbeitskreis Religion und Nation in Osteuropa took part in a helpful critique of my research.

Before embarking on my journey to Europe I had been warned about the travails of researching in foreign archives and libraries. Happily, my experience proved otherwise. I encountered knowledgeable and friendly professionals at every research institution I visited. I would like to acknowledge the efforts of the personnel at the Archiwum Państwowe, the Archiwum Archidiecezjalne, and the Biblioteka Raczyńskich in Poznań, as well as those at the Staatsbibliotek and the Geheimes Staatsarchiv Preußischer Kulturbesitz in Berlin. I also would like to thank Brian Welch, a former employee at Harvard University's Widener Library, for his extensive and invaluable assistance.

A number of institutions provided me with generous financial backing. I would like to thank all of those involved in the important work of the Kościuszko Foundation, the Deutsche Akademische Austauschdienst, and the Martin Marty Center at the Divinity School of the University of Chicago.

Finally I would like to acknowledge my parents and the many friends and family members who were unflagging in their encouragement over my long scholarly sojourn. Special thanks go to Gordon Rudy, who supplied abundant good counsel. This book is dedicated to my wife, Andrea Hoelscher. In accompanying me to Poznań and Berlin for my research, taking photographs, editing rough drafts, and lending an ear to both my inspirations and complaints, she helped make my project both possible and worthwhile.

Introduction

This book examines the relationship between religion and nationalism in Poznań from 1793 to 1848. Currently located in western Poland, Poznań long has ranked as one of the largest cities along the linguistic and cultural borderland that separates the German-speaking regions of Central Europe from the Polish-speaking regions to the east. Relations among the city's ethnic populations were never exactly warm. They grew more strained over the first half of the nineteenth century, a period in which German and Polish Poznanians developed strong attachments to their respective national identities. I explore how religion influenced this process.

Over the past several decades the idea that religion and nationalism can and do mix has been obvious to anyone who reads the newspaper. Around the world a series of powerful movements have sought to redefine societies and rework international boundaries in ways that emphasize the importance of religion within the political logic of nationalism and nation-states. Examples are abundant: the agenda of Hindu nationalists in India; the increasing centrality of Buddhism in the political discourse of the Sri Lankan government; the demands of "fundamentalist" Jewish groups that the Israeli government and society adhere strictly to Jewish law and the boundaries of the ancient Israelite kingdom; the powerful dovetailing of religious and ethnic identity that helped fuel the carnage in the former Yugoslavia; and drives across the Muslim world to bring governments into greater accord with the teachings of Islamic law. Such developments inspired the sociologist Mark Juergensmeyer to write a widely read study in which he argues that the encounter between older "secular" nationalisms and newer "religious" nationalisms has emerged as the most troubling source of conflict in our time. In its early incarnation in eighteenth- and nineteenth-century Europe, he argues, nationalism was secular in nature, "based on the idea that the legitimacy of the state was rooted in the will of the people, divorced from any religious sanction."[1] The secular nationalist ideology became hegemonic in the West and eventually spread around the globe, particularly during the era of decolonization in the 1950s and 1960s. Religious nationalism, in which religious identity is integral to the concept of nation, is a more recent phenomenon, he asserts, typically developing in the non-Western world as a conscious reaction to the perceived failures of secular nationalism to deliver on its promise of modernization and prosperity.

In building his argument, Juergensmeyer draws upon the received wisdom of scholars engaged in the study of nationalism. Although evaluations of the subject are many and diverse, most scholars have articulated versions of the "modernist" argument. According to this argument, nationalism is a distinctly modern phenomenon, originating in Europe in the late eighteenth and early nineteenth centuries, stimulated by the powerful forces that were transforming European society at that time. Some analysts, such as Anthony Giddens (1985) and John Breuilly (1982), focus on modern political change as the root cause of nationalism. Others, such as Tom Nairn (1977) and Michael Hechter (1975), emphasize developments associated with industrial capitalism. Still others, such as Ernest Gellner (1983), Karl Deutsch (1966), and Benedict Anderson (1991), point to the role of modern forms of education and communication. While differing over primary causes, adherents of the modernist view tend to view nationalism—at least in its early phase—as indelibly linked to the liberal values associated with the modern era. Premodern European society was rigidly hierarchical, and its highest echelons claimed as their birthright a preponderant share of wealth and political influence. Nationalism represented a new and more egalitarian understanding of community. Its proponents championed the view that national heritage trumped all other forms of social identity. The status of one's parents, be they noble, bourgeois, or peasant, paled in comparison to one's nationality, and the boundaries of nation included all who exhibited its telltale characteristics. Nationalism thus served as a powerful tool for challenging the privileges of the elite establishment and pushing for more democratic forms of government. Summing up the predominant view of early nationalism, Anthony D. Smith writes: "At the outset, nationalism was an inclusive and liberating force. It broke down the various localisms of region, dialect, custom and clan, and helped to create large and powerful nation-states, with centralized markets and systems of administration, taxation and education. Its appeal was popular and democratic. It attacked feudal practices and oppressive imperial tyrannies and proclaimed the sovereignty of the people and the right of all peoples to determine their own destinies."[2]

A great many scholars also include secularism among the modern values associated with early European nationalism. Under the ancien régime, the argument often runs, Europe's ruling dynasties allied themselves with the dominant church or churches of their realms in order to enhance their power. The churches were granted numerous privileges, and in exchange church officials encouraged followers to believe that the political elite ruled according to God's all-wise design. In their struggle against the social and political order of the ancien régime, early nationalists also took on organized religion, dismissing its political theology as so much superstition, unsuited for the progressive new era that was thought to be unfolding. Scholars often have portrayed early nationalists as secular-minded urban sophisticates, disenchanted with the religious worldview with which they had been raised. Anthony D. Smith argues, for instance, that had secularization not taken place in the nineteenth century, the educated middle classes might have made peace with their lack of political influence by taking "refuge in traditional religious consolations." But a religious worldview "could not be reconciled with science and rationalism," leaving many educated Europeans receptive to nationalist ideologies.[3] Benedict Anderson reaches a similar conclusion:

> In Western Europe the eighteenth century marks not only the dawn of the age of nationalism but the dusk of religious modes of thought. The century of the Enlightenment, of rationalist secularism, brought with it its own modern darkness. With the ebbing of religious belief, the suffering which belief in part composed did not disappear. Disintegration of paradise: nothing makes fatality more arbitrary. Absurdity of salvation: nothing makes another style of continuity more necessary. What then was required was a secular transformation of fatality into continuity, contingency into meaning. As we shall see, few things were (are) better suited to this end than an idea of nation.[4]

At the same time scholars have sought to explain the striking affinities between early nationalist practices and traditional religious piety. The sacred aura surrounding nationalist symbols and their capacity to evoke devotion and self-sacrifice from adherents have led many observers to identify nationalism as a kind of ersatz religion. Perhaps the earliest proponent of this thesis was the French sociologist Émile Durkheim. In his seminal work *The Elementary Forms of Religious Life* (1915), Durkheim argues that religions serve a primary and perennial human need: to affirm and reinforce the communal bonds that allow societies to function. He suggests that in modern Western societies, where the significance of religion has waned, nationalism has begun to fulfill this enduring need. Similar arguments have been articulated by subsequent scholars. They include Carlton Hayes, one of the more influential voices in the field during the mid-twentieth century, whose argument is pithily summarized in the title of his work, *Nationalism: A Religion*. In his own words:

> Since its advent in western Europe, modern nationalism has partaken of the nature of religion. . . . Everywhere it has a god, who is either the patron or the personification of one's patrie, one's fatherland, one's national state. . . . Nationalism, like any religion, calls into play not simply the will, but the intellect, the imagination, and the emotions. The intellect constructs a speculative theology or mythology of nationalism. The imagination builds an unseen world around the eternal past and the everlasting future of one's nationality. The emotions arouse a joy and ecstasy in the contemplation of the national god.[5]

According to this view, the typical early nationalist may have been estranged from traditional religion, but he or she still experienced spiritual needs long associated with religion, such as a sense of moral purpose and a comprehensive worldview. Nationalism helped fill the void created by the loss of traditional religious faith. The currency that this argument still carries is evidenced in recent works on nationalism by Josep Llobera (1994) and John E. Smith (1994).

The modernist argument has dominated the study of nationalism for good reason: its adherents have marshaled an impressive body of evidence in its favor. In this study I have found many aspects of the modernist argument to be especially helpful in making sense of Poznań's changing social order. Where I part company with many modernists is over the supposedly secular quality of early European nationalism. It is indeed true that many high-profile nationalist leaders from this period were avowedly secular, and the fiercest opposition to their agendas often came from religious sources. One can cite the struggles between the Jacobins and the Catholic Church in France, or between Giuseppe Mazzini and the Papal See on the Italian peninsula. But nationalism mattered in the late eighteenth and early nineteenth centuries because it resonated with large numbers of people and manifested itself repeatedly in mass movements of no small revolutionary potential. Yet Europe's population of secular urban sophisticates remained rather limited; secularization was only beginning to take its toll on traditional religious practice. In other words, most of the Europeans who rallied behind early nationalist appeals still maintained their traditional religious affiliations.

This work develops a nuanced and variegated portrait of the relationship between early European nationalism and religion. While many early nationalists were in fact estranged from organized religion, it was not uncommon for adherents of this new ideology to remain faithful to their religious traditions and to draw from these traditions in articulating their nationalist visions. Religion and nationalism could peacefully coexist and fruitfully interact with one another on a number of levels, as I demonstrate through a detailed study of one fascinating case: the city of Poznań in the first half of the nineteenth century. During this time Poznań emerged as an important center of Polish and German nationalist ferment as residents explored their heritage and agitated for a new political order based upon their nationalist assumptions. These processes culminated in an uprising during the "Springtime of Nations" in 1848, a period of revolutionary enthusiasm across the continent that stands as a touchstone of early nationalism. In Poznań in the years leading up to and including 1848, calls for greater political enfranchisement and national self-determination routinely intersected with the symbols, offices, and concerns of organized religion.

I am not alone in challenging the conventional wisdom concerning the supposedly secular quality of early nationalism. Recent studies by Liah Greenfeld (1992), Adrian Hastings (1997), and Anthony Marx (2003) have argued that evidence of nationalist sentiment can be found well before the eighteenth century, and that during their formative phases early nationalisms drew nourishment from more established religious identities. Other scholarly treatments, such as Wolfgang Altgeld's study of German nationalism (1992) and Miroslav Hroch's comparative analysis of smaller-scale European nationalist movements (1985), have exposed complex and often complementary interplays between early nationalism and religion. Despite these valuable contributions the conventional wisdom on the matter continues to exercise a pervasive influence, as Juergensmeyer's work demonstrates.

In exploring the relationship between religion and early nationalism, this book also contributes to an understanding of the evolution of nationalism. To account for the developmental trajectory of nationalist movements, historians long have drawn binary distinctions between early nationalism and its later manifestations. In its early phase, commonly reckoned as extending well into the second half of the nineteenth century, nationalist movements typically were spearheaded by liberal bourgeois elites, whose political interests and values set the tone within such movements. Sometime around 1870, however, the tenor of nationalism started changing. Conservative political establishments across Europe, long opposed to the revolutionary principles associated with nationalism, adopted new strategies vis-à-vis the phenomenon. Rather than resisting nationalism, they co-opted it and made it serve their reactionary ends. In this later phase, the rhetoric of nationalism demonstrated a greater sympathy for premodern values and institutions. It tended toward chauvinism as well, highlighting the virtues of the nation by disparaging ethnic or religious outsiders such as Jews, minority groups, or foreign workers. Such tendencies tapped into the xenophobia of the masses, greatly expanding the popular appeal of nationalism.

An influential example of this typology can be found in Eric J. Hobsbawm's *Nations and Nationalism since 1780* (1992). Hobsbawm describes the years from 1830 to 1880 as the "classical period of liberal nationalism," when nationalism was viewed by both its supporters and detractors as a new and progressive force closely associated with the liberal ideology that had emerged during the era of the French Revolution.[6] But in the decades following 1880, nationalism changed considerably. Most notably, it "mutated from a concept associated with liberalism and the left, into a chauvinist, imperialist and xenophobic movement of the right."[7] In his recent study of Polish nationalism, Brian Porter reiterates this same progression. Early Polish nationalism, he argues, was an inclusive movement focused on the emancipation of Poland and the rest of humanity from oppression of various forms. In the 1870s and 1880s, though, a much narrower conception of the nation emerged that was defined by a conscious hatred of outsiders. This animus was employed to promote the disciplined adherence to national values in the face of outside threats and to buttress established hierarchies of power.[8]

I do not deny the utility of generalizing about the differences between early and later forms of nationalism, especially when theorizing on a grand scale as Hobsbawm does. It is important, though, to consider counterpoints that remind us of the gap between the ideal type and historical reality. The actual development of specific nationalist movements routinely violated the explanatory models later developed to describe them. As my study demonstrates, the attempt by conservative establishments to commandeer nationalist movements was not strictly a late-nineteenth-century phenomenon. The Prussian regime and conservative nobles sought the same goal before 1848. Likewise, early nationalist leaders employed a rhetorical range that extended well beyond calls for equality, self-determination, and international solidarity. Events in Poznań make clear that Polish and German nationalists understood how the demonization of ethnic and religious outsiders could motivate core supporters.

In addition to addressing larger questions surrounding religion and early European nationalism, this book serves as a local history of Poznań and the Prussian-Polish borderland. There is very little scholarly literature in English on the nationalist conflict in this part of the world. The one notable study is William Hagen's *Germans, Poles, and Jews: The Nationality Conflict in the Prussian East, 1772–1914* (1980). Hagen's work is sweeping in scope, covering a broad region and long time span. As a result he treats cursorily, if at all, the issues I explore in depth.

Not surprisingly, there are dozens of historical monographs on the subject in German and Polish. Some of these monographs are of high quality, and I have relied on them extensively for parts of my argument. And yet there are gaps and shortcomings within this literature as well. While there are many studies of the nationalist conflict in Poznań, none attempt a comprehensive examination of religion's role in the matter. There are a number of works on the Catholic Church in Poznań and the larger region at this time, but they focus almost exclusively on the institution itself, with little attention to laity. Meanwhile, the authors of these works tend to wear either their sympathy for the church or their anticlericalism on their sleeves.[9] Little of scholarly substance has been written about Poznań's Protestants in this period.[10] Another challenge one encounters frequently in the Polish and German literature is the nationalist inclinations harbored by the authors themselves. The Polish-German conflict grew especially bitter in the nineteenth and first half of the twentieth centuries. Those scholars who have chosen to write about it often have sympathized with one side or the other, and their prejudices are readily apparent.

My work is intended to provide a substantial addition to the German and Polish scholarship on Poznań and the surrounding region. I pursue a comprehensive approach to the religious life of the city, examining Catholicism and Protestantism in and of themselves and in relation to one another. I explore these faiths both as institutions and as communities of like-minded individuals, paying close attention to the neglected voices of the laity. Taken as a whole, my study offers insights into how religion colored the emergence of nationalism in the city. As an outsider with no immediate connection to the region, I endeavor to present a balanced assessment of the issues in question.

Poznań's Jewish community is one ethnic and religious group that I do not consider at length. This community was quite substantial, composing roughly a quarter of the city's total population in the late eighteenth century and playing an economic role of inordinate importance. But it was not central to the question of religion and nationalism in our time period. Scholars generally agree that nationalist consciousness among Europe's Jewry emerged only in the second half of the nineteenth century. As Jacob Katz notes, for Jews before the 1850s "the national idea was still overshadowed by the idea of social and political emancipation," and it was widely believed that "national aspiration . . . was contrary to the struggle for full citizenship."[11] I limit my examination of this population to the extent to which it affected the nationalist self-understandings of Poznań's German and Polish populations.

I have restricted my focus to just one city in order to facilitate a probing analysis of the texture of life in Poznań and the attitudes of its residents. At the same time I recognize that the city did not exist in isolation. Its residents were in perpetual contact with the surrounding region, the overarching state, and the continent, and these wider associations are considered throughout the book. My approach can best be described as cultural history. I cast a wide net, approaching my subject from a variety of overlapping contexts, including regional and international politics, socioeconomic development, cultural life, and the space and time of the city. Such an approach is well suited to the study of nationalism. Although it has been explored within discrete contexts (political, socioeconomic, psychological, and so on), such approaches cannot fully appreciate nationalism's complexity. Identity formation is the result of the long-term interplay of diverse influences, and the process can best be understood by considering the many forces at work.

This history has been crafted in large measure from primary source materials. Drawing upon the archival records of various bureaus within the provincial government in Poznań and the national government in Berlin, I have scoured a wealth of correspondence and decrees concerning religious affairs in Poznań. While of tremendous historical value, such resources have their limitations. This material mainly consists of correspondence between government officials and thus is dominated by the perspectives and concerns of Prussia's bureaucratic class. To broaden my frame of reference, I also have consulted the records of several religious congregations in the city, including the Lutheran Cross Congregation, the German Catholic community known as the St. Anne Brotherhood, and the Catholic St. Mary Magdalene's Parish. Although much of this material revolves around the minutiae of day-to-day administration, occasionally its pages yield provocative insights into the values of ordinary Protestants and Catholics.

In addition to archival materials, this study draws from a variety of memoirs, travelogues, and treatises written by Poles and Germans with direct knowledge of the state of affairs in Poznań during the first half of the nineteenth century. Of incomparable value is *Przechadzki po mieście* (1957), a massive, two-volume memoir by Marceli Motty (1818–1898), a Polish intellectual who recorded his recollections of nearly everyone who was anyone in his day. His observations are balanced with German voices, including those of the upper-level bureaucrat Eduard Flottwell, the writer Heinrich Heine, and the scholar Heinrich Wuttke.

Defining nationalism is notoriously challenging, as the myriad manifestations of the phenomenon tend to resist abiding under one limited set of attributes. It would be useful nonetheless to offer a working definition. I understand nationalism to be a compelling sense of identification with other members of one's linguistic and cultural group and/or political system, and a sense of collective sovereignty over the territory inhabited by one's fellow nationals. In other words, a German nationalist is one who feels intimately connected to all those who were raised with the German language and "German culture." In places with diverse ethnic populations like the United States, allegiance to a shared political system (American democracy, for instance) can stand in for language and culture to provide the requisite focus for a given group's ardor.

I agree with the majority view that nationalism is a distinctly modern phenomenon whose origin is tied to political, cultural, and socioeconomic developments unique to the modern era. And yet I dissent from the current vogue, inspired in particular by the postmodern approach of Benedict Anderson, of seeing national identities as raw inventions. Nationalisms have been capable of invoking intense passion in part because often they lay reasonable claim to preexisting ethnic identities and historical and cultural legacies that are of genuine, compelling substance.

Some scholars, the German historian Thomas Nipperdey among them, have proposed a more exacting definition of nationalism than my own, identifying it as an intense emotional bond that surpasses all other communal affiliations. Operating from such a premise, Nipperdey is led to doubt whether Germans with other strong ties beyond the national (such as the allegiance nineteenth-century German Catholics felt toward the pope) could be classed as nationalists.[12] The problem with this definition is that it requires the scholar to judge the ultimacy of a subject's social commitment—a difficult feat, even with ample resources upon which to draw. It also ignores the fact that humans readily maintain multiple allegiances with varying degrees of intensity. It is easy to imagine, for instance, a German Catholic who might pulse with patriotic fervor during a period of national crisis, only to give way to feelings of intense religious piety with the coming of the Easter holiday.

The second part of my definition emphasizes the relationship between members of a nation and a given stretch of territory. I agree with the geographer George W. White that despite its central importance, the spatial dimension of nationalism is often given short shrift by scholars.[13] The identities of national groups are molded greatly by their relationship to a specific terrain. Moreover, territory has almost always been at the source of nationalist conflict. My study explores the space of Poznań, searching there for clues to the impulses and attitudes of its inhabitants. The urban environment is the work of human hands, and as such it is an expression of human needs and modes of thought. Once formed, this same environment exerts a powerful influence over its inhabitants, controlling access, directing motion, and focusing collective activity. The space and the people of a city cling together in a tight embrace, the one continuously molding and being molded by the other. The Poznań of brick and mortar thus bears a revealing impression of the Poznań of bone and blood.

Like most historical arguments, mine is essentially comparative, evaluating one place in time against another and illustrating similarities and contrasts between them. My first chapter presents a broad, synchronic portrait of Poznań around 1793, the year Prussia invaded the area and wrested sovereignty over it from Poland. I discuss the city's material form, its political, legal, and socioeconomic organization, and the main contours of its cultural life, including the significance of religion. I conclude that the city remained largely true to modes of thought and action established deep in the past. Poznań was still a premodern town, with a precapitalist economy dependent upon the rhythms and requirements of its agrarian hinterland. Its social order reflected this. Poznanians oriented themselves by the enduring boundaries within which they were born: their "caste" (social rank and/or economic function), confession, and immediate vicinity. Such an environment hardly lent itself to the cultivation of broader forms of identity like nationalism.

My three middle chapters are diachronic, tracking changes in Poznań over the first half of the nineteenth century. Chapter 2 presents the city's transition from several vantages. I review relevant political developments on a local, state, and international level, and I sketch an outline of the profound social, economic, and cultural metamorphoses that were taking place. I conclude that Poznań, along with much of Europe, began crossing the threshold of the modern era during this time. My purpose is to demonstrate how the city's modernization helped propel the rise of nationalist movements there.

Ernest Gellner's thought is particularly helpful for interpreting Poznań's evolution in this regard. Gellner situates the emergence of nationalism within a typological reading of history, dividing human experience into several broad epochs. These include the "agrarian epoch," characterized by a strict social hierarchy of clearly defined castes. Each caste exists within its own particular sphere, and the boundaries between castes and the patterns of production and exchange that enable society to function are heavily laden with sacred meaning to ensure their continuity.

Superseding the agrarian epoch in Gellner's scheme is the "industrial epoch," with rationality serving as the central characteristic of the age. Its actors strive for logical coherence, consistency, and efficiency in thought and action. This rational spirit animates capitalism, as business people employ the most efficient means to achieve their ends, dismantling established traditions that formerly regulated production and exchange. This innovative spirit perpetually reconfigures the economic landscape. Modes of production become more complex, intricately linking larger numbers of people engaged in highly specialized tasks. Individuals are forced to become more flexible and mobile, capable of adapting to new demands, and once-sacrosanct barriers of caste erode. What makes the industrial epoch so significant for the study of nationalism is its demand for a "universal high culture." The industrial economy requires of its workers a modicum of general education, enabling them to quickly warm to a variety of tasks. It is no coincidence, then, that wherever a modern capitalist economy has emerged, it has been accompanied by the push for universal education and extensive educational infrastructures. Universal education and the dismantling of old caste divisions work in tandem to lay the foundations for broader forms of culture, such as nationalism. In many respects Poznań's socioeconomic development from the late eighteenth to the mid-nineteenth century parallels Gellner's typology.

I also have been influenced by the work of Benedict Anderson and Karl Deutsch. Anderson has argued persuasively that large-scale printing in vernacular languages was critical to the emergence of nationalist consciousness. It created "unified fields of exchange" in which those who could read a certain language were led to identify with all members of their linguistic group, while recognizing clear boundaries between their groups and others.[14] Lively print cultures helped reify linguistic groups into powerful models of social belonging. To account for the rise of nationalism, Deutsch emphasizes the importance of developing "wide complementarity of social communication" on an ethnic level.[15] For Deutsch, boundaries between groups are primarily about the relative facility of communication. We identify with those with whom we share a common linguistic, iconic, and behavioral vocabulary, and we feel alienated from those with whom communication is difficult. Nationalism can thus be defined as the group consciousness that emerges from the ease of social communication within ethnicities. I have found the arguments of both of these scholars useful in evaluating Poznań's cultural life.

My conclusions in chapter 2 confirm some of the dominant expressions of the modernist paradigm. Many of the city's most prominent nationalists were products of the modern era: well-educated, enterprising representatives of the bourgeoisie who flourished in the new economy, championed a more egalitarian political system that honored individual achievement over family status, and were ambivalent toward the beliefs espoused and functions exercised by organized religion. But this element was only one part of the phenomenon. Most Germans and Poles in the city remained passionately committed to their religious parties. And as it turns out, these religious commitments often facilitated their gravitation toward nationalist modes of thought.

Chapter 3 charts the changing place of Catholicism in Poznań and the leading role it played in the emergence of Polish nationalism. The Catholic Church as a whole took a dim view of nationalist movements, recognizing them as dangerous influences on Europe's social and political order. But in Poznań the matter unfolded quite differently. The Prussian takeover of the region proved particularly taxing to the church as an institution. The process alienated many church officials from the state, souring them on their traditional role as buttress to the status quo and encouraging their engagement in subversive politics. At the same time, Polish intellectuals were beginning to articulate a new vision of Polish national identity. With the disappearance of the old Polish state and many of its institutions, the Catholic Church emerged as one of the best resources for nationalists to draw upon. The interests of the church and the nationalist movement thus dovetailed, and by the 1840s representatives from both camps were working in unison, encouraging Poles to imagine themselves as integral parts of the Catholic Polish nation and to fight for an independent political existence.

Chapter 4 turns to Poznań's Protestant churches and the impact they had on the development of German nationalism. The advent of Prussian rule had tremendous consequences for the Lutheran and Reformed churches in the city. The state sought to remake them in the image of their counterparts in the rest of Prussia. The effort succeeded handily, and as a result Protestants in Poznań were pulled into ever greater communion with the vibrant culture of Protestant northern Germany. One of the more influential ideas they encountered here was a distinctly Protestant variant of German national identity that stressed the nation's world-historical mission to complete the Protestant Reformation. Through such appeals to their core values, Protestant Poznanians were persuaded to identify with this vision. During the same period Protestant-Catholic relations in Poznań deteriorated, and the resulting antagonism offered Protestants all the more reason to renounce their long ties to the predominantly Polish Poznań region and to identify foremost with Protestant Germany.

Chapter 5 returns to the synchronic approach of chapter 1, painting in broad strokes a portrait of the city on the eve of the 1848 revolution. I draw parallels with the city in 1793, illustrating many facets of its transformation. The confines of caste and locale lost much of their appeal during that period, with German and Polish nationalisms emerging in their stead as modes of social identity more attuned to the circumstances of modern life. These new modes gained ground not in opposition to, but rather in conjunction with, the dominant Christian confessions. Christianity remained relevant in this period in part because it had adapted to the logic of nationalism. A dialogue had emerged both between Catholicism and Polish nationalism and between Protestantism and German nationalism. As a result, the Christian churches were incorporated into the compelling orbit of the nationalist vision, and the transcendent claims of the nationalist movements were burnished through religious associations.

I illustrate my conclusions through an extended look at the 1848 revolution in Poznań. That year's Springtime of Nations was the paradigmatic expression of early European nationalism. From Paris to Vienna and from Berlin to the Piedmont, the continent was abuzz in the early months of 1848 with florid demands for liberty, equality, and international fraternity. The revolution in the Poznań region was animated by this same agenda. At closer examination, however, we observe how integral the interests and perspectives of the Christian confessions were to the events that unfolded. The revolution was not merely a clash between German and Pole, but also between Protestant and Catholic, for domination over the region. These two modes of identity, nationalist and confessional, had become integrally related.

I close with a final note on language. As with any multilingual region, the question of place names along the German-Polish borderland can be difficult to navigate. When a distinct English variant exists (Warsaw, for example), I have used it. Otherwise, I have generally employed the name used by the majority of the inhabitants in the early nineteenth century. I refer to Breslau, for instance, even though today that city is part of Poland and is known as Wrocław. I have included alternative names in parentheses.

Religion and the Rise of Nationalism

1

On the Threshold of a New Era

Evaluations of the state of affairs in Poland in the late eighteenth century have conflicted sharply. Up through the Second World War, German authors tended to regard the situation in Poland as dismal. They emphasized the dysfunctional nature of Poland's political order and the stultification of its culture. In German circles, the phrase "Polish economy" *(polnische Wirtschaft)* long signaled a ludicrous oxymoron. Such assessments were used to justify, directly or indirectly, Prussia's role in the partitioning of Poland. If it can be argued that Poland was a failing state, then Prussia emerges as its redeemer, introducing stability and the flowering of civilization to the territories it absorbed.[1]

Polish authors usually offer different readings. While quick to admit the many problems besetting the country, they tend to emphasize the great strides made during the final decades of the eighteenth century. According to this view, Poland was solving its problems and evolving into a strong, progressive, constitutional monarchy. Its very success, in fact, led to its demise. Because reactionary, autocratic neighbors feared that Poland's transformation could destabilize their own regimes, they crushed the experiment.

Both perspectives can draw comfort from the historical record. Certainly Poland, or the Polish-Lithuanian Commonwealth, as it was known at the time, was burdened by enormous challenges, and the process of reform ignited bitter conflicts that threatened to rip the fabric of the state apart. At the same time, it made some impressive strides forward. In the twilight of its existence the commonwealth, long a study in torpor, displayed uncharacteristic vitality. Driven by the very real threat of dissolution, its leaders undertook bold measures. Its residents, suspended between despair and hope, persevered as best they could.

This chapter portrays the complexity of this dynamic era in one corner of the commonwealth: the city of Poznań. I introduce some of the individuals, landscapes, institutions, and beliefs that comprised the city. In keeping with our central subject, religion and nationalism, I concentrate on the social organization of the city, examining how Poznanians understood themselves in collective terms. The issue is approached from several vantages, including the city's material form, its socioeconomic organization, and its legal, cultural, and religious life.

For all of the noise of this tumultuous period, life in Poznań proceeded in large measure according to long-established patterns. Its residents stood poised on the cusp of revolutionary change, but they were only beginning to experience its effects. The city's medieval heritage remained very much in evidence, from the layout of its streets to the laws that helped maintain order, and from the economic functions of its inhabitants to the comforts they enjoyed. Poznań in the late eighteenth century was a premodern, precapitalist society, where the circumstances of an individual's existence were still determined largely by the particular socioeconomic niche into which he or she was born. Its population was fragmented into dozens of insular communities with few occasions for generating an overarching sense of *communitas* across the urban area, let alone wider expanses. Regarding nationalism, the climate of late-eighteenth-century Poznań was not conducive to such forms of identity. Its inhabitants continued to find meaning and their widest sense of social belonging within the confines of their particular locale, caste, and confession.

Great Poland's Capital City

Whenever foreign travelers in the eighteenth century explored Great Poland (Wielkopolska), the westernmost province of the Polish-Lithuanian Commonwealth, they invariably took note of Poznań. In a region dominated by either farmland or forests and dotted with numerous small, often shabby towns and villages, Poznań easily ranked as its largest city. Rising up from the region's undulating plains, the city appeared deceptively large. In the 1790s one German tourist wrote: "[Poznań] could be counted among the more important midsized cities in Germany, but on account of the great number of churches and towers it enjoys a higher place than others in its class."[2] The Prussian official Karl Friedrich von Voss, who traveled through the area early in 1793 and evaluated what he saw with a jaundiced eye, excluded Poznań from his general assessment: "Of the region's 245 cities, there are hardly ten that deserve the name, the rest qualifying as nothing more than villages. As for those ten, with the sole exception of Poznań, they are so poorly built that almost every year several burn to the ground."[3]

Johann Erich Biester, director of the Royal Library in Berlin and coeditor of the *Berlinische Monatsschrift* (Berlin monthly), spent some time in Poznań in the early 1790s and was quite impressed. He was struck by the planned form of the city center, which he described as "built in an entirely German manner."[4] The center was in fact planned by German settlers back in the thirteenth century. At that time there were towns already established on the island of Ostrów Tumski, as well as a handful of small suburbs and villages nearby. In 1253, the duke of the province authorized the building of a new city on the western bank of the Warta River, the region's largest natural artery. Enjoying state patronage, its builders had the luxury of planning the new city on a grand scale. A large square measuring roughly 140 meters by 140 meters formed the center of the design. Three evenly spaced streets were planned to branch off perpendicularly from each side of the square to form a regular, rectilinear network of passageways. A final element in the composition was a defensive wall enclosing the entire complex. The rhythmic design and generous proportions of the new city proved both practical and popular for centuries to come. The spacious square provided ample, secure space for periodic trade fairs and other events. Its well-planned urban core accommodated a population density capable of supporting a diverse array of goods and services.

Poznań was a dynamic city, evolving according to the practical needs and aesthetic tastes of its residents, as well as to unexpected natural and military disasters. But as successive waves of building or renovation took place, they generally adhered to its original organizing principles. The center of Poznań in the early 1790s remained much as it had for centuries, accommodating the bulk of the area's population on the same basic template. This continuity testifies to the remarkable planning of the city's designers as well as to the city's stable function as a trade and service center for its agrarian hinterland.

As Biester strolled along Poznań's streets, he noted with approval the handsome appearance and generally good condition of the city center. He admired the town hall, a "spacious, pretty, bright building in the old style" situated in the eastern corner of the market square.[5] The most distinctive of the city's architectural landmarks, the Renaissance-style building, designed in the sixteenth century, was topped by a Baroque tower from the 1780s. Nearby, in the western corner of the square, stood the recently built guardhouse (1787), a single-story stone structure ranking among the finest examples of classical

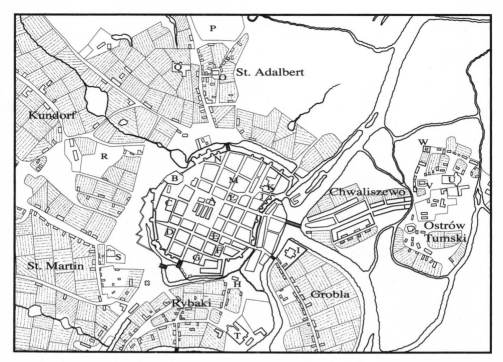

Map 1. Poznań, 1780s. A: town hall; B: castle; C: Franciscan cloister and church; D: Theresan women's cloister and church; E: Benedictine women's cloister and church; F: Konwencianki women's cloister and church; G: Parish Church (Fara); H: All Souls' Chapel; I: Cross Church; J: Dominican women's cloister and church; K: Dominican men's cloister and church; L: Chapel of the Most Sacred Blood of Jesus; M: Jewish Quarter; N: Catherinian women's cloister and church; O: St. Adalbert's Church; P: Protestant Cemetery; Q: St. Joseph's Church; R: Jewish Cemetery; S: St. Martin's Church; T: Bernardine Church; U: Poznań Cathedral; V: Church of the Virgin Mary; W: Lubrański Academy.

architecture in Poland at this time. These buildings were ringed on all four sides by the largest, most attractive houses in the city.

Biester also discovered many architectural gems along the side streets. Walking northwest from the square up Franciscan (Franciszkańska) Street, he passed on his left the Franciscan St. Anthony's Church, whose restrained exterior belied a riot of Baroque ornamentation within. To the right, perched upon a hill, stood the castle, the site of the provincial archives and court and the official residence of the king when he visited the city. The castle had been recently rebuilt (1780–83), replacing the previous structure that had lain in

1. Poznań's Old Market Square, 1838. Julius Knorr's painting centers on Poznań's graceful city hall. To the right stands the city scales building. Well-known Poznanians are represented in the crowd. Courtesy of the Muzeum Narodowe w Poznaniu.

ruins for decades. Looking down Jesuit (Jezuicka) Street from the southern corner of the square, Biester's eye trained on the magnificent Baroque façade of the Parish Church (Fara). He undoubtedly admired the elegant buildings of the former Jesuit college nearby, as well as the preponderance of new brick or half-timbered houses at every turn.

As a foreign tourist Biester saw Poznań at one moment in time, and the immediacy of his experience condensed the many layers of the city's development into a unified impression, an appreciation of a discrete space in the present tense. How different were the impressions of city residents, whose perceptions were colored by decades of personal experience and oral histories passed down from earlier generations. For them the elements of the city held stories, and the whole composition followed a dynamic trajectory. It was common knowledge that many of its finest monuments were remnants of a time when the city was much grander and wealthier. In the sixteenth century Poznań had had a population nearly twice as large as during its late-eighteenth-century incarnation, and it was ranked alongside Cracow as one of the two

2. The Parish Church (Fara). Photograph by Andrea Hoelscher.

prettiest cities in Poland.[6] It was also commonly known that in the seventeenth and eighteenth centuries a series of misfortunes had reduced Poznań's infrastructure to a catastrophic state. What Biester viewed as a handsome city was seen by residents as a remarkable transformation. Starting in the 1760s, thirty years of relative peace and stability, combined with sound policies on a city and national level, encouraged residents to invest in their town.[7] Some of the area's leading nobles and bourgeoisie commissioned a series of fine structures, which helped recreate a measure of the city's old luster. The sharp rise in the construction of private residences was matched by a similar trend in public buildings, such as the renovation of the town hall and royal castle. The late eighteenth century was a time of considerable optimism in Poznań. On a national level reformers were working to heal their gravely ailing state. The most tangible experience of these efforts for most Poznanians was the refurbished face of their city.

The intramural city easily ranked as the wealthiest and most urbane part of Poznań. Most of its houses were multistoried stone structures, and it boasted the largest concentration of public institutions, the wealthiest sector of the population, and the best shops. But it was only one of many parts within the wider urban fabric. Eighteenth-century Poznań contained within its immediate orbit a patchwork of distinct localities. The area encompassed eight or nine different municipal units, most of which, however minuscule, boasted their own town halls and legal arrangements. Unofficial religious and socioeconomic boundaries crisscrossed the area as well. At a time of limited mobility, these divisions were of considerable consequence. They helped define the horizons of those living within their confines.

Just north of the town square, the dense cluster of houses along Jewish (Żydowska), Cobbler, and Wronki Streets composed the Jewish Quarter. Although standing within the city walls and adhering to the same thirteenth-century grid, Jews and non-Jews alike regarded the quarter as a completely separate entity, a city within a city. Its mostly Jewish population followed its own laws and customs. Despite their close proximity, Jews and Christians lived almost completely divorced from one another, restricting their contact primarily to commercial transactions. Owing to legal restrictions that prevented all but the wealthiest of Jews from living anywhere else, the population of the quarter was by far the densest in Poznań. This, in combination with a primitive sanitation system, prompted Biester to note that Jewish Street "stinks horribly even from afar."[8] Its housing was of poor quality, with structures more often of wood than of stone. The quarter bustled with commercial activity. Its first language was Yiddish, and Hebrew characters adorned the many shops, announcing the wares or services on offer. While the quarter was comfortably familiar for Jews, for most Christians it remained darkly exotic.

Beyond the city's walls, the spatial organization and infrastructure of Poznań's suburbs and surrounding villages differed markedly. The streets, paved with stone in the center, gave way to dirt. The rigid logic of the grid receded into meandering paths that followed the demands of the natural environment. Freed from spatial limitations, buildings generally contained just one or two stories and were set further apart.

During his stay, Biester ventured out from the center to visit the Poznań

Cathedral. Walking eastward on Broad (Szeroka) Street, he soon reached the
Warta River. At this time, only the Chwaliszewo Bridge linked Poznań's western and eastern banks. It ran from Broad Street eastward to the island of
Chwaliszewo. Crossing the bridge, Biester found himself on a poorly maintained road hugged on both sides by ramshackle houses. One of the densest
areas outside of the center, Chwaliszewo was home to dozens of relatively
poor, predominantly Polish craft families, a large portion of whom were engaged in cottage-scale shoe manufacturing. Along streets and inside court-
yards, young children played, farm animals wandered, and older children and
parents pursued their respective crafts.

Continuing along the street, Biester eventually crossed over to a different
island, Ostrów Tumski. Around the turn of the first millennium, Ostrów
Tumski was an important political and economic center of the fledgling Polish state. Eclipsed by the new city on the western bank, the island gradually
shed its diverse civic functions and evolved into the administrative center of
the Catholic Church in the region. To the north of the island stood the
Lubrański Academy, a prominent seminary. Situated around the cathedral
were the archbishop's palace and the residences of numerous clergy.

3. Ostrów Tumski in 1798. The cathedral dominated the island of Ostrów Tumski.
The large building to the left is the Lubrański Academy. The brick church to the right
is the Chapel of the Virgin Mary. Courtesy of the Muzeum Narodowe w Poznaniu.

Biester's explorations also took him to the island of Grobla. Walking southeastward from the market square on Water (Wodna) Street, he passed over a small bridge to the island. Beyond the Jewish Quarter, Poznań was regularly punctuated with the symbols and sanctuaries of its dominant religion, Roman Catholicism. Grobla was the one exception. Although Protestants lived in various parts of Poznań, they were especially concentrated here. To the north of the island rose Grobla's chief landmark, the Lutheran community's newly built Cross Church (Kreuzkirche). Nearby stood the rectory and the Lutheran school. Alongside the island's one main road rose the houses, farms, and workshops of its generally well-to-do residents, who, according to Biester, consisted of "German craftsmen almost exclusively."[9]

Many other settlements filled out the Greater Poznań area. To the east of Ostrów Tumski lay settlements of modest economic note, including Śródka, Zawady, and St. John's. On the western bank, several communities encircled the center to the north, west, and south. The suburbs of Kundorf and Nowe Ogrody developed into relatively exclusive enclaves of attractive garden residences. The suburbs of St. Adalbert, St. Martin, and Rybaki, meanwhile, were home to simpler houses and poorer populations. In a wider periphery, a ring of villages operated in close association with the city. They often varied by language, with Poles dominant in Winiary, Żegrze, and Sołacz, and Germans prevalent in Wilda, Dębiec, and Rataje.[10]

The large majority of Poznań-area residents spent most of their lives in their immediate vicinity. Individuals commonly worked in or near the home, and their extended families often lived closed by. Obstacles such as distance, lack of public transportation, and the Warta River complicated matters, and legal and cultural differences between areas strengthened loyalties to one's locale. But there also existed points of centripetal attraction. The commercial opportunities of the city center drew residents of outlying areas, especially during the fairs that periodically ignited the city's economy. The municipal and provincial political structures located in the center also obliged their participation, as did certain religious and cultural events.

Society and Economy

The material forms that defined Poznań—its walls, passageways, and open spaces—had eminently practical functions. They helped regulate the endeavors of the city's large population. The main reason for the endurance of these material forms was the relative stasis of Great Poland's largely agrarian economy, in which Poznań served as the primary marketplace and service center. The stability of this economic system encouraged the replication of the inherited social order within each new generation. The countryside continued to be dominated by a small group of wealthy landowners and was worked primarily by a broad mass of disenfranchised peasants. The urban core remained the domain of merchants, craftspeople, and professionals, each caste maintaining its own internal hierarchy and modes of control. Certainly the region's economy and social order had evolved over time. The rising commercial prominence of the Jews and the declining economic fortunes of cities are examples of long-term changes over the seventeenth and early eighteenth centuries. More recent developments like the introduction of cash rents, the appearance of larger-scale industrial enterprises, and the expansion of an urban protoproletariat suggest the first stirrings of an even more fundamental shift toward a modern capitalist economy. Still, in social and economic terms Poznań in the late eighteenth century was defined more by continuity than by change.

Having contracted during the Northern Wars (1700–21) and the plague of 1709–10, the population of the city hovered at around 5,000 throughout the first half of the eighteenth century and then gradually expanded. By 1777 it had risen to an estimated 8,355, and in 1794, shortly after the city was absorbed into Prussia, the population stood at around 15,000.[11] Of these residents, Łukaszewicz concludes that around 60 percent were Catholic, 24 percent were Jewish, 15 percent were Lutheran, and 1 percent were either Reformed Protestant or Orthodox. Assuming the accuracy of these figures, one can extrapolate roughly the ethnic composition of the city. Around one-quarter of the town's residents were ethnically Jewish, as there was a nearly absolute correlation between religious and ethnic identity within this population. Considering that nearly all Lutherans in Poznań were ethnic Germans and that there was a sizable community of German Catholics as well, the percentage of ethnic Germans in Poznań was somewhat over 15 percent. The percentage of ethnic Poles, almost all of whom were Catholic, was somewhat under 60 percent. Other ethnic groups were statistically insignificant.

Agriculture employed large numbers of area residents, either directly or indirectly. Although there were some independent farmers, most farm operations belonged to larger units such as villages, which often were just one part of the vast holdings of the region's landowners. Income from agriculture served as the primary source of wealth in Poland, and the state's thin stratum of fabulously wealthy nobles owned large numbers of villages.

Poznań owned most of the villages in its immediate hinterland, and the cash income, produce, and labor extracted from them provided critical support for the city's many functions.[12] Cash rents became increasingly common in the eighteenth century, but payment in the form of produce and labor remained a fixture of the rural economy. Every year, for instance, the nearby village of Baggerowo provided its landlord, Poznań's Franciscan cloister, with the grain it used to make beer and bread, the twin pillars of the monks' diet.[13]

If agriculture helped fill the coffers of the city, its institutions, and wealthy landowning residents, it also sustained many of Poznań's merchants. From door-to-door selling to large-scale wholesaling, trade provided a livelihood for a significant portion of the city's population. A substantial percentage of their business consisted of marketing raw products and supplying finished goods to the city's agrarian hinterland.

Christian merchants in Poznań remained organized, as they had been for centuries, into two merchant brotherhoods. The brotherhoods operated like guilds, training new generations of merchants, fighting for exclusive rights to lucrative trading opportunities, and offering members a measure of security against misfortune. The brotherhoods once were large organizations whose members enjoyed numerous advantages over outsiders. Their fortunes declined over the course of the seventeenth and early eighteenth centuries.[14]

Brotherhood members weathered not only the disruptions of war and precipitous drops in population and demand but also stiff competition from Jewish merchants. Jews began moving into areas once dominated by the brotherhoods in the early seventeenth century. Despite numerous legal disadvantages, Poznań's Jews steadily gained ground. They came to dominate commerce with the surrounding countryside and to control nearly all trade between the nearby markets in Frankfurt/Oder, Stettin (Szczecin), and Leipzig.[15] Critical to their success were the well-developed trading networks between Jewish communities. Another, more ambiguous advantage was their overconcentration in the field. Around half of all gainfully employed Jews worked as merchants in some capacity, and heavy competition forced them to accept thin profit margins. This kept their prices low, but it locked large numbers into perpetual poverty.

Regardless of confession, Poznań's merchants enjoyed an expanding economy in the second half of the eighteenth century. Between 1740 and 1792 the city's trade grew ten times in volume, experiencing especially dynamic growth starting in the 1780s. Its traders once again established relationships with a variety of distant markets, including those in Warsaw, Lithuania, Russia, and Hungary.[16]

The third pillar of Poznań's economy was craft. As in trade, craft production took place under the aegis of guilds, some dating back to the fourteenth century. In theory, guilds provided a system for training youths, preserving technical expertise, and providing for the welfare of their members. In practice, their effects were often more odious, leading to monopolies that stifled innovation, social mobility, and fair prices. If the dismantling of guilds is taken as a key element in the emergence of modern capitalism, then Poznań at this time still had some distance to travel. When the state-sponsored Good Order Commission made efforts to improve the area's economy in the 1760s and 1770s, it revitalized the guild system. By 1779 there were thirty-nine guilds in Poznań, the highest number ever.[17]

Guild organizations followed the religious and jurisdictional boundaries of the city. Jewish craftspeople were categorically denied entrance to the guilds of Christian Poznań. Up until the 1760s, religious differences among Christians often manifested in separate guilds for each party or rancorous disputes within the same guild. When the Good Order Commission revised guild statutes, it usually added clauses of religious toleration between Christian confessions. There were similarly sharp distinctions between Poznań's guilds and those of neighboring communities such as Chwaliszewo.

An important development in this period was the emergence of early capitalist modes of production. The central figure in this respect was Jan Jakub Klug, an ambitious merchant from Cracow. In 1785 he established wool and silk factories in Poznań. Employing foreign specialists, local workers, and the capital investment of various nobles, Klug's wool factory employed around fifty people and produced high-quality cloth at low prices, prompting futile protests from members of the cloth guild. Other early capitalist ventures produced leather goods, soap, candles, playing cards, tobacco, and rope. Altogether these factories employed around two hundred fifty people, a small percentage of the city's workforce. Their significance would grow over time.[18]

Beyond Poznań's three main economic fields—farming, trade, and craft—other career paths rounded out the economic landscape. A small group of nobility lived part or all of the year in Poznań. The wealthier among them invested their capital and pursued careers appropriate to their high station, such as governmental or military service, arts patronage, or philanthropy. The petty nobility were by necessity more flexible in terms of the living they pursued. Some joined representatives of the bourgeoisie in forming a modest body of professionals who provided a range of necessary services in the city.

Their ranks included religious specialists, teachers, and a handful of doctors, pharmacists, and midwives.

Gathering at the other end of the spectrum were the makings of a proto-proletariat, a group not owning property or performing a traditional profession. Many had no stable domicile and lived a marginal existence, working as day laborers or servants. Some sustained themselves through crime, prostitution, or begging.[19] A Prussian report from 1793 provides anecdotal evidence suggesting that large numbers had gathered at the bottom of the social ladder: "Begging among this population has not yet been eliminated. On the contrary it is richly sustained by the regular support of prosperous citizens, hospital funds, and the cloisters, as evidenced by the many disgraceful scenes of beggars settled in along the alleyways and bridges. Perhaps I am mistaken when I conclude that, as in Italy, the beggars are so numerous here because they enjoy a very comfortable existence."[20]

The Rule of Law

A city requires commonly accepted rules in order to function, and Poznanians lived according to a large number of them. As an ensemble the rules lent coherence within groups and established the boundaries that defined Poznań's society. Like the material city and its socioeconomic composition, this thick web of rules exhibited remarkable endurance. Indeed, many were centuries old. Their longevity played an important role in maintaining venerable modes of organization.

The majority of area residents lived under the legal jurisdiction of the city of Poznań, which in the late eighteenth century included most of the intramural city, the island of Grobla, and parts or all of the suburbs immediately surrounding the city on the western bank. Remarkably, the legal obligations governing city residents continued to be defined in large measure by Magdeburg Law, the legal charter granted to the city at its founding in 1253. According to this law, the city agreed to defend the area and make annual payments to the king in exchange for a large degree of autonomy. The primary tasks of city officials included enforcing justice and maintaining security within their jurisdiction. They oversaw the upkeep of the town walls and earthworks, maintained a small police force, and operated a court of law. Most law-abiding, productive males within the city limits enjoyed the privilege of citizenship. A gathering of citizens periodically came together to elect from their ranks representatives to unpaid, one-year posts on a governing council headed by a mayor. The council managed city and police affairs. A local judge dispensed justice in the first instance. The responsibility of government was a matter of great pride, and leading citizens embraced the opportunity to contribute.

In Germany, the birthplace of Magdeburg Law, cities began losing their cherished autonomy toward the end of the sixteenth century as kings or princes exercised ever greater control over urban wealth and productive capacities.[21] In Poland, where the power of the nobility came to overshadow that of the king, a challenge of a very different nature emerged. Using the National Assembly (Sejm), which they controlled, as an instrument, the nobility passed legislation that systematically undercut the influence independent cities once had had on the national level, as well as the privileges that had allowed them to flourish. The purpose was not to control these cities so much as to undermine their economic power, thus benefiting those cities and villages owned by the nobility. Over time, the number of independent cities dwindled as many lost their status or sunk into economic insignificance. Poznań managed to cling to its independence, and the actual statutes defining city governance changed very little from their original medieval formulation. It lost its earlier right to send delegates to the National Assembly, however, thereby depriving residents of any say in the affairs of state.

The nobility also passed laws that reinforced divisions between nobles and town dwellers. Town dwellers were forbidden to own land in the countryside, and nobles were discouraged from practicing an urban profession under penalty of losing their titles. What is more, the nobles exempted their property and actions within cities from the jurisdictions of these cities, a development that had a negative impact on the financial health and decorum of urban areas. In Poznań in 1729, nobles owned 47 of the 525 buildings within the city walls.[22] City officials were deprived of tax revenues from these properties and from a share of the economic production that occurred there. One example is the brewery and distillery operated by Itzig Pincus in the 1780s and early 1790s on the island of Grobla. While technically within the city, his operations were located on property owned by a noble named Kęczicki, and thus beyond the city's reach.[23] City officials likewise stood by helplessly when nobles flouted the public order. Enjoying immunity before city courts, any claims against nobles were tried before their more sympathetic peers, a prospect that generated little fear of serious repercussions. Needless to say, their own legal disadvantages disposed ordinary Poznanians poorly toward the nobility as a caste. The nobility responded to such resentment with an equal measure of disdain.

Other laws defined the many powers and prerogatives of the Catholic

Church. Beyond the official limits of the city, church institutions exercised by far the greatest legal control in the Poznań area. Over the centuries church institutions established their authority over the towns of Ostrowek, Śródka, and Zawady on the eastern bank, the island of Chwaliszewo, and parts of the St. Adalbert and St. Martin suburbs. Residents of these areas generally paid their taxes and rents to church officials and resolved legal disputes in church courts. The church was also well represented in the city; it owned eighty houses in the center of town by 1729.[24] Like the nobility, the church had managed to exempt its holdings and officials from city taxes and courts, thereby weakening the city and arousing the animosity of townspeople. Indeed, many among the city's Catholic majority found themselves in the ambiguous position of opposing any expansion of the church to which they belonged. In the seventeenth century, the Carmelites sought to buy a house on Jewish Street in order to turn it into a chapel; city leaders fought unsuccessfully to block the effort in order to prevent the further erosion of Poznań's tax base.[25]

The city's Jewish community occupied yet another zone in Poznań's legal patchwork. At the local level, Poznań's Jews were legally and politically autonomous. A small group of male Jews led by the head rabbi constituted the *kahal,* the body that governed the internal life of the Jewish community. The *kahal* enforced standards of hygiene and operated schools. It collected taxes, policed the Jewish Quarter, and adjudicated disputes between Jews. It had extensive powers, including the exercise of the death penalty. It was answerable only to the *voivode,* the regional representative of the Polish crown. Beyond the city, Poznań's Jewish community belonged to regional and national structures. Nationally Poland's Jews maintained the Four Land Council, an institution unique in all of Europe, in which Jews from various regions in the state (Great Poland, Little Poland, Red Ruthenia, and Wolhynia) regularly gathered. Besides administering the collection of the flat tax owed by the entire Jewish community to the Polish king, the council regulated Jewish congregational life and pursued Jewish interests at the highest levels.[26]

Despite written guarantees from a series of kings, the precise limits of Jewish rights were a matter of intense disputation. City residents and officials resented the fact that Jews lived within the city walls but were not subject to its authority. Christian merchants and craftspeople feared the sophistication of their Jewish counterparts and despaired over the consistently lower prices in Jewish shops. Deep-seated prejudices based on religious differences facilitated the distillation of such insecurities into moral outrage. At their most charitable, Christians perceived Jews as unscrupulous and guilty of persistent violations of the law. At their worst, they regarded Jews as a malignant, magical force, ultimately responsible for fires, plagues, floods, and other disasters.

Eager to assuage public sentiment, city officials attempted to limit the economic activity of Jews and the number of houses they controlled. Much more serious was the enmity of the Catholic Church. Enjoying broad authority over matters related to religion, Catholic officials encouraged laws that limited Jewish activity on Christian holy days and forbade Jews from trafficking in goods such as Catholic books.[27] Moreover, when they determined that a Jew had violated the "sacred order" in some way, earthly laws offered the accused little refuge. Poznań's historical record is littered with alleged sacrilegious offenses committed by Jews, ranging from host desecration to ritual murder. The idea of such offenses disturbed the Catholic sense of the cosmos and could easily develop into furious orgies of holy rage.[28]

The influence of the Catholic Church over Poznań's political life ensured that Catholic values were often translated into legislation. Non-Catholics were legally obliged to show respect to the Catholic faith. A person who insulted the Virgin Mary, for instance, could meet with a monetary fine or worse.[29] The religious obligations of Catholics were often reinforced by municipal laws. An excerpt from the statutes governing residents of the villages Żegrze and Rataje illustrates this point: "Every orthodox Catholic farmer living in Żegrze and Rataje should fear God; he should not, through sinning, offend God, who punishes evil in hell and rewards good in heaven; he should fulfill the obligation of the Catholic Church to confess at Easter and to take Holy Communion annually; he should avoid work and attend church on Sundays and holidays."[30]

Such an environment placed Protestants in potential jeopardy. The Catholic Reformation in the Polish-Lithuanian Commonwealth stripped most Protestant communities of the protections that had earlier allowed them to flourish, leaving them much more exposed, in legal terms, than the Jews. On the other hand, they were spared the degree of hostility that rendered Jewish rights so ineffective. Protestant well-being thus depended in large measure on amicable relations with the Catholic majority, and their community was very adept at getting along. Protestants took great pains to accommodate themselves to the sensibilities of Catholics, quietly fulfilling their religious obligations and rarely challenging their neighbors on matters of symbolic import.

One reason why Poznań's legal affairs were so fractious was the lack of an effective central government.[31] Centuries earlier the nobility had emerged as the main power in the Polish-Lithuanian Commonwealth, rendering the king dependent upon the National Assembly, which they alone controlled. But the assembly itself was hamstrung by the *liberum veto,* a provision that required complete unanimity for the approval of any legislation. The dissent of one member was sufficient to scuttle a bill, which made the process exceedingly difficult to navigate. As a result, the central government grew impotent, unable to respond adequately to demands placed upon it. This suited many leading nobles, who opposed any threat to their "golden freedom" and welcomed the devolution of power to the regional level, where they could influence matters more directly.

In the international arena the commonwealth was overshadowed militarily by more powerful neighbors. Supporters of the status quo reasoned that this weakness was the state's best defense: as its neighbors had nothing to fear from the commonwealth, they would respect its territorial integrity. Not everyone agreed. A political reform movement gradually emerged in the middle decades of the century, and it managed to have one of its own elected to the throne in 1764. The new monarch, Stanisław August, and his supporters believed that if the commonwealth were to be saved, its legal affairs had to be fundamentally reworked. The process met fierce resistance from those nobles loathe to relinquish any of their powers and conservative church officials suspicious of the Enlightenment-era of the reformist camp, including its endorsement of religious toleration and its boundless confidence in human reason. In 1772, the neighboring states of Prussia, Russia, and Austria took advantage of the commonwealth's weakness and internal division, forcing it to yield some 30 percent of its territory, which they divided among themselves. This has come to be known as the first partition. Two others would follow, in 1793 and 1795, leading ultimately to the dissolution of the Polish-Lithuanian Commonwealth.

Before those lethal blows, however, King Stanisław August and his reform-minded allies exploited a brief window of opportunity to secure their crowning achievement, the Constitution of 3 May 1791. Remarkably progressive for its time, the constitution centralized power once again in the person of the king, eliminated the *liberum veto,* and opened the National Assembly to a wider cross section of the population. Friends and foes alike acknowledged the soundness of its principles and potential to restore the commonwealth as a regional power. The Prussian minister Hertzberg noted the following regarding the new Polish charter: "The Poles have given the coup de grâce to the Prussian monarchy by voting a Constitution much better than the English. I think that Poland will regain sooner or later West Prussia, and perhaps East Prussia also. How can we defend our state, open from Memel to Cieszyn, against a numerous and well-governed nation?"[32]

The reform era reverberated in Poznań in numerous ways. It brought the formal guarantee of religious toleration for Protestants and an effort to ameliorate the abuses levied against the Jewish community.[33] Voivode Kazimierz Raczyński, an avid supporter of reform, sought to augment the central government's profile in the city by restoring the royal castle and outfitting the town hall with symbols of the Polish state.[34] The constitution itself invested city residents with a greater voice in state affairs and had the potential to unify Poznanians behind shared interests at the state level, thereby softening the many sharp boundaries that divided the city. Before this instrument had time to exercise its full effects, however, the Polish-Lithuanian Commonwealth was picked apart.

Community Life, Culture, Ideas

In his influential study of nationalism, Karl Deutsch defines culture as "a common set of stable, habitual preferences and priorities in [a group's] attention, and behavior, as well as in [its] thoughts and feelings," a common bond that renders communication within the group easier than communication beyond its confines.[35] Working from this definition we could say that there were as many cultures in Poznań as there were clusters of individuals bound together by a distinct set of perceptions, shared experiences, and interests. Whether at home, at work, or in their leisure, Poznanians established patterns of behavior and belief that facilitated cooperation and communication. Once established, these cultures exhibited tremendous power, providing models of action, modes of viewing the world, and, to borrow Maurice Halbwachs's useful formulation, the "collective memory" upon which emotional bonds of solidarity are built.[36] Every Poznanian belonged to several of the dozens of overlapping cultures operating in the area, ranging from the intimacy of family to larger collectivities such as neighborhood or profession. The broadest forms of culture were found within the confines of caste and confession. It is impossible to speak of a strong, widely shared national culture in the Polish-Lithuanian Commonwealth at this time.

One consequence of the central government's weakness was the stunted development of institutions capable of fostering a normative or "high" culture in the commonwealth. At this time in Europe strong central governments constituted the primary arbiters of high culture within their realms, funding the institutions that allowed scholarship and the arts to flourish, the press organs that helped coordinate public opinion, and the structures, spaces, and rituals of the widest symbolic effect. The commonwealth's noble elite maintained their own forms of cultural expression, which had a certain normative quality on account of the wide geographical scope and political power of their caste. Noble culture found its primary expression in the complex ceremonies, customs, and endeavors that took place within the upper echelons of the army, the palaces of Warsaw, and the manor houses scattered across the countryside. Poznanians with the requisite wealth and lineage could find access to this cultural milieu, but the horizons of the large majority rarely extended beyond their immediate vicinity. A thin network of poorly maintained roads and the absence of a regular postal service inhibited the traffic of people, goods, and information to and from the city.[37] Poznań boasted no public venues for the arts and no newspapers or journals for the transmission of ideas.

When King Stanisław August and his allies came to power, they sought to strengthen the centripetal pull of the state. Their crowning achievement was the creation of a national education system, which coordinated existing Catholic institutions into a unified structure based on common standards. They also created a national cadet academy for the training of officers and launched a press organ, the *Monitor,* which served as a sounding board for their Enlightenment-era values. The king's efforts undoubtedly found a warm reception among the small coterie of "enlightened" Poznanians. But as Jerzy Jedlicki argues, the reformists' program struck most residents of the commonwealth as foreign, and it was relatively easy for conservative forces to arouse the public's antipathy toward it.[38] With time such innovations may have achieved their desired effect, but rapid progress could hardly be expected on such ambitious goals.

As in all societies, the boundaries of language and custom in Poznań formed important bases of social belonging. Poznań's historical record is replete with examples of how the city's three main national groups—Poles, Germans, and Jews—tended strongly to support their own and discriminate against others. Clearly, a common nationality provided an important source of social identity for city residents. It would be wrong, however, to identify such sentiments as nationalist in the modern sense of the word. Some important elements were lacking.

German Poznanians remained keenly aware of their national and linguistic heritage. While it cut them off from certain rights and privileges, it also locked them into a clannish minority that generally fared well in the commonwealth. German craftspeople and merchants in Poznań, as in cities across the realm, long ranked among the wealthiest and highest skilled, and new generations found ready access to this status. The same was true in the countryside, where German farmers, on average, labored under more promising conditions than their Polish counterparts. Awareness of their heritage, however, did not translate into reliable knowledge of—or a sense of kinship with—the German-speaking peoples of Central Europe, who were at that time scattered across dozens of independent states. Even Germans living squarely within the territory we now know as Germany were usually quite ignorant of the customs and mores of their Teutonic cousins living in closely neighboring states.[39] Such ignorance was all the more acute in Poland. German Poznanians had little knowledge with which to flesh out the abstract concept of "Germany," let alone enough to develop a sense of personal identification with such a concept.

Among the Polish-speaking population, a profound cultural, economic, and political gulf divided the slight ranks of Poland's elite from the large majority of their would-be conationals. Heinrich Heine noted the disparity during his visit to the area: "The humility of the Polish farmer before the Polish noble is shocking. He bows his head almost to the feet of the merciful sir and ritually announces: 'I kiss your feet.' Whoever wishes to see obedience personified, simply look at a Polish farmer before a noble; the wagging tail of a dog is alone missing."[40] An ideology known as Sarmatism reinforced and justified the disparities. Most nobles in the Polish-Lithuanian Commonwealth, be they of Polish, Lithuanian, or some other ancestry, fancied themselves the descendants of the Sarmatians, a mythical race of conquerors from the Black Sea region, who according to legend had invaded the Polish territories centuries earlier and ruled over its native residents ever since. The differences in Polish society thus were based not only on circumstance but on blood. The nobility considered themselves a class apart and zealously defended their birthright. Among the most powerful nobles, the magnates, the notion emerged that they were more elite still, having descended from the ancient Romans.[41] The Polish peasantry and urban lower classes, disenfranchised, economically and culturally impoverished, and poorly educated if at all, had little grounds for identity beyond their immediate family and village, let alone beyond their castes. The lot of the Polish bourgeoisie was marginally better, but they formed an insignificant fraction of the total Polish population.

In some respects the communal sentiments of Poznań's Jews approximated modern nationalism. This group identity extended to all Jews, an inclusiveness grounded on a shared ancestry. It was buttressed by a deep sense of group history, a common destiny, and a rich cultural and social life distinctly at odds with their larger surroundings. One element central to modern nationalism and lacking in Jewish identity, though, was a tangible territory upon which to affix shared political aspirations. Jews in Poznań and across Europe continued to dream of an eventual return to the Holy Land, but that place remained much more of a spiritual than a political reality, as far removed from their practical experiences as it was geographically. However intangible it may have been, the Holy Land loomed large enough in Jewish minds to alienate them from their immediate surroundings.[42] Even for Jews with deep roots in Poznań, the city remained a land of exile.

The bulk of Poznań's Christian residents continued to find meaning and belonging within the venerable institutions of the city and their respective professions. Ferdinand Braudel identifies the medieval town as Europe's first fatherland, and the same spirit of shared identity and interest continued to stir in Poznanians a profound commitment to their city.[43] Civic pride found its symbolic locus in the beautiful town hall and harmonious lines of the market square, and it was nurtured through the performance of political ceremonies and obligations on the part of its members. It helped bridge distinctions between merchant and craftsperson, German and Pole, Catholic and Protestant.

For those belonging to the various guilds and brotherhoods in the city, their commitments usually extended well beyond the workday. Beyond participation in the administration and ritual life of the organization, members often shared their free time at public houses to drink, trade opinions, or play games of chance.[44] Membership anchored their lives firmly within a group orbit, molding their perspectives and self-understandings around the profession or craft they practiced.

Of all the cultures in Poznań at this time, those grounded on religion ranked among the most powerful and pervasive. Expansive in scope, they insinuated themselves into nearly every aspect of their members' lives, stretching throughout and beyond the bonds of family, city, caste, and nation. Ambitious in purpose, they maintained cadres of well-trained professionals whose mission it was to mold the worldview, collective memories, and life course of the souls under their charge. The prescriptions of faith and the boundaries between religions decisively shaped the social order in Poznań. In what follows we will explore in greater depth the respective cultures of two of the city's main religions, Roman Catholicism and Protestantism.

Catholic Poznań

With roughly 60 percent of the area's population under its mantle, Catholicism was by far the largest religion in Poznań. Its adherents belonged to the official religion of the commonwealth, which was served by a thick network of professionals and institutions. The insufficiency of the commonwealth's own institutions magnified the church's significance. The church was positioned like no other organization to influence the functioning of the state and to shape the cultural horizons of its members. All Poznanians, regardless of confession, regularly encountered the church's broad authority. Likewise all Catholics, regardless of the depth of their piety, carried with them the effects of their religious formation.

Poles long have identified the political origins of the Polish state with 966 A.D., the year Mieszko I, a tribal duke from the Poznań region, accepted baptism and allowed the Catholic Church to propagate the faith among his pagan subjects. His decision helped put Poland on the map of Christendom and provided his fledgling state with some important resources, including writing, tested organizational methods, and an ideology conducive to centralized authority. In return the Catholic Church gained a position of great privilege and influence over a broad swath of new territory. It retained this position until the final dismemberment of the Polish-Lithuanian Commonwealth.

Unlike European states such as France and England, where strong central governments managed to force the church into a position clearly subordinate to secular authority, no corresponding effort succeeded in the commonwealth. Although many among the nobility resented the privileges and wealth of the clergy, they never managed to curtail the church in any substantial way. Rather, the nobility and the church found a basis of common interest upon which to build a political alliance. Since the mid-sixteenth century, the nobility increasingly accepted the church as a central and exclusive element in the life of the state. The ideology of Poland as a Catholic bulwark against heathen and barbarian loomed ever larger in the political consciousness of the elite.[45] So, too, did Catholic political thought, which at this time posited religious homogeneity as the ideal condition of a state. This principle overshadowed the nobility's earlier tendency to tolerate diversity in matters of conscience, earning the commonwealth a reputation for religious persecution by the eighteenth century.[46] Only late in the eighteenth century was the central role of the church in state life drawn into serious question. The actual reforms enacted during this time were modest by the standards of the day.[47]

If, in the main, the noble establishment accommodated the priorities of the church, so too did the political activity of the church reflect the interests of the nobility. Positions within the upper echelons of the Catholic hierarchy were the exclusive reserve of the nobility, and candidates were required to be trained not only in theology but in the culture of polite society as well. Higher church officials lived like nobility, maintaining vast landed estates and even small armies, and made the rounds within elite social circles. While owning a palace next to the cathedral, for instance, Poznań's bishops often resided on their country estate in Ciążen or in family palaces in Warsaw. Not surprisingly, bishops were inclined to transmit the perspectives and expectations of the nobility to their Catholic subjects.

In a state suffering from a stunning paucity of centralized authority, concomitant bureaucratic structures, and a sizable intelligentsia, the church offered a disciplined network of relatively well-trained individuals eager to manage the country's business. Catholic officials dominated the field of education and played leading roles in cultural and political life. The parish system provided them with an unparalleled degree of access to the Catholic population. In Poznań alone well over a hundred priests were employed across the city's six parishes in the mid-1790s. Education and the mantle of office afforded the clergy tremendous influence within the Catholic community. Their monopoly on the keys to salvation greatly magnified their authority. The threat of denying the Eucharist or a proper Catholic burial—occasionally made to persons whose actions were considered morally reprehensible— proved powerfully persuasive.

The political fissures within the Polish-Lithuanian Commonwealth were also readily apparent in the church. In the reform camp surrounding Stanisław August, Enlightenment-era priorities found some of their most articulate proponents among the Catholic clergy. Catholic officials on the other end of the political spectrum supported movements opposed to political reform and the toleration of other religions. In 1792 several bishops and numerous clergy joined the ranks of the Targowica Confederation, a counterrevolutionary movement of a conservative Catholic nature intent on undoing the recent gains of the reform movement.[48] On the whole, it was the conservative spirit of Targowica rather than the liberal faith of the Enlightenment that oriented the majority of the clergy. For all of the state's problems, conservative Catholic officials could take comfort in the degree of their influence at a time that seemed so unpropitious to faith in many corners of Europe. Their resistance to the reform program only grew as the French Revolution unfolded and news of its strong anticlerical dimension reached the commonwealth. In Poznań and throughout the state, Catholics were consistently reminded of the dangers of republican ideas as well as the virtues of their traditional political system.

The extent of the clergy's political influence over the laity varied. Johann Erich Biester echoed a common observation when he noted that "educated Catholics, and particularly those in large cities, do not speak about their religion with the appropriate respect. . . , whereas the simple folk are deeply devout and enjoy religious ceremonies enormously."[49] However ambivalent some of Poznań's more educated Catholics may have felt about the church, very few renounced their ties to the institution altogether. Even the most skeptical usually recognized the value of allegiance within a society that privileged Catholics, not to mention Catholicism's usefulness in promoting harmony between social classes. A large majority managed to balance anticlerical sentiments with genuine religious faith.

As in politics, the Catholic Church played a prominent role in Poznań's social and economic life. In an environment where religion was so formative and where there existed scant basis for nonsectarian culture or community, Catholics inevitably gravitated toward coreligionists in developing relationships. Here they could expect to find the most common ground and the greatest ease of understanding. Certainly this did not preclude them from establishing bonds of interest, friendship, and even marriage with Protestants, but in these cases religious differences hindered understanding more than they helped.[50] The religious differences separating Catholics and Jews, meanwhile, were practically insurmountable.

At a time when caste distinctions posed rigid boundaries difficult to cross, the Catholic Church helped build bridges and regulate relations between groups. The parish created a forum in which all Catholics within a given territory, regardless of rank, gathered together regularly to reaffirm a common faith. Religion provided Catholics a rare opportunity to identify with others beyond their particular caste. This solidarity, however, did not rest on equality. Economic and social distinctions were given formal expression within the context of religious observance. Nearly every church building contained memorials to its leading patrons in the form of epitaphs, altars, or even chapels. In important rituals such as baptisms, marriage ceremonies, and funerals, every priest involved and every bell rung had its price.[51] The elaborateness of such rites of passage varied considerably, rendering them partly into testimonies of an individual's significance.

Although it represented status in its material and ritual forms, the church sought to alleviate tensions based on social and economic inequality through its teachings. It encouraged the poor to accept their fate without protest, repeating the assurances of Jesus that meekness is a virtue and that the poor shall have their reward in heaven. It reminded the wealthy of their moral obligation to the poor, and it provided ample channels for charity. Throughout the city and suburbs, the church operated at least eight different hospitals, where poor, infirm, and aged Catholics could find aid. Under its aegis, wealthier Catholics gathered into two different brotherhoods that sought to alleviate the suffering of less fortunate residents.

The economic commitment of ordinary Catholics to the church extended well beyond the arenas of status and charity. Catholics were obliged to pay church taxes, often to their consternation. Many gave above and beyond that which was required, motivated by the desire to strengthen the church's institutions, to satisfy a sense of moral obligation, or to prompt a fortuitous chain of cosmic cause and effect. It was de rigueur, for instance, for the city's many guilds and brotherhoods to have Catholic saints as patrons, and they routinely sponsored masses at altars to their holy protectors.[52] A well-venerated saint, it was assumed, would see to the prosperity of the organization as a whole. Individuals and families sponsored priests to say masses for departed loved ones in the hope of speeding their passage to the heaven.

To be Catholic in Poznań was to be steeped in a particular culture. Members of the church were encouraged to perceive the world in a uniquely Catholic way, and to develop a cluster of tastes, expectations, and motivations that distinguished them from Poznanians of other faiths. Priests instructed Catholics about the nature of the universe, human responsibility, the purpose of life, and the rewards or punishments in store after death. In church they absorbed a sense of aesthetics and of the sacred. Some Catholics enjoyed the privilege of more formal education, which was also provided under the aegis of the church. Poznań's St. Mary Magdalene's Parish maintained the only Catholic elementary school of any note in the area.[53] In the 1780s the National Education Commission turned the city's former Jesuit College into a Catholic gymnasium (high school). By 1793 this institution encompassed 10 teachers and over 240 students engaged in a six- or seven-year course of study.[54] Young men interested in the priesthood could receive their training at the Lubrański Academy.

Acculturation to Catholicism brought with it a distinct sense of space and time. In the complex spiritual landscape of the faith, the seen world was but one thin plane of existence sandwiched between layers of the unseen. Below lay the fires of hell, and above the heavens. Divine and diabolical forces from these other worlds regularly erupted into the mundane plane. These forces sometimes operated in ways that confounded human reason. At other times they responded directly to human action. Worthy actions or earnest pleas could bring welcome results, just as immoral behavior could meet with swift retribution. The stakes were high—eternal life itself hung in the balance!— and constant vigilance was required. These many unseen forces found their material echo in the large number of sites dedicated to their honor. Nearly thirty Catholic churches made their mark on Poznań's skyline. Within each a sometimes bewildering array of altars, niches, and statuary signaled the presence of saintly patrons, both in spirit and in the form of relics. At these points devout Catholics could attain a comforting proximity to the patron of their choice.

While most Catholics conducted their religious obligations at their own parish church, many churches had particular valences that attracted outsiders on appropriate occasions. On All Souls' Day Catholics from the Poznań area streamed to the dilapidated All Saints' Chapel, located just south of the city center, in order to pray for the souls of their dead. On August 2, the anniversary of the Portiuncula Indulgence, the Franciscan church welcomed a flood of pilgrims, who for their efforts were assured the complete forgiveness of sins. The same church also contained a purportedly miraculous painting of the Virgin Mary that regularly drew the devout and the desperate. Ill or handicapped Catholics often ventured to the Dominican church and its relic of St. Jacek, famed for its healing powers.[55]

Several Catholic churches attracted large numbers of worshipers, in part because of their impressive size and beauty. First among them was the Poznań Cathedral, a soaring structure that dominated the eastern bank of the Warta. Dating back to the tenth century, the building's age was masked by a series of thorough renovations in which its exterior form passed through Romanesque, Gothic, and Baroque phases in turn. The Parish Church—known as the Jesuit Church before that order was disbanded in 1773—ranked as the most prominent religious structure in the center of town. The Jesuits had at their disposal a rich endowment and spared no expense, importing Italian architects and building specialists, noble materials, and fine works of ecclesial art. Built in the late seventeenth century, it stood within an impressive complex of buildings, including apartments, a grand hall, a library, and a pharmacy. Perhaps the greatest testament to the grandeur of the complex was the fact that when invading armies occupied Poznań, their commanders usually opted to reside here.

The Parish Church was one of many fine structures built for the various religious orders in the city. Several of these buildings were tied to the painful history of local interreligious strife. In the seventeenth century the calced Carmelites (an unreformed branch of the order whose members wore shoes) built St. Joseph's Church and an adjacent cloister on a hilltop just north of the city, a site where a Protestant group known as the Bohemian Brethren once worshiped in wooden churches that were burned down repeatedly by Catholic mobs. For many Catholics, the calced Carmelite complex represented a triumph over heresy.

To the south of the city stood the Corpus Christi Church. This church was built in the fifteenth century for the discalced Carmelites, a reformed branch of Carmelites whose members went barefoot or wore only sandals as a sign of their commitment to poverty. Corpus Christi was well known throughout Poland for the miracles that purportedly took place there in 1399. According to legend, three Jewish elders surreptitiously procured three blessed hosts, which they attempted to desecrate by stabbing them with knives. The hosts began bleeding, and the frightened elders tossed them into a swamp south of town. But the hosts rose from the swamp in the form of a shepherd boy, and many miracles occurred. Responding to the outrage of the Catholic population, city authorities arrested a rabbi and thirteen Jewish elders and burned them alive as punishment.[56] The Corpus Christi Church was built to memorialize these events. Inside, three golden hosts were placed at the pinnacle of its high altar, and in the middle of the main aisle sculptural representations of the three elders symbolically recreated the sacrilege.

A new chapter in the legend of the three hosts was written in 1620, when someone claimed to have discovered the table on which the Jews allegedly stabbed the stolen hosts. The table was in the basement of a house on Jewish Street, in the heart of the Jewish Quarter. The discalced Carmelites bought the building in the early 1660s and turned it into the Chapel of the Most Sacred Blood of Jesus. They had the ceiling decorated with a fresco cycle, parts of which depicted the host desecration story.

Catholicism pervaded the public spaces of Poznań. The statue of St. John Nepomuc on the market square was just one of many shrines sprinkled throughout the city. On Catholic holidays, quotidian endeavor on the city's streets, byways, and squares gave way to ritual practices befitting the occasion.

4. Chapel of the Most Sacred Blood of Jesus, ceiling.
The fresco cycle painted on the ceiling of the chapel
contains scenes from the alleged host desecration of
1399. Photograph by Robert E. Alvis.

Most Catholics were keen to cultivate their religious obligations within the
public space of the city. Honoring the holy was central to a moral life and encouraged the favor of God and the saints. For Catholics of intolerant or superstitious inclinations, a corollary was also true: just as Catholic observance
brought favor, the simple presence of non-Catholics brought destruction to
the entire community. In times of distress many Catholics automatically
blamed non-Catholics and demanded retribution, often forcing the alleged of-
fenders to contribute to the propagation of the Catholic faith. In 1725 when
the towers of the cathedral suffered damage in a fierce storm, Protestant pas-

tors and teachers throughout Great Poland were obliged to pay for its restoration.[57] It was the Jews, however, who suffered most from this logic.

The large majority of Poznań's Catholics rarely ventured beyond the immediate area and had little firsthand knowledge of the province, let alone the state. Their religious affiliation, however, instilled within them a particular sense of their geopolitical circumstances. Their leaders regularly struck upon the theme that Poland was a Catholic country. A central motif in Catholic piety of the time identified Mary—and the image of the Black Madonna at Częstochowa in particular—as queen of Poland and the state's chief protector. Moreover, Catholic leaders warned their followers of the great spiritual dangers at the commonwealth's gates. Orthodox Russia to the east and Protestant Prussia to the west threatened to overwhelm the state and undermine the Catholic religion.

This Catholic geopolitical understanding was founded on a knot of collective memories that were taught in school and preached from pulpits. Since at least the sixteenth century, Catholics were inculcated with the belief that their state served as the gatekeeper of Christendom. Poised on its eastern border, Poland was destined to defend the rest of Europe from the godless Asiatic horde. The classic examples cited in this argument were the repulsed Mongol invasions of the thirteenth and fourteenth centuries, as well as the key role of King Jan Sobieski's Polish army in stopping the Turks before Vienna in 1674. The Swedish "Deluge" of the 1650s provided a new dimension to this tradition. Having overrun practically the entire state, the Swedish army failed to capture the fortified cloister at Częstochowa, where monks used the image of the Black Madonna to bolster the morale of the cloister's defenders on the ramparts. News of the Swedish failure spread throughout the state, emboldening natives to drive out the invaders. The Black Madonna was later crowned queen of Poland, and the conviction emerged that so long as Catholics remained faithful to the Virgin Mary, she would deliver Poland from foreign aggression.

This sacred history offered Catholics a profoundly meaningful time frame in which to understand their lives. More powerful still was the liturgical year, the annual ritual reenactment of the life and death of Jesus and the triumphs of the church. The Catholic calendar largely determined the rhythm of life in Poznań. While workdays demanded up to sixteen hours of productivity, on Sundays and Catholic holidays the call to labor gave way to an entirely different set of obligations and customs. Prior to 1775 Catholics in the Poznań area celebrated dozens of religious holidays that, along with Sundays, consumed more than a quarter of the year. In 1775 Pope Pius VI eliminated twenty-four of them, but many continued being unofficially observed.[58] The observance of holidays usually combined measures of religious piety with frivolity and drunkenness, varying in proportion according to individual propensity and the season of the year. The period from Christmas to Ash Wednesday was particularly lighthearted, while the forty days of Lent called for sacrifice and repentance.[59] Non-Catholics were expected to show respect for the holidays, and any display to the contrary could lead to trouble.

Catholicism also molded the life course of the individual. Its rituals of baptism, confirmation, marriage, and burial punctuated the passing years, lending coherence to the mysteries of life, aging, death, and destiny. The church inculcated within its members a distinct vision of the future beyond death, which more than any other factor underlined the central importance of membership and moral living. In belonging to the church and following its strictures lay the promise of eternal life in paradise, while the tortures of purgatory or hell awaited those outside the fold. This sense of destiny conditioned Catholic perceptions of non-Catholics, especially the Jews. Many felt a moral imperative to promote their faith to outsiders, either through persuasion or more forceful means.[60]

Protestant Poznań

Protestants occupied a liminal zone within the city's religious landscape. They were clearly not Jewish, but from the perspective of the Catholic majority neither were they fully Christian. Rather they were dissenters from the true faith, baptized in the name of Christ but obstinately committed to false churches. Legally they lacked the diverse privileges guaranteed the Jews, but they were spared the degree of mistrust that rendered Jewish rights so insecure. While their religious affiliations may have exposed them to numerous disadvantages, it also locked them into a particular political, socioeconomic, and cultural sphere to which their members were fiercely committed. As with the Catholic community, the religion of Poznań's Protestants extended far beyond articles of faith to permeate nearly every aspect of their lives.

By 1520, just three years after Luther first hammered his theses onto a church door in Wittenberg, the Protestant movement made itself felt in Poland. The call for reform in the church resonated with many, and the state's relatively tolerant climate initially allowed Protestant faiths to grow. Poznań eventually emerged as one of the most important Protestant centers in the country. A community of Bohemian Brethren—a movement originating in the Czech lands in the fifteenth century—arrived in Poznań by 1548 and won many adherents. They settled in the St. Adalbert suburb under the protection of Jakub Ostrorog, a powerful noble and faithful supporter of the movement, and with time their community contained two churches, a hospital, and a cemetery.[61] Polish- and German-speaking Lutheran communities emerged in the early 1560s. They flourished under the patronage of the Górka family and held religious services in the Górka palace just off the market square.

However fortuitous its start, the Reformation suffered a series of major setbacks later in the sixteenth century. Representatives of the Jesuit order arrived in the city and introduced vital new currents into the Catholic faith. They applied themselves just as vigorously to undermining the Protestant churches, in particular by wooing Polish nobles back into the Catholic fold. Protestant Poznanians lost their most powerful champions when the last of the Górkas died childless in 1592. Shortly thereafter city officials forbade Protestant worship within the city. The Lutherans joined the Bohemian Brethren in the St. Adalbert suburb, and for a time they managed to maintain their marginal religious lives in relative peace. Increasingly fiery rhetoric from Catholic pulpits and presses, however, spoiled their hopes. Encouraged to root out the scourge of heresy in their midst, bands of Catholics repeatedly turned the Protestants' modest wooden churches to ash.

Early-seventeenth-century legislation on the local, regional, and state level rendered allegiance to these faiths a distinct liability. After 1616 Protestants in Poznań were not allowed to rebuild their churches. In 1619 they were barred from city citizenship, and in 1628 they were denied access to guilds and merchant brotherhoods. In 1632 the National Assembly granted tolerance to existing Protestant churches, but forbade the building of new ones. Protestant nobles still enjoyed remarkable freedoms, however, and under their patronage many Protestant communities across the country were able to survive and even flourish. Certainly their situation compared favorably to that of religious minorities in other European states at the time.[62]

In Poznań the Bohemian Brethren and the Polish-speaking Lutheran community faded away. Only the German Lutherans survived in any appreciable number. Denied a place of worship in the city limits, they attended services in neighboring towns under the protection of Protestant nobles.[63] They were allowed to continue burying their dead in their cemetery in Poznań, provided that the ceremonies took place in the evening without fanfare and that the priests at St. Adalbert's and St. Martin's Parishes were paid. They had to turn to Catholic priests to baptize children and marry consenting adults. As well, they often fell under the jurisdiction of the church when they ran afoul of the law.

The sharp decline of the commonwealth's fortunes in the early eighteenth century disposed its Catholic establishment to more repressive political measures against Protestants. The National Assembly passed legislation that compromised the rights of non-Catholic nobility and limited their ability to defend their coreligionists.[64] Poznań's Lutheran community endured several decades of hardship, exposed more than ever to the wrath of radical Catholics. Their situation improved later in the century, when, under pressure from neighboring states, the National Assembly approved the Warsaw Tractate of 1768. The tractate restored wide-ranging freedoms to religious minorities in Poland, including the freedom to practice their religion unhindered, to hold public offices and honors, and to appeal to a confessionally mixed legal body in cases of religious conflict.[65]

Their difficult history molded Poznań's Protestants into a tightly knit minority, sustained by systems of mutual support and bound by a common religious culture. The congregation formed the bedrock of their solidarity, and church officers served as de facto leaders of the community. Poznań's Lutheran congregation was administered by the elders, a small number of distinguished male members. The wealthy merchant Andreas Ackermann functioned as chief elder in the final, tumultuous decades of the commonwealth. He represented the congregation at the negotiations leading to the Warsaw Tractate, and he oversaw the building of a new church in the 1770s and 1780s. The liberalization of 1768 also allowed a small Reformed congregation to take shape in Poznań. It emerged in 1772 and consisted primarily of newcomers to the city.[66] Although young, the congregation was eager to claim for itself the legacy of the Bohemian Brethren in Poznań.[67]

The congregations constituted informal political and legal bodies, and each member was expected to uphold the values shared by the community, to deal fairly with coreligionists, and to contribute according to one's means to the common good. It was the duty of religious leaders to enforce these obligations. Disputes naturally arose, and Protestant leaders took great precautions to resolve them quietly within the confines of the congregation, fearful lest they find their way into the public sphere dominated by Catholics. The opinion of other members and the ultimate threat of exclusion from the community offered most Protestants sufficient reason to conform to communal expectations.

Poznań's Protestants belonged to regional bodies composed of Lutheran and Reformed congregations throughout Great Poland. These organizations provided occasion for leaders to jointly address matters of doctrine and practice, to solve problems plaguing their communities, and to pool resources for greater effect. Neither congregation belonged to larger religious networks, but they did maintain informal contacts with coreligionists beyond the province. On the local level, Lutheran and Reformed Protestants in Poznań recognized one another as allies and maintained warm relations.

Congregation members helped maintain each other not only spiritually but economically as well. During the long period of religious discrimination, during which time Protestants were barred from participation in city organizations, the congregation provided an important forum where fellow members could establish networks of economic exchange. Considering that Protestants often ranked among the leading merchants, craftspeople, and urban professionals in the region, such alliances afforded them numerous advantages and a healthy measure of influence. Evidence of this cooperative economic spirit can be seen in the Lutheran community's effort to build a new church. The Lutheran banker Jan Klug lent the community the funds for the project, and leading Lutherans operated the brick factory that provided materials for the construction. The economic commitment of Protestants to the congregation was also demonstrated at their deaths. Lutheran leaders made regular entries in the church journal describing the financial contributions listed in the wills of deceased members. Samuel Durenfeld (d. 1790) was particularly generous. He left six hundred florin to the Lutheran church and three hundred florin to the Lutheran hospital.[68] Mutual support extended to the poor and infirm. At a time when there was little public help for individuals unable to fend for themselves, Lutherans and Reformed Protestants considered it their obligation to aid their less fortunate coreligionists.[69]

However much they may have cooperated with each other economically, Protestants remained very aware of caste distinctions within their ranks. A number of Protestant nobles wielded a disproportionate amount of influence over the congregations in the province. They typically dominated secular positions of authority within both confessions. Their status as nobles granted them greater influence in Polish society, making them effective advocates for their fellow Protestants. It also availed them to certain privileges. Poznań's Lutheran community, for instance, offered plots in its cemetery to noble Protestants regardless of which confession or congregation they belonged to, a right normally reserved for local congregation members. In urban centers like Poznań, wealthy members of the bourgeoisie also played key roles.

Culturally and ideologically, the Protestant congregation ranked as one of the most homogenous environments its members knew, and a large portion of the congregation's work had the express purpose of replicating this homogeneity. Shared religious faith caused people to think and act in many of the same ways. They held common views on the nature of the world and of humanity, common understandings of life's purpose and its ideal course, and common expectations for the afterlife. In church they gathered regularly to reinforce the faith that bound them.

The education of children ranked as one of the principal tasks of the Protestant congregations. In Poznań all education was sectarian, and for most Protestants the very notion of sending their children to Catholic or Jewish schools was unthinkable. They viewed education as a process of moral formation, through which their children would develop into conscious, committed members of the faith. Protestant leaders took great pains to find qualified teachers, interviewing a variety of candidates drawn from across the province. By 1793 both Protestant confessions operated elementary schools that offered a rudimentary education.[70]

Most Protestant children received no education beyond elementary school. A fortunate few continued their studies at one of the state's several Protestant gymnasia. An even more select group went on to earn a higher degree. No such Protestant institutions existed in Poland, compelling students to turn to foreign universities. Many among the Protestant elite spent years of study abroad, where they were exposed to the cultures of Protestant Europe. They brought their experiences back to Poland, opening a window to new intellectual currents developing there, such as pietism and the Enlightenment.[71]

Another factor that affected the cultural horizons of Poznań's Protestants was language. Knowledge of German—the first language of the large majority—allowed them access to German-language books printed abroad and foreign newspapers. It also facilitated cultural and economic connections with Germans in other lands. When the Lutheran congregation wanted to have an organ built for its new church, for instance, it turned to a master craftsman based in Stettin, Prussia.[72]

The city's Lutheran and Reformed members maintained a distinctly Protestant sense of space and time. Within the city they tended to concentrate on the overwhelmingly Protestant island of Grobla and in the city center. Very few lived in the settlements to the east of the Warta River, which were controlled by the Catholic Church. These patterns underscored the ambiguous position Protestants occupied within a predominantly Catholic population.

While their relations were harmonious in the main, occasional displays of intolerance kept Protestants on their guard, and they sought safety in numbers.

A telling example of this ambiguity occurred in June of 1769. At that time an army belonging to the Confederation of Bar, an alliance of nobles leading an armed rebellion against the reformist government and the newly won religious freedoms of Protestants, was closing in on Poznań. The city's Protestants were terrified. As the Lutheran chronicler notes, "We poor Poznanian dissident Christians experienced more confusion, anxiety, and fear by this unexpected turn of events than anyone with a quill could adequately describe in words." Their fear was well founded. When the confederates finally occupied the city, Protestants suffered numerous indignities and had to pay staggering sums of money to avoid still worse fates. Andreas Ackermann, well known for his advocacy of greater tolerance toward Protestants at the 1768 National Assembly, was thought to be in particular danger. Ironically, as the confederate army approached, Ackermann sought refuge in the Jesuit cloister, where the priests "willingly took him in and treated him in a friendly and Christian manner." Long vilified as archfiends by Protestant polemicists, the Jesuits, like many Catholics, could be moved to brave acts of compassion on behalf of their Protestant neighbors.[73]

Prior to 1771 the only officially Protestant space in the city was the Lutheran cemetery, located at the foot of Winiary Hill north of the city. The space of their collective memory, however, was more extensive. Protestants clung to the legacy of their forebears. They maintained a lively oral history, recalling how Protestant services were once held in the Benedictine convent (formerly the Górka palace), or how in the early 1530s Professor Krzysztof Hegendorf zealously spread Reformation teachings at the Lubrański Academy. They recalled with bitterness where their wooden churches used to stand, and how the churches were thrice burned. Perhaps they enjoyed the irony that members of the Górka family—some of the greatest champions of Protestantism in Poznań—were entombed with honor in one of the Poznań Cathedral chapels.[74]

The building of the Cross Church signaled the start of a new era. The congregation chose a site on Grobla, in accord with the city's requirement not to build within two hundred ells of a Catholic church.[75] Lutherans sacrificed tremendously to see the project to completion. The biggest contributors included the cloth and silk merchant Friedrich Goebel, who donated four thousand ducats, and the goldsmith Martin Endemann, who donated one thousand ducats. Reminding them of how easily their wooden churches had once burned, an influential Protestant noble named Stanislaus August von der Goltz convinced the congregation to construct their new church out of brick and stone.[76] Set in the middle of a Lutheran enclave and surrounded by a wall, the structure epitomized the cautious but growing confidence of Poznań's Protestants.

The cornerstone of the church was laid 1 July 1777, and by 1786 services began to be held inside. The building, which still stands, is rectangular in form, running lengthwise north to south. A modest tower, rising above the main entrance on the western side of the structure, distinguishes the staid exterior. Inside, the pews on the main floor and the balcony form ovals, organized around the pulpit and altar in the middle of the eastern wall. The congregation was

5. Cross Church, circa 1850–60. Courtesy of the Muzeum Narodowe w. Poznaniu.

tremendously proud of their church, which, as one member noted, was "ad-mired by strangers."[77] As one of only two explicitly Protestant public spaces in the city, it was put to a variety of practical functions. Everything from elementary school final exams to piano recitals took place here. The church's door served as the Lutheran bulletin board, where important information was published. Meanwhile, its carefully organized interior performed a symbolic function, reifying in its design the congregation's social order. The space was divided by gender, with women on the ground floor and men in the balcony. On both levels, seats were rented to individuals, with those in the front fetching substantially higher rents.[78] One's position at worship thus served as a means of displaying one's financial worth. However equal members may have been in the eyes of God, human eyes witnessed their inequality every week.

Beyond the city, the spaces with which Protestants primarily identified themselves were the overlapping spheres of German language and Lutheran or Reformed faith within Great Poland. For the more optimistic among them, these spaces fit comfortably within their preferred vision of the Polish-Lithuanian Commonwealth: a multinational, multiconfessional state in which the majority tolerated minorities. During the reign of Stanisław August, Protestants encountered considerable cause for optimism in this regard, and it strengthened their patriotism.

In their enthusiasm for the 1768 Warsaw Tractate, the Lutheran community in Poznań had an ode written and published in honor of the king that sheds light on its political self-understanding. Two of the eight stanzas read as follows:

> You who offered peace and gave peace, o King!
> Your grateful people, who forget their own dead
> And neglect to honor the memory of their dead with incense,
> Your people will never neglect your memory, Stanislaus Augustus!
>
> Whoever does not love the king, product of Sarmatian blood,
> He does not recognize freedom; in him glows not a manly heart
> With noble sentiment; on his frozen breast is not written
> In flaming script, Stanislaus Augustus![79]

Invoking the ideology of kingship, Lutherans identified themselves collectively in the ode as subjects of the Polish king. As subjects they owed him respect and love, much as a child would a parent, and in return they hoped for fair treatment and generosity. In the second stanza they acknowledged the Sarmatian myth. Residents of Poland were not one people but rather a society divided by blood between ruling and servile classes.

As committed as they may have been to the commonwealth, Protestants remained keenly insecure about their place within the state. They regarded radical Catholics as the greatest threat to their well-being, perceiving in them a tremendous capacity for intolerance and cruelty. The depth of their fear emerges time and again in the journals the Lutheran community maintained. Some entries soberly record improbable hearsay information about Catholic excesses, which the author obviously regarded as factual. During the period of the Confederation of Bar's insurrection, for instance, the chronicler lamented the purported plan of the confederates to deliver all Protestants, Jews, and Orthodox Christians "into lifelong slavery to the Turks."[80] In a subsequent entry the chronicler recorded the case of a certain Malachowski, a monk from a nearby discalced Carmelite monastery who abandoned cloister life in 1768, fled to Berlin, and converted to the Reformed faith. When Malachowski returned to the Poznań area a year later, the Carmelites supposedly seized him, spirited him off to a monastery, and walled him into a tiny basement cell, providing only a small hole for air and minimal sustenance. He would have suffered there indefinitely had not a contingent of Russian troops under General Roenne passed by the monastery. Hearing foreign voices, Malachowski cried out in French for help and was saved.[81]

This story is difficult to verify, but it illustrates aspects of the Protestant sense of place in Poland. They saw themselves surrounded by a religion as mysterious and towering as the churches and monasteries that Catholics built. Although most Protestants knew little about what actually went on within such churches and behind monastery walls, they were quick to believe the worst. The story also highlights the geopolitical perspective of Poznań's Protestants. They had long placed their faith in neighboring non-Catholic states to keep the commonwealth's Catholic establishment in check. Just as the Russian general Roenne had freed Malachowski, so had Poland's neighbors helped secure greater religious freedoms for minorities. In the eighteenth century Russia, Prussia, Sweden, and Denmark had all pressured the commonwealth in this regard. At the same time Protestants also shared a measure of the Catholic population's ambivalence toward neighboring states. During the Confederation of Bar rebellion, Russian troops occupied Poznań on more than one occasion. They committed numerous excesses against the civilian population, thereby dampening Protestant enthusiasm for their supposed defenders. The Lutheran chronicler took a still dimmer view of Prussia. The author identified Prussia's successful attempt to destabilize the commonwealth's economy in this period as a "second confederation," comparing it to the loathed Confederation of Bar.[82]

However anxiously they may have monitored their political situation, for the devout the powers of earth paled in comparison to those of heaven. Poznań's Protestants inhabited an enchanted universe in which God actively engaged in human affairs. They petitioned for divine assistance in their endeavors and assigned the victories and tragedies they encountered to God's inscrutable wisdom. The Lutheran chronicle is full of references to divine power. It was a "higher hand," for instance, that brought to naught the confederates' plan to turn all non-Catholics into Turkish slaves. Like Jews and Catholics, Protestants believed they stood in an ideal relationship with God and enjoyed God's special favor. Not only did they live under the new dispensation introduced by Christ, their understanding of this dispensation was free of the many corruptions introduced by the Roman church.

Just as their faith molded their perceptions of space, so too did it instill within them a distinct sense of time. Theirs was a history in which the providential hand of God was at work, even if at times this work unfolded in mysterious ways. They believed that the life of Jesus inaugurated a new covenant with all people, in which God availed grace to the faithful in order that they might live more in accord with the divine will. Early Christian communities had managed to do that, but corrupt leaders within the Catholic Church twisted the terms of the covenant. Christendom was plunged into darkness, and centuries passed before the reformers managed to restore the light.

Whereas Protestants living under Protestant rulers might have found reason to believe that their corner of the earth partly reflected the glory of God's kingdom, until 1768 Protestants in Poland could not share this optimism. Their collective memories of persecution in the seventeenth and eighteenth centuries prompted many to equate their circumstances with the periods of foreign domination and exile endured by the ancient Israelites. Their newly won freedoms, in turn, filled them with tremendous hope for the future. The Lutheran chronicler resorted to the Bible to intuit the deeper historical significance of the Warsaw Tractate, quoting a passage from Isaiah, chapter 12: "You will say in this day: I will give thanks to you, O Lord, for though you were angry with me, your anger turned away, and you comforted me."[83]

If their sense of history contained radical swings, Protestants found peace in the rhythms of their religious observation. The three bells of the Cross

Church, rung according to a carefully planned schedule, reminded them of their weekly obligations.[84] The weekly routine, in turn, gave way to days of heightened religious significance such as Christmas, Good Friday, Easter, and Easter Monday, holidays honored by Lutheran and Reformed groups everywhere. Having lived for so long in a predominantly Catholic environment, however, Protestants gradually came to observe a number of Catholic holidays with no basis in Protestant tradition.[85] In a telling example of how Catholic time had become second nature for them, more than once the Lutheran chronicler referred to the feast days of Catholic saints to identify the date of notable events in the congregation. The dominant rhythms of the city had become theirs as well, and this common calendar helped build bridges with their Catholic neighbors. Shared holidays offered occasions for generating a sense of *communitas*. Just as important, they helped avoid stirring up divisive reminders of religious differences.

2

A Half Century of Change

On 22 January 1793 the Prussian army poured over the Polish border at six different points and fanned across Great Poland. After months of secret preparation, the second partition of the Polish-Lithuanian Commonwealth was under way. The invaders were relieved to encounter next to no resistance from the native population. Count Karl von Hoym, one of the Prussian ministers in charge of the takeover, informed the king that while some of the commonwealth's nobles were incensed by recent developments, many remained calm or even indifferent, and the rest of the population seemed to welcome the new regime. "The townspeople and farmers," he claimed, "praise the day when Your Majesty took control of their districts and liberated them from the oppression under which they previously suffered." [1] In Poznań residents responded as passively as did the rest of the region, opening the city's gates to the Prussian army. Having lived through numerous occupations in recent decades, city leaders hoped that their peaceful cooperation would spare them from wanton destruction.

In 1848 a revolution of a very different nature engulfed the city. In February of that year the fall of the Bourbon royal house in France emboldened leftist political groupings across Europe and set conservative governments on a panicked edge. Metternich's government in Austria soon collapsed, and in Prussia King Friedrich Wilhelm IV conceded to popular demands for fundamental political reforms. When the news reached Poznań, Polish leaders responded with a call for Polish independence. Large sectors of the population erupted in spontaneous celebration. Prussian military and government representatives in the city stood by passively as separatist leaders occupied the town hall and replaced the Prussian flag with the red and white standard of Poland.

Fifty-five years elapsed between these two revolutions and the vastly different responses they generated. During this time the city changed dramatically. Its population nearly tripled. To accommodate the growth, its material form extended upward and outward. Meanwhile its functional profile adopted characteristics of a modern provincial capital, including an array of government bureaucracies, an expansive service sector, and a diverse cultural life. The worldviews of Poznań's residents evolved in tandem. In particular, the city's German and Polish populations grew more inclined to perceive the world through nationalist lenses. The stronger their nationalist commitments grew, the more their political aspirations diverged.

An exploration of the complex genesis of nationalism in Poznań requires an examination of the phenomenon in three overlapping contexts: political, socioeconomic, and cultural. In the first section, therefore, I sketch a rough political history of Poznań from 1793 to 1848. My purpose is to trace the impact of nationalism as a political ideology on the attitudes of Poznanians. The central drama in this regard was the conflict between Prussia's defense of ancien régime principles of government and the gathering momentum of revolutionary demands for new bases of political legitimacy and investiture. This same scenario played itself out across much of Europe at this time, but in Poznań it took on a particular flavor owing to the city's position along the German-Polish ethnic divide.

Next I consider the city's socioeconomic evolution through the interpretive lens developed by Ernest Gellner, who emphasized the centrality of social and economic modernization in the development of nationalist consciousness. During this period there emerged in Poznań many of the hallmarks associated with modernization, and I consider to what extent these changes proved conducive to wider forms of social identity.

I then explore nationalism's cultural dimension. In this era, nationalist interpretations of culture became popular among the educated elite of Europe. Adherents of this view believed that each nation was distinguished by unique forms of expression inherent to it. The cultural expressions of a nation, whether in folklore or fine literature, everyday customs or monumental achievements, represented the distilled essence of its character and a measure of its political viability. Many nationalist-minded Poles dedicated themselves to the preservation and propagation of their cultural heritage, believing that their efforts provided the moral grounds for a future Polish state. Similar concerns were developing within German circles. Their political aspirations usually centered on justifying the unification of the many German-speaking states of Central Europe. Both forms of cultural nationalism, the Polish and the German, began resonating in Poznań at this time. Opposing them was the

Prussian state itself. Purssia was one of the largest states in Germanophone Central Europe, but its leadership was generally opposed to German nationalism and the drive for German unification. This was partly the result of the disturbingly liberal political orientation of many German nationalists, and partly a reflection of the enduring commitment the Prussian establishment felt to the heritage and traditions of the Prussian kingdom.

The Shifting Political Landscape

The second partition of the Polish-Lithuanian Commonwealth was the direct result of that state's successful efforts at internal reform. Fearing a resurgent neighbor, not to mention the Jacobin sympathies spreading among its elite, Russia and Prussia opted to carve the commonwealth down to a still smaller size. Running roughshod over the rights of a sovereign, nonaggressive state, however, required some explaining. Despite the expanding currency of Enlightenment-era ideals among its ruling elite, in the late eighteenth century Prussia remained a fairly typical ancien régime state in which political and military power was concentrated in the hands of the ruling monarch and society was hierarchically arranged into different estates.[2] Coming on the heels of the French Revolution, the political change afoot in the Polish-Lithuanian Commonwealth seemed to many Prussian observers to have the potential to follow the French model. In its official propaganda Prussia justified the second partition in terms integral to ancien régime principles. It argued the necessity of opposing "the ever growing revolutionary spirit" in the commonwealth, which was threatening to destroy "all civil, political, and religious bonds."[3] It also made the extraordinary claim that Prussia's royal house, the Hohenzollern dynasty, was descended in part from the Piast dynasty that had ruled Poland in the early Middle Ages, and therefore the Prussian king had a hereditary right to rule over its Polish territories.[4]

After the Prussian occupation, most Poznanians resigned themselves to a seemingly irreversible fait accompli. Few residents were actively engaged with international politics, and they were primarily concerned about the local ramifications of the invasion. Firsthand knowledge of Prussia was rare, and the stereotypes in circulation varied. Some spoke of a colorless land of military conscription and rigid fiscal discipline. Others noted Prussia's military strength and political stability—virtues in the eyes of those who weathered the tumult of the commonwealth's twilight.[5] Faced with the unknown, Poznanians of various stations besieged their new overlords with petitions, requesting the preservation of the privileges that provided their lives a measure of security.[6]

The first organized resistance to the partitions came in 1794. A Polish officer named Tadeusz Kościuszko launched a drive within the remaining portion of the commonwealth to restore the state to its prepartition borders and free it from foreign domination. Kościuszko also hoped to spark an uprising in those territories separated from the commonwealth by the first two partitions. He won support from the two groups that stood to lose the most from the partitions: the nobility and the clergy. In Prussian-controlled Poland, most of the population moved with the prevailing wind. In towns like Poznań where Prussia maintained a military presence, few dared to challenge the state. In areas where Polish nobles organized insurgent militias, few resisted the pressure to enlist or contribute materially to the rebellion.

Kościuszko has since been lionized in Poland's national mythology. Contrary to patriotic accounts, the uprising he led was not so much a spontaneous expression of the popular will as it was a movement orchestrated by a small elite and sustained by the threat of harsh punishment for those who failed to contribute. From the start it was handicapped by a stubborn catch-22. To succeed against the much larger armies of Prussia and Russia, it had to engage the commonwealth's vast peasant population. Yet the most effective quid pro quo—emancipation—threatened to alienate the nobility, whose support was also necessary.[7] In the end Kościuszko's supporters were unable to pull off their audacious gambit. After a couple notable successes, Kościuszko's army was defeated and its commander captured on 10 October 1794. The third and final partition occurred not long thereafter, and the Polish-Lithuanian Commonwealth ceased to exist.

The task of absorbing the Polish territories was enormous. The administrative and legal systems in place in Poland varied considerably from their Prussian equivalents and were regarded as inferior, if not hopeless, by Prussian observers. The state forged Poznań and the surrounding region into a new province named South Prussia. It chose Poznań as the capital and established institutions of government along Prussian lines. True to its ancient régime instincts, Prussia sought to win the loyalty of area nobles and to work with them in governing. Not long after the invasion, the state staged an elaborate ceremony in Poznań, where nobles pledged their fealty to the Prussian king. The king's power was legitimated through the nobility's acceptance of vassalage. Nobles, in turn, enjoyed the favor of the king. At the ceremony in Poznań, some nobles were awarded commemorative medals and the honor of entry into the distinguished Red Eagle Order.[8]

Despite its proximity, most Prussians knew very little about Poland.[9] An abundance of negative stereotypes sustained the ruling elite's dim views of the morality and industriousness of the commonwealth's inhabitants.[10] They had little doubt, though, that exposure to Prussian civilization would gradually improve the population. An official named J. F. Streuensee noted in a published report the following regarding the region's rural population: "We can expect little from the current generation because schools do not exist yet. In my view, the best possible education for these people is the example set by foreign colonists who live with them and demonstrate that thrift and hard work alone bring profit."[11] Through the encounter with Prussian settlers and training in Prussian schools and the military, it was hoped that the region's inhabitants would gradually adopt Prussian values.

This transformation proved difficult to achieve. Residents of South Prussia had to cope with a foreign political culture, higher taxes, a deteriorating economy, and—for the Polish majority at least—a foreign language. These challenges stirred feelings of alienation and acute nostalgia. Streuensee acknowledged that the province had no small supply of "eulogists and defenders of the old days."[12] The disdain many Prussian bureaucrats displayed toward the native population only fanned such sentiments. One Prussian official familiar with the South Prussian era judged that the state's inability to win the population's loyalty stemmed in large measure from the mistakes of its administrators: "The Prussian bureaucrats there were guilty of ignorance and unhelpfulness. They did not understand the new nation, and neither did they try to serve it."[13]

One revealing index of Prussia's failure in South Prussia was the warm response there to Napoleon's invasion in 1806. When news reached Poznań that the French army had crushed Prussian defenses and was advancing eastward toward the city, large numbers joined in spontaneous celebration. Beyond the army and bureaucratic corps, few felt committed to the government in Berlin. Justus von Gruner, a Prussian administrator stationed in Poznań at the time, glumly noted the following in a secret report to his superiors: "One must admit that [public support for Napoleon here] is widespread. No one has dared to avoid participating in it, let alone offer resistance."[14] Napoleon arrived in Poznań on November 27 to a hero's welcome.

After defeating Prussia and Austria on the battlefield, Napoleon stripped them of their Polish territories and resurrected a state there, dubbed the Duchy of Warsaw. A version of his Napoleonic Code served as its constitution, and governing institutions were assembled in short order. Most residents enthusiastically welcomed this development. Despite a surplus of goodwill, though, the duchy was saddled with tremendous difficulties. Throughout its brief history it suffered under staggering financial and personnel contributions to Napoleon's relentless military engagements.

Napoleon's hegemony over much of Europe, however short, transformed the continent's political and social orders. His regime was ultimately responsible for bringing many of the ideas of revolutionary France into the mainstream, particularly in French client states such as Poland. Lacking the traditional foundations of political legitimacy, Napoleon relied on the popular will, of which he was a master manipulator. In the new Duchy of Warsaw the promise of independence stirred the dormant ambitions of the nobility and won their support for his revolutionary agenda. Meanwhile the constitution he prepared for the duchy helped instill a new sense of political investiture for those outside the nobility. It did away with many traditional caste distinctions by abolishing serfdom, fostering parity between confessions, and declaring the equality of all before the law. It even cleared the way for Jewish integration into mainstream society, a proposal that was promptly suspended for ten years in the face of intense Christian opposition.

These legal changes placed the duchy's social order on a much more egalitarian basis than before, at least in theory. All the while, a steady diet of wartime propaganda stoked patriotic sentiments. Bound together by a common cause, its inhabitants demonstrated a solidarity uncommon to a society once rigidly compartmentalized. Ironically, it was in this period of French domination that many residents of the duchy first developed a strong sense of Polish nationalist identity. They came to see themselves as linked to their fellow citizens, regardless of caste and confession, by virtue of a shared belonging to the Polish state.

Napoleon had a similar effect on the Germans. During the decade in which he dominated much of the German-speaking world (1803–13), German nationalist identity began making sense to unprecedented numbers of people. Many grew dissatisfied with the political fragmentation of the German population of Central Europe that rendered it helpless before large states like France. They also started to question the ancien régime models of state and society under which they lived, models that paled in comparison to the new alternatives of human equality and broad political enfranchisement practiced in the United States and France. The dream of a strong united Germany in tune with the political ideals of the age fired their imaginations, particularly in 1813 and 1814 when the tide of battle turned against France.

The Duchy of Warsaw's fate was closely linked to Napoleon's own, and after his disastrous Russian campaign its days were numbered. Russian troops followed on the heels of Napoleon's forces, reaching Poznań on 13 February 1813. Questions of sovereignty were eventually solved at the Congress of Vienna in 1815. Here the rulers of Prussia, Russia, and Austria—known collectively as the Holy Alliance—decided to repartition the Polish territories among themselves. Poznań and most of Great Poland were placed once again under Prussian control. During their deliberations in Vienna the alliance recognized that much had changed during the Napoleonic era. The experience of independence and the tenor of the times had electrified the political ambitions and cultural sensitivities of many Poles. Forcing them now to assimilate wholly into the dominant culture of a partitioning power could backfire badly. For this reason the Treaty of Vienna guaranteed the Poles greater political autonomy and respect for the Polish language and culture.

In keeping with the treaty, King Friedrich Wilhelm III (1797–1840) granted the Prussian portion of Great Poland a quasi-independent status. The region, renamed the Grand Duchy of Poznań, was placed under the symbolic authority of a Polish viceroy *(Statthalter),* Prince Anton Radziwiłł. In the 1820s the king authorized the creation of a provincial congress *(Landtag)*—once again with symbolic authority—in which the region's elite could voice their concerns. Poles also found entry to many lower and midlevel bureaucratic posts and were assured that their language would enjoy parity with German. Prussia was careful, though, to hold on firmly to the reins of power in the grand duchy. High-level posts, such as provincial governor *(Oberpräsident)* and police commissioner, were staffed exclusively by those whose loyalty to the Crown was beyond question.

After so many years of war, the large majority of the grand duchy's population had a tremendous hunger for peace and stability. Initially most Poznanians accepted the resumption of Prussian control with equanimity, if not quiet relief. The Duchy of Warsaw had disappointed the lofty expectations surrounding it and generated a new appreciation for Prussia's virtues, including relatively honest, efficient bureaucracies and a ruler free of megalomaniacal tendencies. It was not long before the new political order took on an air of normalcy and generated either fondness or enmity among those with firm ideological commitments. Conservatives could take comfort in the state's

Map 2. Grand Duchy of Poznań, 1815–48.

defense of monarchal rule, the social hierarchy, and religion. Liberals, by contrast, lamented what they considered to be a reactionary regime opposed to their core values of human equality, constitutional government, and the right of nations to self-determination.

By no means an organized group, conservatives in Poznań spanned nationalities and encompassed divergent concerns. Their ranks included much of the region's wealthy nobility, who benefited handsomely from the status quo, as well as large portions of the peasantry, who tended to be shy of change. They were united in their preference for the Prussian Crown and the rather traditional order it represented over any form of political or social experimentation that might replace it.

Prussia enjoyed the unwavering loyalty of many prominent Polish nobles, including Viceroy Radziwiłł. He was married to the Prussian king's daughter, but his loyalty extended well beyond the familial: Radziwiłł was convinced that Polish interests were best served under the Prussian scepter. During his tenure in office Radziwiłł strove to mold his fellow Poles into model Prussian citizens. Other conservatives included the brothers Edward and Atanazy Raczyński, two of Poznań's most influential citizens. From an early age both were inculcated with a strong sense of their heritage as Polish nobles and an even stronger hatred of revolution. Their grandfather Kazimierz, the former *voivode* of Great Poland, had taught them that the royal house under which they lived, be it Polish or Prussian, ruled by the grace of God, and loyalty was the moral obligation of all subjects. The brothers never wavered from their grandfather's teaching. The revolutionary character inherent in the struggle for Polish independence alienated them from the start.[15]

Liberals were likewise diverse, though their numbers tended to be younger, well educated, and from the bourgeoisie or petty nobility. For Polish liberals, the effort to reestablish an independent Poland resonated both with their political ideals and a burgeoning feeling of national pride. German liberals were drawn to this same cause more by political concerns, recognizing in a resurrected Poland the chance to create a constitutional republic in the heart of conservative Central Europe. The local gymnasium was one hotbed of liberal thought. Polish and German students alike engaged in subversive talk about the need for revolution, talk that eventually prompted Prussian authorities to crack down on the institution. But in general Poznań in the 1820s lacked the kind of forums that nurture political activity. Liberal intellectuals often looked to progressive circles in Warsaw and Berlin for inspiration.

Quite a few Poznanians studied at German universities, and many were deeply influenced by the liberal climate there. One such student was Karol Marcinkowski (1800–1846). Born to a family of modest means in the St. Adalbert suburb, Marcinkowski was able to pursue university study in Berlin thanks to Anton Radziwiłł, who funded the educations of talented, underprivileged boys from the grand duchy in the hopes of fostering their identification with Prussia. Just the opposite happened to Marcinkowski. In Berlin he joined Polonia, a secret society that, in the words of one Prussian minister, maintained as its goal "the restoration of the former Polish kingdom in its geographical and political integrity" and encouraged within members "the belief that they belong more to the Polish nation than to the Prussian state."[16]

As the 1820s wore on, Prussian officials monitored attitudes in the grand duchy with increasing concern. Mounting evidence suggested that many residents nursed the hope of eventual Polish independence. The grand duchy's provincial congress began operating in 1827 and quickly emerged as a sounding board for Polish nationalist concerns.[17] Around the same time Prussian police took note of a variety of suspicious actions, such as a gathering to celebrate May 3, the anniversary of the 1791 Polish-Lithuanian Constitution.[18] Concern turned to outright alarm in 1830 with the outbreak of the November Uprising in the Congress Kingdom of Poland, that part of the former Polish state under Russian control.

The November Uprising unfolded at a time of mounting revolutionary ferment across the continent. In 1830 the Greeks declared independence from the Ottoman Empire, and revolutions toppled governments in France and Belgium. Convinced that the time was right to strike against Russia's grip on the Congress Kingdom, a radical faction in Warsaw hatched a plot late in November to capture the kingdom's Russian commander, Grand Duke Constantine, and the Russian garrison. Both efforts failed miserably, but they set off a chain reaction. Before long the kingdom was in full revolt.

The conflict never spread to the grand duchy, thanks to extensive Prussian measures to maintain order. Many residents openly sympathized with the uprising, however. Despite Prussian prohibitions, some smuggled money and supplies to the revolutionaries. Others stole across the border to join the fight.[19] Such actions disturbed the king and lent credence to hawkish voices in the Prussian government. Determined to stamp out rebelliousness, the king appointed Eduard Flottwell provincial governor (1830–41) and sanctioned a more repressive political course in the province.

The cornerstone of the new policy was a more aggressive Germanization of the Polish population. In a formal *Denkschrift* summarizing his tenure,

Flottwell described his mission as follows: "To strengthen [the province's] ties to the Prussian state, whereby the efforts, habits, and tendencies of the Polish inhabitants to resist such ties are gradually eliminated and the German element in its material and intellectual dimension is increasingly extended, until which point the goal of complete union of both nationalities through the dominance of German culture is achieved."[20] In 1832 the Polish language lost its coequal status in the grand duchy. The state decreed that, with few exceptions, all government and judicial business had to be conducted exclusively in German. German likewise gained greater prominence in the province's schools. The state took pains to encourage German immigration to the grand duchy and subsidized the land purchases, economic endeavors, and cultural efforts of ethnic Germans.

Berlin also reengineered the structures of power in the province. It moved to undercut the influence of the Polish nobility, whose power it feared and loyalty it suspected. In 1833 it reorganized the election process for the provincial congress in order to break the dominance of Polish nobles there.[21] In the same year the state drafted new charters for the so-called *Medienstädte* (cities under the control of particular nobles) in an effort to free their residents from dependency on the nobility. Meanwhile, Berlin cultivated new allies in the region. It worked assiduously to boost the number of German nobles in the grand duchy by taking over financially troubled Polish estates and auctioning them off at attractive prices to Germans. The state hoped a substantial investment in the countryside would favorably impress rural residents. Likewise it anticipated that the *Vorläufigen Verordnung wegen des Judenwesens im Großherzogtum Posen,* an 1833 law that opened up the possibility of naturalization to Jews in the grand duchy, would create a growing body of German-speaking, loyalist Jews who would augment the political power of the province's German population.

The policy shift in the grand duchy had a profound effect on its political landscape. Up to this point the most important dividing lines remained liberal versus conservative, tradition versus revolution. Conservatives, be they Polish, German, or Jewish, usually felt greater political kinship with fellow conservatives of a different ethnic group than they did with liberals of their same ethnicity. Prussia's new approach lent the issue of nationality much greater prominence in the political arena. With time it would come to overshadow other bases of solidarity.

The balance once sought by conservative Poles—to be at once loyal to Prussia and loyal to one's Polish heritage—rapidly lost credibility among the Polish elite. The Polish aristocracy grew alienated from Prussia as their ranks were squeezed out of many government posts. Anton Radziwiłł, formerly a symbol of Prussia's respect for Polish national identity, found himself sidelined by Flottwell in the governing of the grand duchy. Atanazy Raczyński, a diehard conservative, withdrew from Poznań's turbulent climate and accepted posts abroad as a Prussian diplomat.[22]

As loyal Polish Prussians lost heart, their independence-minded compatriots gained in strength. Russia's suppression of the November Uprising in 1831 proved to be only a temporary setback. Many elites there, having compromised themselves politically in the uprising, fled rather than face prosecution. They eventually regrouped in Paris and other Western cities and established a variety of political factions committed to Polish independence. Prince Adam Jerzy Czartoryski directed the more conservative of these factions, the Hotel Lambert out of a Parisian hotel of the same name. His followers wedded their abiding commitment to monarchical government with the call for a constitution, the abolition of serfdom, and the development of a strong, urban middle class. More to the left and much larger was the Polish Democratic Society (Towarzystwo Demokratyczne Polskie), whose platform called for democratic government and genuine social equality.[23] These and other associations in exile created a vibrant political and cultural life. They published a dozen different newspapers and hundreds of books and pamphlets, and their ideas carried considerable influence in the Polish territories.[24]

In the Polish territories, Poznań gradually eclipsed Warsaw as the center of Polish political action. The independence movement found its most effective leader in Karol Marcinkowski, the same man who ran afoul of the law during his student days in Berlin. Marcinkowski returned to Poznań with a medical degree in 1823 and set up a flourishing practice, but he never relinquished his dream of an independent Polish state grounded on liberal principles. When the November Uprising broke out, he defied Prussian restrictions and crossed the border to aid the rebellion. Marcinkowski later returned to his hometown and served time in jail for his crime. Upon his release in 1837, he resumed his political activity with renewed vigor. The central focus of his endeavor was the Organic Work Movement, which he helped found. Marcinkowski had tremendous respect for the scientific, economic, and cultural achievements of the Germans and believed Polish political ambitions were doomed to fail so long as their nation continued to lag behind in these fields. The Organic Work Movement was designed to strengthen the Polish community from within. Its goals included increasing the number of Poles engaged in higher education and urban professions of all kinds.

The Prussian crackdown also had a profound effect upon the city's German community. The community as a whole had long shied away from an active role in political and cultural affairs, tending instead to defer to the leadership of the Polish elite. The more liberal minded in their ranks often were passionately committed to the cause of Polish independence. As they saw it, rebellions like the November Uprising were being waged not just for Poles, but for all who suffered under the repressive regimes of the Holy Alliance.[25] Several months into the uprising, two Prussian police commissioners named Schultz and Hofrichter, dining at the Stiller Restaurant in Poznań, were shocked to overhear a certain Herr Krumrei, an ethnic German and secretary to the Higher Appeals Court, publicly express subversive, pro-Polish sentiments. According to their account he "mockingly enumerated nearly every [Prussian security] measure taken in light of the Polish issue and praised to the heavens the actions and virtues of the Polish rebels, portraying their uprising as an act of justice that must succeed and which no honest man can view passively." What is worse, his comments met with the general approval of the other German officials in his company.[26]

The situation began to change during the Flottwell era. The advantages Germans enjoyed under the policy of Germanization inclined growing numbers of them favorably toward the state.[27] Meanwhile, association with the Polish cause developed into a distinct liability. A new and more divisive chapter was opening in Poznań's long history of German-Polish cohabitation. As several of Flottwell's Polish critics saw it, his policies "built a wall between the Germans and Poles."[28] Rather than looking to the Polish elite for leadership, the city's Germans began taking their cues from the Prussian military and bureaucratic establishment. As one liberal observer wryly put it, conservative bureaucrats enjoyed "more success here than anywhere else" in cultivating a "Philistine sensibility" (read: unflinching loyalty to a reactionary state) among the German population.[29]

Discontent in the grand duchy mounted over the course of the 1830s, convincing many officials in Berlin that aggressive Germanization was driving the Polish population toward outright revolt. The death of King Friedrich Wilhelm III on 7 June 1840 occasioned a debate on the matter, and his son and successor, Friedrich Wilhelm IV (1840–61), agreed with those urging a softer policy toward the province. The new king initiated a series of conciliatory gestures. Eduard Flottwell, widely despised among Poles, was transferred out of the grand duchy (January 1841) and replaced by the much more congenial Count Adolf Heinrich von Arnim-Boitzenburg. The state liberalized its education policy, allowing Polish children once again to be taught in their own language. It also loosened its tight censorship laws and declared a general amnesty for participants in the November Uprising.

The new king's gestures did nothing to slow Polish political activity. On the contrary, it offered Poles greater room to maneuver and emboldened them to press the state for more concessions. Alongside lawful activity like the Organic Work Movement, there emerged two conspiratorial groups that sought to lay the groundwork for an armed insurrection. The first was the Poznań Committee (Komitet Poznański), founded in 1839 by an emissary from the Polish Democratic Society. The committee was headed by Karol Libelt. Like Marcinkowski, Libelt haled from a modest family in Poznań, but thanks to a wealthy patron he was able to study philosophy under Hegel at the University of Berlin. Actively engaged in politics, Libelt secretly ventured into the Congress Kingdom to support the November Uprising. His action rendered him a persona non grata in Prussia, and it was only after the 1840 liberalization that he was able to return to his hometown.

More radical still was the Plebeian Union (Związek Plebejuszy), founded in 1842 by Walenty Stefański. The son of a local fisherman, Stefański learned the printing trade as a youth. In a display of the social mobility that was now possible in the city, he used an apprenticeship at the local Decker Printing Press as a stepping-stone to form his own printing company and a small bookstore. Along the way he had developed something akin to a socialist political sensibility. He rejected the goals of the Poznań Committee as too modest. His vision of the future included not only an independent Poland but a new social order grounded on true equality. Stefański and his supporters in the Plebeian Union aimed their message at the largest sectors of the population, the urban underclass and the peasantry.[30]

The Poznań Committee planned an armed uprising for the evening of 21 February 1846 that was to occur in all three partitions simultaneously. In Poznań conspirators plotted a surprise attack on the citadel, the large military fort to the north of the city. Ludwik Mierosławski, recently returned from exile in France, assumed charge of military operations. Just days before the agreed-upon date, though, police fanned across the city and arrested scores of suspected collaborators. A noble privy to their plan had betrayed them. Libelt, Mierosławski, and other conspirators were arrested and sentenced to long prison terms.

The failed uprising caused German-Polish relations in Poznań to deteriorate still further. Stung by yet another disastrous setback to their ambitions,

Polish leaders grew more insular in their deliberations. Many Germans, meanwhile, had concluded that their interests would be far better served within Prussia than within a future Polish state. They found a new source of strength in an alliance with the city's naturalized Jews, allowing them to bypass entanglements with Polish leaders. Before 1833, the grand duchy's Jews had been barred from participating in local and regional politics. That changed in 1833 when the Jews were allowed to become naturalized Prussian citizens. By the 1840s they emerged as a small but growing political force, and one strongly inclined to sympathize with the interests of conservative Germans. This was clearly demonstrated in 1846, when two Jews were elected to Poznań's city council. They consistently voted with the German faction, thereby depriving the Poles of a majority within that body.[31]

Recognizing the potential benefits of such cooperation, German leaders started cultivating Jewish support. Emblematic of this new strategy is the career of Eugen Naumann (1803–1880), an ethnic German who served as Poznań's mayor from 1833 to 1871. Early in his tenure Naumann adamantly opposed the cause of Jewish emancipation. His actions reflected the concerns of his Christian constituency, which felt little affection for Jews and feared the prospect of Jewish economic domination. By the late 1840s, however, Naumann began supporting Jewish interests.[32] In Poznań's changing political landscape, the antipathy many Germans felt toward the Polish nationalist movement enabled them to shelve their ancient distrust of the Jews.

In the late 1840s a group of German nobles from the grand duchy, led by August Hiller von Gärtringen, took German opposition to the Polish cause one step further. They publicly urged the government to return to the policies of the Flottwell era, calling for the expulsion of Polish dissidents and the selling of their property to Germans, the stricter surveillance of Polish institutions, and the strengthening of Poznań's garrison.[33] Although the effort did not result in any policy changes, it did signal a higher degree of alienation from the Polish population, as well as a stronger commitment to the Prussian state, among the grand duchy's Germans.

Toward a Modern Society and Economy

As we have seen, nationalism in Poznań was a profoundly political development. Yet the political represents only one dimension of the phenomenon. To more fully understand why national identity became so compelling for Germans and Poles in Poznań, it is essential to consider some relevant socioeconomic factors. The Poznań region as a whole remained overwhelmingly agrarian in this period, venturing only slowly down the road to industrialization and modern capitalism. Its capital city, however, was a progressive exception. It constituted the most dynamic center in the province and was beginning to exhibit many of the hallmarks of the modern era. Not surprisingly, it was here that nationalist sentiments reached their most fevered pitch.

One sign of change in this period was the city's rapid population growth. Poznań more than doubled in size, from around seventeen thousand in 1793 to around forty-three thousand in 1848.[34] Poznań's growth was typical of many European cities at this time. Natural increase accounted for part of it, supported in no small measure by the expanded nutritional capacity afforded by the humble potato. Another factor was urbanization. Faced with limited economic opportunities, many among the province's swelling rural population ventured to the city in search of gainful employment. Poznań beckoned as well to German immigrants from other parts of Prussia.

Such expansion laid the basis for a modern capitalist economy. The city was awash in able-bodied workers eager to seize any opportunity that came their way. What they found, increasingly, was an economy that functioned according to new rules. An array of arcane traditions and privileges that once lent stability to economic relations were disappearing, dismissed by their detractors as medieval holdovers unsuited for the modern era. Blind market forces were gaining in influence, awarding success to those who could produce more, provide superior services, or offer lower prices.

In the craft and industry sector almost all of Poznań's production once had taken place in small workshops under the aegis of guilds. While this system provided guild members a measure of security, it tended to stifle the quantity and quality of production. Prussia gradually undermined these monopolies, granting numerous concessions to individuals seeking to practice crafts outside of the guild system. In 1833 it opened up the sector entirely. Guilds were transformed essentially into voluntary associations, diminishing many of the advantages they once provided. One result was a sharp increase in the number of individuals engaged in craft.[35] Competition grew fierce, forcing craftspeople to increase their production and to accept slimmer margins of profit, and threatening many with penury.

Early stirrings toward industrialization also occurred in the city during this period. Several attempts at factory-style production had been made as early as the late eighteenth century, but these ventures had disappeared by 1815, stymied either by more competitive wares from other parts of Prussia or by the traumas of the Napoleonic era. Subsequent attempts to industrialize after 1815 were initially hampered by a nagging recession and new tariffs on exports to Russia, once the leading market for Poznanian products. Matters gradually improved thereafter, and the city experienced modest industrialization in a variety of fields. An area of particularly strong growth was alcohol production. By 1849 the city contained thirty-three distilleries. The first heavy industry in Poznań emerged in 1843 with the founding of a machine factory by Jan Netrebski.[36]

One example of an early successful industrialist was a German named Traeger. Traeger moved to Poznań around 1820 and opened the first tobacco-processing plant in the city. His timing was excellent. After an 1831 outbreak of cholera, doctors recommended smoking as "a means of cleaning the air." The popularity of Traeger's products immediately caught fire, and he became a very wealthy man. Before long, other Poznanians sought to imitate Traeger's success. By midcentury eight additional tobacco-processing plants had sprung up around the city to satisfy the demand.[37]

While the marketplace could create tremendous opportunities for well-positioned producers like Traeger, enduring success required constant vigilance and adaptation. A negative case in point was a Poznanian named Jagielski, who began manufacturing affordable soap and candles from tallow. According to Marceli Motty, for a time Jagielski's wares commanded a wide clientele among the city's Polish population. But competition grew stiffer, especially as imported products made their way into the city's shops. "Jagielski was not clever enough," Motty concludes, "to modify his factory with the times, to diversify his products and embellish them according to the current fashion, and thus his business folded."[38]

Similar processes were at work in Poznań's commercial sector. At the start of the Prussian era, the city's merchants, marketeers, and peddlers operated under a constellation of factors that conspired to maintain the status quo. Laws delineated who could trade in what goods, and organizations like the merchant brotherhoods jealously guarded their prerogatives. Infrastructural limitations such as poor roads and border tariffs buffered the city from extensive contact with the trends and tastes beyond the immediate region. Ingrained, precapitalist attitudes deplored aggressive competition as immoral, and respectable merchants never ventured beyond modest signs to advertise their wares.[39] The purpose of engaging in commerce was to meet the needs of one's family, not to expand market share. It was to provide necessary products, not to stimulate demand.

Poznań's commercial sector evolved considerably over the next fifty years. Modern systems of financing, such as the joint-stock company, made their appearance, heralding the advent of more sophisticated uses of capital. Improvements in transportation and the reduction of trade tariffs did much to stimulate long-distance trade, especially with Central and Western Europe. Important landmarks along the way include an 1818 law that rationalized customs policy within Prussia, and the 1834 creation of the German Customs Union (Deutscher Zollverein) that dramatically reduced tariffs between participating states. The 1833 order allowing Jews to become naturalized citizens simultaneously freed them of many hindrances in the field of trade. The Prussian Shares Law of 1843 simplified the process of founding new firms and expanding existing ones into limited-liability joint-stock companies.[40]

Poznań's changing environment gave rise to a new generation of merchants. Increasingly, those who succeeded in business possessed a capitalist mentality and the agility to adapt within an evolving marketplace. Karol Marcinkowski concluded that to become a proper merchant in his day required a more extensive education than was previously expected, particularly in bookkeeping and foreign languages. Starting in the 1830s business activity in the city gained momentum. The number of shops rose from 143 in 1819 to 349 in 1846.[41] Merchants began selling a wider array of products, including more imports from Central and Western Europe and the colonial world. They also demonstrated a willingness to lure potential customers with novel marketing techniques. In 1845, for instance, the bookseller Jacob Cohn placed in his display window two controversial prints that depicted allegorically the triumph of Deutschkatholizismus (see chapter 3) over the Roman Catholic Church. Cohn's effort earned him the attention he sought, but it also generated threats from angry Catholics and a monetary fine from the police.[42]

Alongside production and trade, Poznań's economy long included modest numbers engaged in other necessary professions, such as medicine, law, government, education, and the service sector. All of these fields experienced rapid increases in the diversity of jobs and the number of individuals engaged within them. The ranks of government officials swelled as Prussia located its provincial bureaucracies in Poznań. The state also established an appellate court in the city, which created the need for a substantial body of judges, lawyers, and other court officials. The expanding educational infrastructure required ever more teachers. With its burgeoning population, Poznań attracted dozens of investors eager to fund services, cultural centers, and amusements of all kinds. The number of hotels and inns, a rarity in the 1790s, soared to forty-three by 1846.[43] Cafés, bars, and restaurants likewise became commonplace. Poznań's new economy not only produced reasonably well-paid professionals, proprietors, and entrepreneurs, it also created thousands of low-paying jobs. Poznań's underclass grew rapidly as large numbers migrated from the surrounding countryside and points abroad. The construction of the city's massive citadel employed more than four thousand workers in the early 1830s.[44] An army of domestic servants, mainly women, also expanded appreciably.[45]

As the capitalist model redefined Poznań's economy, similar forces were at work in agriculture, the region's largest and most conservative economic sector. In the Polish-Lithuanian Commonwealth, the nature of farming and the social order it supported had been dictated by centuries-old traditions. Prussia's invasion of Great Poland in 1793 set the stage for a major transition. Farmers in the Poznań region suddenly were placed in competition with their more efficient Prussian counterparts. They faced increasing pressure to improve their techniques or perish. What is more, agriculture in Prussia and throughout much of Europe at this time was in the throes of a profound transformation. There was a mounting drive to rationalize agriculture and animal husbandry in order to increase production. Capitalist ideas like profit maximization and market analysis were seeping into a field long dominated by almost mystical notions of agriculture as a moral obligation to God and humankind.[46]

The situation forced changes in the lifestyles and thinking of the nobility, who were the primary leaders of the agarian economy. The system that formerly had enriched large landowners, sustained their less fortunate cousins among the petty nobility, and insulated both from the "demeaning" commerce of the cities began showing signs of strain. In order to survive the nobles had to view their lands less as permanent "estates," granted by right of birth and entailing distinct prerogatives, than as property with the potential to generate capital.

One noble who successfully made this transition was Dezydery Chłapowski. After spending his early adult years in Napoleon's army, he returned to Great Poland to assume the management of his family's farms, only to find them saddled with debt and inefficiently run. Chłapowski moved to enforce greater discipline among his staff. In a symbolic gesture, he replaced the family crest above the main door of the manor house with a clock. In 1818 he traveled to England and Scotland to purchase the latest farm equipment for use on his land. In time Chłapowski's operations began turning impressive profits and attracted a stream of pilgrims eager to learn from his achievements.[47]

Other members of the gentry were not so fortunate. Many borrowed heavily against poorly performing estates and eventually had to sell them and turn to other means of making a living. The threat of penury forced some to do what was once considered unthinkable: adopt an urban profession. A certain Polish noble named Mańkowski stooped so far as to open a café in Poznań, a fate he regarded as divine punishment.[48]

Mańkowski offers a dramatic illustration of a larger trend: the narrowing gap between the nobility and the bourgeoisie in the grand duchy. Before the nineteenth century, the nobility generally disdained Poznań and its uncouth inhabitants, preferring the loftier environs of their country estates. That began to change as the city developed into a more vibrant economic and cultural center. Considerable numbers of the region's nobility took an active interest in Poznań, spending more of their time and money within its confines. They also were more inclined to enter into partnerships with the bourgeoisie. When Netrebski sought to raise capital for his machine factory, for instance, he found investors among nobles and non-nobles alike.[49] This same development was unfolding throughout much of Europe. In Prussia it was stimulated by legal reforms such as the October Edict (1807), which eliminated laws that penalized nobles who practiced urban professions and laws that prevented commoners from purchasing landed estates *(Rittergüter).*[50]

If the divide between noble and commoner blurred at this time, so too did the ancient distinctions that tied the peasantry to their servile fates. Peasant emancipation gained considerable momentum over the early nineteenth century. The 1807 Napoleonic Code granted new rights to peasants in the Duchy of Warsaw, and Prussia expanded upon these rights in 1823. The changes did much to transform the social order upon which traditional agriculture was based. Peasants emerged as independent agents, free to work for their own gain. At the same time they forfeited a measure of security, as nobles were no longer obligated to meet their needs.

Utilizing their new freedoms, better-positioned peasants were able to ascend into the ranks of prosperous, independent farmers. In many instances, though, the new economic reality proved just as enslaving as their former lot. Poorer peasants could not afford to buy land and had no choice but to work for other farmers, a very difficult existence that rendered them vulnerable to economic exploitation. For this reason growing numbers migrated to urban centers like Poznań in search of better opportunities.

On account of these many factors, Poznań's society experienced an uncommon dynamism in the first half of the nineteenth century. Here noble and peasant, day worker and entrepreneur, craftsperson and merchant interacted with one another in an environment where old corporate identities were losing their definitive power. To be sure, the city's social order was not evolving into an egalitarian paradise. As traditional distinctions evaporated, new ones rose to the fore. In particular, wealth and education emerged as leading measures of respectability. Embedded within this revised understanding of society was a greater appreciation of the potential within every individual. A life was no longer as predetermined by a fortunate or unfortunate birth. Under the new regime Mańkowski, a noble, could go on to open an urban café, and Karol Libelt, the son of a cobbler, could develop into a noted philosopher and political leader.

The blurring of old corporate boundaries generated both the possibility and perceived need to create broader forms of culture. The Prussian state, eager to provide Poznań's expanding population with a new sense of orientation, expended great effort toward this end. It built a network of state-run schools, sponsored a newspaper, censored all printed material, and encouraged only those cultural forms and associations that reflected its values. At the same time numerous individuals and groups, independent of the state and often at odds with its priorities, pursued their own culture-building agendas (discussed later in the chapter). New and wider bases of solidarity were emerging at this time, including both German and Polish nationalisms.

To fully understand the development of these broader forms of culture, and especially nationalism, it is essential to consider the intersection of socioeconomic change and ethnicity. Eager to transform the grand duchy's capital into a solidly German enclave, the state offered various financial incentives to Germans across the kingdom to relocate to Poznań. These efforts succeeded in dramatically boosting the German population. Official census data at this time recorded confession, and from these records we learn that the city's Protestant community—nearly all of whom were ethnically German— grew from an estimated 15 percent of the total population in 1793 to over 30 percent by 1846. The number of ethnic Germans rises still higher when German Catholics are considered. According to an 1831 count there were 1,678 German Catholics in Poznań, or roughly 12 percent of the city's Catholic population. Poznań's Jewish community also grew, but at a much slower rate. Estimated at around 24 percent of the total population in 1793, it declined to around 20 percent by 1816 and hovered at this point for the next three decades. It is important to note that at this time growing numbers of Jews sought to assimilate into the dominant culture of the realm. Increasingly they were regarded by themselves and others as a part of the German population, and official Prussian statistics eventually treated them as such. Jewish assimilation thus augmented considerably the government's Germanization effort. The rising percentage of Germans in Poznań came largely at the expense of the Polish community. Statistics illustrate how the city's Catholic population dropped from an estimated 60 percent in 1793 to 50 percent in 1846. Assuming that ethnic Germans continued to compose around 12 percent of the Catholic population, ethnic Poles made up around 44 percent of the city's total population by 1846.[51]

What is more, clear correlations can be identified between ethnicity and the accumulation of wealth. Poznań's German community long had enjoyed relative prosperity. Their financial success appears to have expanded over the first half of the nineteenth century. They gained an important advantage as knowledge of the German language grew more valuable, both in higher education and as a means of exploiting booming trade links with German-speaking lands. They benefited from the government's pronounced preference for ethnic Germans in the hundreds of administration, justice, and police jobs so central to the city's economy. Furthermore, the fact that most of the city's Germans were Protestant is not insignificant. Echoing the observations of many scholars before him, historian Thomas Nipperdey has noted that in this era the "mental disposition" characteristic of Protestants seems to have fostered attitudes conducive to success in the new economy. "They possessed a certain spiritual asceticism," he writes, "with a strong emphasis on work, scholarship and performance, planning and saving, and a distaste for the simpler pleasures of life, like playing cards. Protestant restlessness combined with an ethos which held poverty to be scandalous, and wealth the basis of honor."[52]

Poznań's Jewish community also made financial strides under Prussian rule. Unlike the Germans, they were not the focus of the government's largess, but as a group they possessed important strengths relative to the new economy. Medieval restrictions once had limited the economic endeavors of the community to sectors such as trade and financial services, and the expertise they had developed served them well as these sectors grew in importance under capitalism. Gradual emancipation allowed Jews to exploit these strengths to a greater degree. Over the first half of the nineteenth century the number of Jewish merchants in the city rapidly increased, well surpassing the number of German and Polish merchants combined.[53] Linguistic affinities between Yiddish and German enabled them to take advantage of Poznań's expanding contacts with German-speaking lands.

By contrast, the fortunes of Poznań's Polish community suffered many disadvantages in this period. Their noble elite were slow to reconcile themselves to capitalism. Many clung to premodern attitudes, such as an antipathy to commerce and industry and a preference for lavish expenditure over capital accumulation. Meanwhile, non-noble Poles were poorly represented in well remunerated urban professions and had a difficult time ascending into these ranks. The language barrier complicated their passage through higher education and the requisite examinations. Thereafter, they encountered a state suspicious of their loyalties. Their religion constituted yet another disadvantage. In general, the nineteenth-century Catholic Church inculcated within its adherents an abiding mistrust of their "materialistic" age, discouraging them from the very attitudes and activities critical to success.

A variety of evidence suggests the degree to which Germans gained ground financially as Poles slipped behind. By 1840, two-thirds of all private property in Poznań was owned by Germans.[54] Land ownership was important because it determined who could vote in local elections. It is no surprise, then, that by 1848 a mere 115 Poles qualified to vote compared to 315 Germans. Another measure is the fact that in 1847 the Poles, who at the time composed around 44 percent of the city's total population, were responsible for only 23 percent of its tax revenues.[55]

Such discrepancies were quite evident to Poznanians and undoubtedly shaped their loyalties. In his comparative study of the emergence of nationalism within the smaller nations of Europe, Miroslav Hroch argues that nationalist consciousness can only be understood in light of economic interests. In his view, nationalist political agendas gained momentum when they appeared to address the economic grievances of a substantial portion of a given population. Conversely, in ethnically mixed milieux where the members of one ethnic group concluded that their ethnic identity was an economic liability, they often expressed their frustrations by supporting nationalist causes.[56] The example of Poznań supports Hroch's thesis. While economic discontent was by no means the sole factor behind the rise of the Polish nationalist movement, it certainly played a role. Keenly aware of their declining profile vis-à-vis their German and Jewish neighbors, many Poles came to believe that their interests would be better served in a resurrected Polish state than in Prussia. This sentiment was not lost on local Prussian bureaucrats. Not long after the outbreak of the November Uprising in 1830, a Prussian official in Poznań expressed his concern on the matter in a letter to his superior. He noted that because "considerable difficulties are placed in their way during the job search," many promising Polish youth conclude that "they are at a disadvantage in competition for posts against those of German extraction, even when they have a higher education and better qualifications."[57] In his view, this was why many young people were crossing the border to fight for Polish independence.

By contrast, new economic opportunities available to Germans and Jews in Poznań inclined them to pro-Prussian attitudes. It is little wonder that preferential treatment in the allocation of official posts and financial assistance for resettling and buying land in the region should instill within Germans an affection for their generous benefactor, the state. For Jews, it was not privilege so much as the promise of equality that created strong inducements to loyalty. In 1833, after decades of indecision and half-hearted measures, the government availed to Jews in the grand duchy the possibility of becoming naturalized citizens. To qualify, candidates were required to have considerable financial means and an impeccable reputation, and to conduct all of their public affairs in German. Eager to prove their suitability, many Jews openly demonstrated their loyalty to the state and affinity for Prussian mores and customs.[58]

Culture Wars

There was no overarching culture binding together most residents of the old Polish-Lithuanian Commonwealth, and its weak central government lacked unifying mechanisms like a statewide education system and wide-reaching press organs. In so decentralized a state, the broadest forms of culture were found in the bonds of caste and confession. Prussia operated according to a different model. As an absolutist state, the central government exerted its influence over many aspects of its subjects' lives and tolerated no rivals within its borders. This influence extended deeply into the cultural sphere. Prussian officials understood the potential power residing in cultural expression. They tapped this power in order to further the central government's raison d'état: the maintenance of a stable and prosperous state.

After gaining control of western Poland, Prussia sought to harness the riot of competing voices in the cultural sphere. Its first priority was to erase the new territory's distinctiveness from the rest of the kingdom. Only in this way would it become an integral element of Prussia. The primary strategy in this regard was Germanization. In the words of Provincial Governor Johann Baumann: "The goal of the Prussian government is to reach a point whereby a majority if not almost all of the population in the Grand Duchy of Poznań is committed heart and soul to the motherland. To achieve this goal, an amalgamation of the residents of the new province and the rest of the kingdom must take place. It is obvious that the best way to achieve this would not be for Prussians to become Poles, but rather for Poles to become Prussians. The next step toward this goal is the Germanization of the grand duchy."[59]

Germanization entailed much more than making German the dominant language in the region. It meant the cultivation of "German values," such as obedience to authority, thrift, and economic productivity—values that the state believed were nearly absent in Poland, even among ethnic Germans living there. What it did *not* mean was promotion of German nationalism. As the state ideally would have it, its subjects would exhibit German values while maintaining a strong patriotic attachment to Prussia.[60]

The state seized upon education as the most effective tool for achieving its cultural agenda. The educational system inherited from the Polish-Lithuanian Commonwealth had its strengths, but it was not suited for Prussia's goals. From the state's point of view, too few children were receiving an elementary education, too much instruction was conducted in Polish, and curricula were determined mainly by Catholic and Protestant church officials. The Prussian state was not opposed to confessionally affiliated schools per se, but it wanted greater control over the content of instruction. It gradually reengineered the educational system to more closely resemble Prussian models.[61]

During the South Prussian era, progress toward these goals was hampered by the province's lack of funds and personnel. In an effort to raise elementary school enrollment, the state made attendance obligatory for all children, at least in theory. In practice the numbers of schools and teachers were far from sufficient. In Poznań, by 1805 only around 40 percent of the child population attended one of the city's seven elementary schools or received private instruction. In 1803 the government reorganized the city's gymnasium, introducing a typical Prussian curriculum as well as a more prominent role for the German language.[62] Yet another achievement was the establishment of a teacher's college in Poznań.

More progress was made after 1815. Only one of Poznań's elementary schools had survived the Napoleonic era. The government oversaw the rebuilding of this infrastructure, establishing eight additional schools by 1849. In 1825 it enacted more forceful legislation regarding the obligatory schooling of children, penalizing parents who resisted.[63] These efforts bore fruit in the form of increased enrollment and literacy rates. By 1839, around 72 percent of all school-aged children in Poznań were enrolled in school.[64]

Eager to mold the region's elite into proper Prussians, in 1824 the government made German the primary language of instruction for the three upper classes of the gymnasium, a move that stirred heated protest among the city's Polish community.[65] In 1834, in response to that institution's burgeoning size, the state divided the gymnasium into two confessional parts: the original institution, named after St. Mary Magdalene, was reserved for Catholic students, while a new one, named after Friedrich Wilhelm, was established for Protestants. Although the student body at the Catholic gymnasium was overwhelmingly Polish, German continued to serve as the dominant language of instruction. Courses were taught exclusively in German at the Protestant gymnasium.

Beyond education, the state employed other cultural means to achieve its goals. Early in the century the king personally financed the building of a theater in the city. He was persuaded to do so by Prussian officials in Poznań who trumpeted the practical benefits of such an institution: "We would like to observe in all humility that a good German theater house would promote in no small measure the desire to learn the German language. In so doing it would help to gradually amalgamate the two nations that currently inhabit South Prussia, an advantageous development to which Your Royal Majesty is surely not opposed."[66] The state also sponsored the creation of several newspapers through which it could broadcast perspectives favorable to its ends.[67]

As the state plied its cultural agenda, it found itself faced with a swelling chorus of competing voices. The population was growing larger and more literate, which meant that the city was home not only to more consumers of culture but to more producers as well. During the first half of the nineteenth century the cultural life of Poznań evolved substantially, as the old boundaries of locale, caste, and confession that once defined the limits of meaningful social interaction began declining in significance vis-à-vis ethnic boundaries. This is especially clear in the spheres of scholarship and the arts, where a diverse array of explicitly German and Polish endeavors invited city residents to reimagine their social identities in ethnic terms.

Educated members of the many German-speaking countries of Central Europe have felt for centuries a sense of connectedness based on a common cultural foundation. Already in the sixteenth century humanist intellectuals living in the Holy Roman Empire were demonstrating an interest in the ancient Germans and writing works of history with a distinctly German focus.

This perception of a shared heritage, however, was restricted mainly to language and culture, bearing none of the political ambitions associated with modern nationalism. Neither was this perception very inclusive. For educated Germans of the sixteenth century, the "nation" encompassed only those people of higher station. The rest of the population was regarded as wholly different, ill bred and dangerous.[68] In the eighteenth century expressions of German nationalist identity grew more elaborate and compelling. One factor behind this development was the Enlightenment's recognition of all humans as worthy rational beings, a perception that challenged once-sacrosanct hierarchical social models and opened the possibility of wider forms of social identity. Also at work was the desire of many German intellectuals to resist the cultural hegemony of France. They displayed a growing appreciation of the German language and culture in scholarship, literature, and the arts.

National identity came to be seen by many German intellectuals as a spiritual force that animates the expression of those who possess it. Of signal importance for the development of such ideas was the work of Johann Gottfried Herder (1744–1803). Herder argued that humankind consists of many diverse expressions of one divine order. Every nation has its own unique characteristics and purpose. That uniqueness rests in large measure on the formative power of language, which conditions how a nation encounters the world. To discover the truest essence of a nation, Herder recommended looking to simple people in the countryside who live in relative isolation from foreign influences.[69]

It was Napoleon's domination of the German-speaking world that allowed German nationalist ideas to find a broad and passionate reception. Lofty descriptions of the binding power of language and culture won eager adherents in a region whose political fragmentation had exposed it to the grandiose machinations of the diminutive emperor. And in a period when all things French became synonymous with foreign exploitation, many Germans took newfound pride in the exalted conceptions of German culture formulated by nationalist theorists. Such sentiment motivated a new generation of scholars and connoisseurs to sound the depths of the German soul. The effort proceeded on many fronts, ranging from the collection of German folk legends and sayings à la the brothers Grimm to lively debates over the "Germanness" of various architectural styles.

The idea of a shared culture binding together all Polish people followed a similar trajectory. Unifying factors such as language and history were long acknowledged, but they were overshadowed by more immediate differences.

The gulf between noble and serf was particularly difficult to bridge, as were regional affiliations. Poles could point to a common political history, but even this heritage was complicated by the tremendous diversity that characterized the Polish-Lithuanian Commonwealth. It was only after the dissolution of the commonwealth that notions of Poland as a unified cultural entity generated more compelling interest. Faced suddenly with life under foreign crowns and the wholesale liquidation of Polish traditions and institutions, many Poles grew intensely nostalgic about the past. Meanwhile, new ideas such as Herder's cultural definition of nation were in circulation and, to borrow Benedict Anderson's memorable phrase, "available for pirating."[70] Polish thinkers expended great efforts defining the essence of the Polish nation, and growing numbers of Poles found orientation therein.

Polish nationalists placed great emphasis on Poland's status as a "historical nation" with a legacy of political independence stretching back to the early Middle Ages. As a result, there was, in the first half of the nineteenth century, an extensive engagement with Polish history. A new generation of historians, including Joachim Lelewel and Jerzy Samuel Bandtkie, endeavored to depict the nation's past and explain its tragic fate in the modern era. History also provided the inspiration for much of the period's literature. Along with a host of largely forgotten writers, more enduring figures like Julian Ursyn Niemcewicz transformed elements of the Polish past into dramatic, engaging narratives.[71] Nationalist-minded organizations emerged, such as the Society of the Friends of Scholarship (Towarzystwo Przyjaciół Nauk), founded for the purpose of preserving the Polish language and historical legacy. Philosophers weighed in as well, attributing to the Polish nation a world-historical mission. Perhaps the most influential figure in this regard was the poet Adam Mickiewicz, who described Poland as a Christ among nations, crucified according to a providential plan that would lead to the redemption of the world.[72]

Early in the century the uncontested center of Polish cultural activity was Warsaw. Although growing, Poznań remained something of a provincial backwater. The region's nobility infused the city with a degree of sophistication, but many nobles tended toward more cosmopolitan tastes. Atanazy Raczyński, for instance, was a devoted connoisseur of German art and was more likely to communicate in German or French than he was in Polish, even with his own Polish relatives. Another area noble, Bernard Potocki, demonstrated similar preferences. In his memoirs, Motty recalls that Potocki "gave the impression of being a foreigner, especially because he spoke almost exclusively in French, and when he spoke Polish his pronunciation and diction betrayed foreign influences." He never took part in any of the region's Polish institutions or cultural endeavors and openly displayed an "ambivalence toward our people."[73]

With time, however, growing numbers of Polish Poznanians developed passionate commitments to what they perceived as their national culture. This process gained considerable momentum in the 1830s, in part as a response to the state's Germanization campaign. Faced with the likely decline of their cultural heritage, many Poles rallied to its defense. This impulse found still greater expression in the years 1840–46. With the relaxation of censorship laws, nationalist-minded Poles turned to the printing press to promote their causes. They were joined by an influx of Polish intellectuals from Russia, Austria, and Western Europe, drawn to Poznań's newly tolerant climate. Virtually overnight the city emerged as the cultural capital of the Polish-speaking world.

In this era a number of Poznanians made significant contributions to the burgeoning field of Polish historiography. They included Edward Raczyński, whose projects included a two-volume history of Great Poland.[74] More importantly, he financed the publication of many original documents illustrative of the Polish past, including a twenty-volume collection of journals, letters, and other material from the eighteenth century.[75] Jósef Łukaszewicz (1799–1873) wrote a number of highly respected historical monographs while promoting the understanding of history as a teacher at the Friedrich-Wilhelm Gymnasium, as municipal archivist, and as chief librarian at the Raczyński Library.

This interest in Polish history and culture extended well beyond scholarly forays into the archives. Poznanians celebrated significant anniversaries, like May 3, the date the Polish-Lithuanian Constitution of 1791 was ratified. Some prominent nobles, including Jósef Napoleon Czapski and Seweryn Mielżyński, demonstrated their cultural commitments by donning traditional (and very outmoded) forms of dress such as the *kontusz,* a long robe worn by men.[76] In the spirit of Herder, many Poznanians displayed a newfound interest in the culture of the Polish peasantry. After settling in Poznań in 1843, the celebrated poet Ryszard Berwiński (1819–1879) set off on extended rambles through the surrounding countryside to record the folklore and fairy tales of its inhabitants. Around this same time a local publisher issued a collection of Polish folk songs gathered by Oskar Kolberg.[77]

The Polish language and literary tradition also won devotees. Tomasz Szumski (1778–1840), a teacher and bookseller by trade, promoted an informed appreciation of his native language through the publication of several books on Polish grammar. Jósef Muczkowski (1795–1858), a professor of Polish and Latin at Poznań's gymnasium from 1819 to 1827, also published a guide to Polish grammar and edited a collection of poems by Mikołaj Sęp Szarzyński, a sixteenth-century Polish writer who had faded into obscurity before Muczkowski helped raise his profile.[78] Meanwhile, contemporary writers found in Poznań a wellspring of support for those aspiring to add luster to the nation's literary legacy. As the young Adam Mickiewicz was building his reputation in Warsaw in the 1820s, 365 wealthy residents of the Poznań region contributed to the publishing of a four-volume collection of his work.[79]

In the field of theater, Polish aspirations were hampered by infrastructural limitations. The city's one stage was dominated by German plays, and the state was reluctant to permit the building of a second theater for Polish productions. Polish theater enthusiasts had to content themselves with occasional performances by visiting troupes from Warsaw and Cracow or local, amateur efforts. Heinrich Heine noted that during his stay in the city, such events usually generated great interest and packed houses: "All the Poles in Poznań visited the theater out of patriotism. Most of the Polish nobility with estates in the area traveled to Poznań to witness plays in Polish."[80]

In the 1840s Poznań emerged as an important center of Polish philosophical thought, which at this time was consumed with questions pertaining to nationhood. Enlivening the scene was the arrival of August Cieszkowski, regarded as one of the most important Polish philosophers of his day. Another eminent philosopher, Bronisław Trentowski, had hoped to settle in Poznań as well but was blocked by Prussian authorities. He maintained strong contacts in the city, though, and in 1840 Edward Raczyński, Karol Marcinkowski, and others collected funds to support his work. Concerned that most major philosophical texts by Polish authors were published in German, they supplied Trentowski with a yearly pension to enable him to write an important philosophical work in Polish. Trentowski eventually completed a four-volume study of "national pedagogy" published—in Polish!—in 1842.

Polish cultural activity in Poznań blossomed in tandem with a growing cultural infrastructure. In the 1820s Edward Raczyński funded the building of the Raczyński Library, a stately structure modeled after the Louvre in Paris. In addition to serving as the city's first public library, Raczyński intended the institution to house a salon that would nurture a body of sophisticated artists and intellectuals. Another critical resource was the emergence of numerous Polish-language journals. Titles included *Tygodnik Literacki* (Literary weekly), a sophisticated forum for the discussion of literature, history, philosophy, and society that quickly emerged as the leading Polish publication of its kind; *Orędownik Naukowy* (Scholarly advocate), which included a similar range of material from a more conservative political perspective; *Rok* (Year), a philosophical and political journal produced by the democratic camp; and *Przeglądem Poznańskim* (Poznanian review), founded by a group of wealthy, conservative Catholics as a sounding board for their perspectives. These publications created lively forums where literate members of the Polish community shared common concerns and interests.

As the above list of periodicals suggests, the cultural scene among Poles in Poznań was fractured along political lines. There were those who favored a loyalist course toward Prussia and those who secretly plotted insurrections, those who defended tested social models and those who envisioned egalitarian utopias. What united them was the mounting conviction that they were one people, linked together by the powerful bonds of history, language, and character. These bonds were regularly described in metaphysical terms. In an open letter to Flottwell, an anonymous group of Poznanians launched their condemnation of his policies with what they regarded as an obvious proposition: "You will grant us that every nation, regardless of its political situation, exists according to the Creator's law and design, and therefore has to reach its foreordained place in the order of nations."[81] And indeed by this time such a proposition was considered obvious among most educated Poznanians. It was a deeply attractive message, an invitation to belong to something truly great, something that accorded with God's masterful plan for the world. As Poles adopted this worldview, their sense of self adjusted accordingly. They came to honor their native tongue as a thing of wonderment, an irrevocable passport for the journey toward Poland's divinely ordained destiny. The present began to resonate in sympathy with an illustrious past. Time-tested customs evolved into rituals of great solemnity.

Prussia's new king, Friedrich Wilhelm IV, underestimated the commitment to national culture among Poles in the grand duchy. The concessions he made early in his tenure were intended to eliminate Polish grievances. His basic position on Polish nationalism, however, was not so removed from that of his father. In 1841 he sent a formal statement to the provincial congress gathered in Poznań in which he condemned the separatist tendencies cultivated by Polish leaders. Employing the language of Hegelianism so in vogue at the time, he argued that the antitheses *Polish* and *German* should find a higher synthesis in a strong Prussian identity. It was the obligation of all residents to put aside divisive national allegiances and focus their loyalties on the Prussian Crown.[82]

The king's statement was not well received by the Polish community. Provincial authorities in Poznań heard reports of widespread disgruntlement. When the provincial congress met again in 1843, one of its delegates, Andrzej Niegolewski, delivered a formal response to the king that captured the sentiments of many Poles: "No, Sire, in terms of nationality we are not Prussians. . . . Language, custom, and memories of the past—these are the foundations of nationhood. . . . What is more, I will state simply that I do not know of the Prussian nationality at all, for I see in this country neither a unique language, nor unique customs, nor historical memories shared by all of its provinces."[83]

The king's statement and the response it engendered underscore the widening gap between the state's cultural ambitions and Polish grassroots efforts. Despite Prussian attempts to mold them into German-speaking, Prussian-thinking citizens, many Poles pursued contrary agendas with growing determination. Nowhere were these cross-purposes so evident as in the field of education. Here where the state placed its greatest hopes, challenges began arising at every turn. In the 1840s the Catholic gymnasium was the site of a series of disturbing violations. In the wake of the failed uprising early in 1846, the institution's director, Father Jacub Prabucki, and four of its Polish professors were fired for not supporting the government's efforts to stifle dissent. In April of 1846 concerned Prussian officials filed a report to the king regarding recent problems at the institution. They described a school rife with subversive political activity. The situation was so dire that, in their view, the temporary closure of the gymnasium appeared justified: "It is not a matter of just a few students engaging in illicit political activity. Rather there is a general spirit throughout the institution that flies in the face of discipline and obedience."[84] A year later Aleksy Prusinowski (1819–1872), a priest who taught religion, Latin, and Polish at the gymnasium, was fired for what provincial officials regarded as subversive pedagogy. He had his students read "On the Necessity of Learning One's Mother Tongue," an essay condemning Prussia's language policy in the grand duchy. He also led his students through Mickiewicz's epic *Konrad Wallenrod,* which, in the eyes of Prussian authorities, "seethes with hatred of the Germans from beginning to end."[85]

In comparison with the Poles, the cultural endeavors of Poznań's German community lagged well behind. Traditionally they had deferred to the Polish elite for cultural leadership, a pattern that continued well into the nineteenth century. In his history of the city even the German scholar Moritz Jaffe, whose sympathy for Poznań's German population is abundantly clear, accused them of "philistinism" *(Spießbürgerlichkeit)* in terms of arts and letters.

He writes, "Not one of them made a distinguished name for themselves, either in scholarship, in art, in the civil service, or in a bourgeois profession."[86]

Poznań's Germans not only lacked a tradition of cultural striving, they were also slow to respond to the call for a national culture. The short, sad career of Julius Maximilian Schottky (1795–1848) in Poznań offers a good example. Schottky was born in Upper Silesia and studied law in Breslau before pursuing a degree in German studies in Vienna. He first arrived in Poznań around 1822, the same year Heinrich Heine graced the city with an extended stay and memorialized it in an essay. Heine was clearly impressed with Schottky, who, from Heine's vantage, was engaged in groundbreaking research into the medieval history of the German people. By Heine's account, Schottky recently had spent six years in Vienna poring over restricted archives, and in the process he had amassed a huge collection of material, including poetry, songs, and folk sayings, illustrative of the German past. As a Romantic, Heine was suspicious of Schottky's arid academic approach, but the sheer quantity of material Schottky had gathered offered tremendous insights into the German heritage. For this reason Heine was not only surprised but concerned as well that so eminent a scholar should end up in Poznań. The city lacked the scholarly resources Schottky would need to advance his research. More importantly, as Heine saw it, "One must live in Germany proper if one is engaged in a project that requires a total immersion in the German spirit and the German essence. The whispers of German oaks must surround the researcher of German antiquity. There is a danger that passionate enthusiasm for things German will cool off or disappear completely in the Sarmatian wind."[87]

Heine's observations were prescient. The Prussian government appointed Schottky as a professor of German language and literature at the gymnasium, believing that he would be able to kindle the interest of the restive student body. But his curriculum fell flat in an institution dominated by Polish sympathies, and his lack of pedagogical skill led to chaos in the classroom. Motty was enrolled at the gymnasium at the time and recalls in his memoirs how his fellow students would chatter among themselves, run from bench to bench, and hide behind the furnace while Schottky tried to teach. On one occasion the professor entered a classroom full of uncharacteristically silent students, only to discover that they had placed upon his lectern a herring ringed with potatoes, along with a note that read: "Out of herring tails and potatoes is Schottky's laurel wreath composed."[88] Schottky lasted there just two years. Neither was he particularly successful at his other endeavor, the founding and editing of a German-language journal titled *Vorzeit und Gegenwart* (Past and present).

The journal, whose subject matter included history, literature, art, and poetry, was designed to chart connections between the German heartland and Germans living in the mainly Slavic East. *Vorzeit und Gegenwart* attracted very few readers, and before long Schottky was forced to find a new publisher, change the name of the journal, and publish a more popular range of material in both German and Polish. These measures failed to make the journal profitable, and less than a year into the venture Schottky resigned.[89]

More typical of Poznań's German intelligentsia in the early nineteenth century was another professor at the local gymnasium, Michael Stotz. Stotz was first hired in 1814 to teach history, geography, and Latin. He served as director of the institution from the 1820s to 1842. Stotz never earned a reputation as a serious scholar or pedagogue. He published little, and, according to Marceli Motty's memoir, when he taught, "the greater part of the hour normally would pass in light banter about the news, recent events inside and outside of school, and historical anecdotes." Despite his shortcomings, Stotz was beloved by his students, Germans and Poles alike. His popularity rested in large part on his appreciation of the region's cultural diversity and his ability to navigate with ease between the German and Polish spheres. In marked contrast to the nationalist focus of Schottky's scholarship, Stotz was, in Motty's words, "utterly indifferent to matters concerning nationality and politics." Although he spoke German at home and socialized mainly with Germans, Stotz was equally at home among the city's Polish majority, leading Motty to conclude that Stotz was "a Pole in spirit and instinct." Like many long-term German residents of the Poznań area, Stotz was a product of the region's cultural blending. In fact, his students used to joke that he would begin every lecture with the phrase: "We Poles, we Germans. . . ."[90]

Not counting newspapers, Schottky's journal *Vorzeit und Gegenwart* was the only German-language periodical produced in Poznań in the first decades after 1815. Not until the 1830s would there be other attempts, all of which proved ephemeral. Of these, only one, the *Provinzial-Blätter für das Großherzogtum Posen* (Provincial papers for the Grand Duchy of Poznań), had any bearing on the national question. Founded by Ernest Günther, *Provinzial-Blätter* was decidedly liberal in tone and sought to ensure that "knowledge and the general tendency toward progress not be limited by language and nationality." Despite such lofty ideals, the journal lasted just twelve issues.[91]

Also during the 1830s a handful of mainly German associations were created. The impetus behind these groups came primarily from the state, which sought to lure Poznań's Germans out from the Polish shadow and to create a

cultural infrastructure that would make life more tolerable for Prussian bureaucrats and military officials. The Beautification Society (Verschön-
erungsverein) and the Philharmonic Society came into being in 1832. Failing
to command much interest, both were short-lived. More successful was the
Art Society of the Grand Duchy of Poznań (Kunstverein für das Großherzogtum Posen), an organization created by Flottwell in 1836 that sponsored
art exhibitions from Berlin and other parts of Germany. Flottwell undoubtedly saw the society as a way of winning adherents to German culture. But
such intentions certainly were never stated publicly, for a good portion of the
society's membership consisted of Poles.[92]

In the 1840s a strong German cultural identity and institutions in the grand
duchy came to be recognized by both outsiders and natives alike as a critical
need. Forcing this conclusion was the flurry of Polish cultural activity and, in
1846, the foiled uprising. From his home in Leipzig the scholar and publicist
Heinrich Wuttke began issuing a series of newspaper articles, alerting anyone
who would listen of the need "to enliven and strengthen the national feeling"
of Germans in the region.[93] There is evidence that some Germans in the
grand duchy were beginning to reach the same conclusion. When Gärtringen
and his allies among the local German gentry called on the government for
greater support of German interests, many of their demands were cultural.
They urged the state to promote more forcefully both the German language
and German culture.[94]

3

Catholic Poznań

The first half of the nineteenth century brought profound changes to Poznań. Shifting political boundaries were just the most dramatic of a series of fundamental realignments that were transforming the city and the lifestyles and attitudes of its population. These changes helped create a climate conducive to nationalist ideologies. Though often underestimated, another factor in the rise of nationalism was religion. Throughout the period most Catholics and Protestants in Poznań regularly fulfilled their religious obligations and remained fiercely loyal to their respective confessions. Their religious commitments, in turn, continued to influence the determination of social belonging and exclusion. Poznanians rarely assessed their allegiance to nation in isolation. Religion figured prominently in their judgments concerning identity.

This chapter focuses on the intersection of religion and nationalism among Poznań's Catholic population. The Catholic Church as an institution was drawn into the same vortex of change as that affecting the entire city. From the start the church fit poorly into the Prussian state, and their marriage only grew more difficult with time. Prussia was steadily reducing the church's property, personnel, and power. Among church officials, early despondency gave way to a growing willingness to oppose the state and its policies.

Such murmurings within the institutional church did much to sour ordinary Catholics on the Prussian state. Yet they found their own grounds for discontent as well. Having lived in the Polish-Lithuanian Commonwealth, where Catholicism was the official religion, many found life under the Prussian government deeply disturbing. The state's policy of parity among Christian confessions ensured that many of the prerogatives Catholics once took for granted were no longer tenable. Worse still was the state's vigorous promotion of the Protestant faiths. The Protestant population in Poznań not only had expanded, it also seemed to be enjoying special favors from Berlin.

Many Catholics concluded that their religion rendered them into second-class citizens.

As the period progressed, this discontent would provide fertile ground for the cultivation of a powerful strain of Polish nationalism built upon Catholic foundations. A growing number of the educated Polish Catholic elite began reconciling their religious faith with nationalist principles. Abandoning the rigidly hierarchical social order once so integral to the Catholic worldview, they embraced a new vision of the Polish people as a homogenous nation bound by language, culture, and Catholicism, and enjoying the special favor of God. Drawing on the church's extensive legacy in Poland, they disseminated compelling portraits of this vision to an increasingly receptive audience. In so doing, the Polish Catholic elite channeled the religious sentiments of Polish Catholics toward a comprehensive national identity. They seized upon Catholic frustration with Prussia's religious policies, using it to generate greater resistance to government-sponsored Germanization and to build enthusiasm for a future Polish state.

The inflamed religious passions of the Catholic population and the authority enjoyed by Catholic leaders impressed more secular-minded Polish nationalists. Many concluded that Catholicism could help the nationalist movement win the broad appeal it needed to succeed. In the 1840s the sympathies and strategies of Catholic leaders and secular nationalists began to dovetail. While this expanded the nationalist movement, it also created new divisions. It alienated many secular Germans, who had once supported the Polish cause on political grounds. Meanwhile Polish and German Catholics found that ethnic differences were overshadowing their common religious bonds.

Submitting the Church to the State

After its seizure of Great Poland in 1793, Prussia was eager to win the favor of Catholic leaders. As a Calvinist dynasty ruling over a largely Lutheran and substantially Catholic state, the Hohenzollerns long had recognized the political wisdom of religious toleration. No amount of goodwill, however, could negate the troubling realities looming over the future of church-state relations. The absolutist Prussian state had no room for the large degree of influence and independence the Catholic Church had come to expect in the old commonwealth. Prussia claimed ultimate authority over most aspects of life and actively exercised its right to intervene in matters large and small. Even its most impious leaders supported the work of the three officially recognized churches of the realm (Lutheran, Reformed, and Catholic). In exchange for this benevolence, however, the state expected the churches to serve its raison d'état. It regarded the clergy as state bureaucrats, whose chief responsibilities included instilling their flocks with "the fear of God, respect for the law, loyalty to the state, and honesty toward their fellow citizens."[1] In the South Prussian era the government attempted a delicate operation: to reduce the power of the Catholic Church down to a more manageable level without damaging its instrumental value. It sought to strip the clergy of authority while preserving their loyalty, and to wean lay Catholics from their dependency on the church while not offending their sensibilities or disabling their moral compass.

The government focused its efforts first on the church's immense wealth of real estate. By claiming a share of it, the government could enrich its own coffers while rendering the church financially dependent, and thus more malleable to the state's wishes. Early in 1796 the state claimed outright ownership of all church properties and rights to 50 percent of the rents and agricultural revenues from these lands, leaving their former owners to survive on the remaining 50 percent.[2] Prussia also curtailed the church's wide legal jurisdiction and punitive authority, restricting clerical courts to cases related to religion. When appealed, such cases now ended up before a secular court.[3] The state exercised its authority even over church affairs, exhibiting reserve only on those matters limited exclusively to Catholic cultus and sacramental life. It subjected the appointment of priests to careful scrutiny, seeking to advance those candidates sympathetic to its political ends.[4] It required its own imprimatur on all pastoral letters and religious publications. It began to micromanage the church's economic affairs, creating complex price tables for all church taxes and fees.[5] Because the international nature of the church impaired the state's ability to control Catholic institutions and officials within its realm, Prussia imposed tight restrictions on clerical communication with the outside world. It forbade direct contact with the Vatican, requiring church officials to transmit all communications through Prussian channels.[6] Similar logic guided the decision requiring priests to obtain government permission for local and international travel. Such permission was granted sparingly.

Through its policies Prussia sought to create a streamlined infrastructure of parishes and schools operated by a loyal cadre of priests. It had no such vision for the region's many monks and nuns. In an era permeated with the "enlightened" embrace of reason and mercantile economic principles, cloister residents were accused of a cardinal sin: they had no use-value. While consuming precious resources, they did little to encourage morality and foster obedience. Women's cloisters, moreover, siphoned off potential mothers who might otherwise contribute to the natural increase of the population. The Prussian government moved rigorously to undermine the foundations of cloister life. It slashed cloister income, leaving just enough for the monks and nuns to survive while depriving them of the rich endowments that had once enhanced the appeal of monastic life. It also changed the rules for entrance, raising the age requirements to twenty-five years for men and twenty-one years for women. These new regulations ensured that cloisters would have difficulty attracting new members.[7] In 1803 the government raised the bar still higher, requiring cloister applicants to take a formal examination.

Prussian church policy sent shock waves throughout the Catholic establishment in the Poznań area. Once so successful at defending their privileges and properties, church leaders found themselves suddenly powerless as the political order they once knew dissolved. The Prussian state proved stubbornly unresponsive to their persuasions. Their frustration inclined many to participate in the Kościuszko Uprising in 1794. In the various pockets of rebellion throughout South Prussia, priests, monks, and nuns aided the rebels' cause. After the uprising many tried to exonerate themselves by claiming that their participation had been forced, but Prussian investigators gave little credence to this line of defense, concluding ultimately that a rebellious spirit was widespread among the clergy.[8]

The Prussian government's aggressive response to insurrection convinced Catholic officials of the virtues of obedience. Recent developments in other parts of Catholic Europe, such as the Revolution in France, Josephinism in Austria, and the failing viability of the Papal States, offered little succor. A mood of despondent resignation settled over many priests, monks, and nuns. Even those most affected by Prussia's policies dared to do little more than complain. The prioress of the Theresan women's cloister in Poznań, Sister Augustina Hęszycka, showered her scorn upon Prussian bureaucrats for driving her house into financial ruin, noting in a letter that she and her fellow sisters "must suffer from hunger and want unknown under the Polish government."[9] But like the leaders of other cloisters, she limited her protest to words.

While discontent was widespread, a portion of the clergy responded with unalloyed loyalty to the Prussian government. In a 1793 letter to the king, one cloister abbot wrote, "The benevolent providence of God, which we wish to constantly praise, has freed us from anarchy and its evil consequences and placed us under Your Majesty's glorious rule, a rule under which so many nations live with the greatest satisfaction and from your just scepter enjoy justice, freedom, and the secure possession of their property." [10] Clearly the author hoped flattery would secure favorable treatment from the government, but one should not discount the authenticity of his sentiments. Having lived through the tumultuous final decades of the Polish-Lithuanian Commonwealth, some Poznanians appreciated the stability and discipline characteristic of Prussia and welcomed their introduction to the region.

The loyalty of others rested on ideological grounds. The most prominent embodiment of this was Ignacy Raczyński, bishop of Poznań from 1793 to 1807 and archbishop of Gniezno from 1807 to 1818. Raczyński's commitment to the Prussian Crown stemmed in large measure from his conservative political orientation. He was a monarchist and viewed the Prussian king as the new legitimate ruler of the Poznań region. His sentiments were strengthened considerably by his loathing for the Revolution in France and its political and religious ramifications. Like many, he believed the same revolutionary spirit had animated the reform movement in the old commonwealth and continued to fuel underground opposition to the partitioning powers. In his eyes, this revolutionary spirit threatened to undermine the Catholic religion and push Europe headlong into anarchy. Raczyński proved a faithful friend to the Prussian government. In 1794 he came out strongly against the Kościuszko Uprising. And as Prussian policy toward the Catholic Church in the Polish territories unfolded, he posed little opposition. He seems to have measured any disagreement he may have felt against the need to support the established political order. He also knew full well that, on account of the general fragility of the Catholic Church internationally at this time, he would be fighting any battles from a position of weakness. [11]

Raczyński's political orientation was not uncommon among the higher clergy. Although Prussia had dismantled much of their power, the clergy continued to educate and minister to their adherents with few limitations. Certainly their situation was preferable to that of the clergy in France. Their old freedoms seemingly lost forever, many learned to adjust to the realities of their new circumstances. This attitude was readily apparent when Napoleon's armies began advancing on Poznań. Catholic Church leaders generally did not share the enthusiasm that gripped much of the city. Despite his recent concordat with the Vatican, Napoleon's reputation for cavalier manipulation of the pope and the Catholic Church preceded him. Justus von Gruner, a Prussian bureaucrat who remained in Poznań during the first few months of French occupation, recorded his assessment of the hierarchy's orientation toward the invasion. He noted that "the larger part of the higher clergy" had been "forced" to voice their support for the new regime.[12]

The actuality of the freshly minted Duchy of Warsaw proved bitterly disappointing to church officials. Although it recognized Catholicism as the official religion of the state, the duchy lacked Prussia's conservative orientation and the incumbent impulse to encourage piety. Archbishop Raczyński waged a fruitless struggle to improve matters. In an 1808 letter he accused the government of forsaking its responsibility to the church: "Blasphemy against God, the holy, and the eternal life of the soul goes unpunished. . . . The commandments of God and the church are violated, adultery openly practiced, markets and fairs held on Sundays and holidays. Public officials neglect attending Holy Mass and Easter services, and the common folk look on and follow in their footsteps."[13]

While Catholic leaders struggled in vain to extract concessions from the government of the duchy, parish priests and cloister residents struggled for survival. The state's military obligations translated into crushing taxes and other obligations levied on all church institutions. At the same time, revenues dried up.[14] The church entered a period of impoverishment, undermining its internal discipline and operations. Raczyński presented the matter bluntly in an 1807 letter to the minister for internal affairs: "The previous government, although Protestant, was better to the clergy. Presently, under a Catholic government, they are being squeezed by taxes, financial charges under various names, and the quartering of soldiers, and the oppression never lets up." Two years later he complained that the clergy were "short on food" and "not in a state to hold church services, let alone pay their staffs and taxes."[15]

The Napoleonic era left church officials greatly impoverished and demoralized. After the Congress of Vienna returned the Poznań region to Prussia, the king opted for a relatively liberal approach toward the Catholic Church. Most of Prussia's goals for downsizing the church had already been met. To solve some outstanding issues the government, local church officials, and the Vatican entered into talks that eventually resulted in the papal bull *De salute animarum* (1821). Another high priority for the state was the reform of the seminaries in Poznań and Gniezno. Both government and church officials long had recognized the need to improve the situation, which included instructors with no university education, students with inadequate formal education, and an outmoded curriculum. The state introduced stricter standards, requiring a university education for instructors and a *matura* examination for students.[16]

Though freed from the burdens of wartime, church officials in the grand duchy continued to struggle with financial and personnel shortages. While the professed goal of seminary reform was to produce better-trained priests, a more immediate result was the exacerbation of the priest shortage. According to an 1826 report, a quarter of the Poznań diocese's parishes lacked priests. "The poor seminaries in Poznań and Gniezno, disorganized and barely functioning. . . , are far from sufficient to the pedagogical task at hand and the needs of the church in the region."[17] The situation of the region's cloisters was even worse. The traumatic years of the Duchy of Warsaw had decimated their ranks, and the Prussian king was determined to finish the job.[18] By 1830, there were just forty-one residents in five cloisters in Poznań, or roughly one-eighth of the city's prepartition monastic population.[19] They were joined by a new cloister, the Sisters of Mercy, invited by the king to perform the "useful" task of caring for the ill.

The troubled state of the church factored into diverse acts of rebellion by its members during the 1820s. Some clergy engaged in subversive political activity. Father Adam Loga, a popular instructor at Poznań's gymnasium, belonged to an underground nationalist group during his studies at the University of Bonn, an affiliation that nearly prevented his admission to the Lubrański Academy.[20] Faculty at the academy quietly opposed the government's Germanization efforts, planting seditious seeds in their young charges' heads.[21] A government report later concluded that the seminary "amply nourished the [rebellious] tendencies of the Catholic clergy and in particular their Polish identity."[22]

The nationalist activities of Loga and the faculty at the Lubrański Academy were not isolated phenomena. According to Marceli Motty, "a new generation of clergy" who harbored similar sentiments was coming of age at this time. In his memoirs he describes one such cleric, Father Franciszek Bażyński, whom he knew personally. Bażyński grew up in Poznań, and after his ordination into the priesthood in 1824 he served for a time in the St. Adalbert Parish. Bażyński began engaging in underground political organizing partly out of patriotism and partly in defense of his religion. As he saw it, in a province where the Polish nation and the Catholic Church seemed to be under siege, the fate of both entities was linked together. "In those whose Polish consciousness grows cold," he felt, "Catholic passions likewise will recede." Bażyński eventually paid a heavy price for his actions. In 1836 he was arrested and spent a number of years behind bars.[23]

Berlin gradually lost faith in the Catholic Church as a reliable ally in the task of governing. As its attitude regarding the province as a whole began to harden toward the mid-1820s, so too did its religious policy. Some advisers to the king, concerned that the local Polish church hierarchy commanded far too much authority over the large majority of a potentially wayward province, proposed subsuming the archbishopric under the authority of the more ethnically German archbishopric of Breslau.[24] Circumstances beyond their control foiled the plan.[25] The Prussian government sought as well to hinder the election of the politically suspect Teofil Wolicki as archbishop. This effort also came to naught.

Just as the November Uprising of 1830–31 inaugurated a shift in Prussia's governing style, so too did it open a new, more divisive chapter in church-state relations. Reports emerged from all corners of the province accusing clerics of supporting the uprising. In Poznań priests were charged with offering masses for the success of the rebellion and of trying to persuade "young people from the lower classes" to cross over the border and fight alongside the insurgents. Vicars Loga, Kropiwnicki, and Brzezański from the Poznań Cathedral and Vicar Balcerowski from St. Martin's Church came under suspicion for secretly venturing into the Congress Kingdom.[26] Prussian authorities concluded that many among the Catholic clergy had disregarded their obligations to the state. Retribution promptly followed. The state prosecuted those clergy found guilty of supporting the uprising. It also adopted bold new measures designed to further curtail the church's influence over the Catholic population.

Bent on incorporating Germans into the church hierarchies at Gniezno and Poznań, the government scored its first success in 1832 when it had Joseph Regenbrecht named to the Poznań capitalate. The state also introduced a new order requiring the archdiocesan consistory to conduct all official business primarily in German. Convinced that the Poznań seminary fostered nationalist attitudes among its Polish candidates, the state sought to Germanize the institution. Its efforts resulted in an all-German faculty by the mid-1830s, who taught every subject in German. Not satisfied with these results, the state made plans to erect a new seminary in Breslau connected to the university there, where candidates would undertake their theological studies in a thoroughly German environment.

Prussia's new policy doomed the last of the city's original cloisters. An 1833 order declared that all remaining cloisters were to be secularized within three years. By the end of 1836, the only cloister still in operation was that of the Sisters of Mercy. The government also turned a blind eye to parishes in financial trouble. One such institution was St. Mary Magdalene's, Poznań's central parish. Officially it ranked as a *collegiat,* an elite status supported by a special endowment that conferred prestige and a higher income to its member priests and obliged them to conduct holiday services of unusual grandeur. These services drew large crowds from the Greater Poznań area. Over the course of the early nineteenth century, the endowment shrank as many of its constitutive elements (primarily real estate) were damaged, destroyed, or contested in court. Hard-pressed to fulfill their obligations, the parish's priests turned to the government for help. Karl von Stein zum Altenstein, the minister of religious affairs (1817–40), and Flottwell rejected the request, suggesting instead that the parish's *collegiat* status be eliminated. As they saw it, "If the clerical personnel were reduced and the pomp and circumstance limited, many of the church's visitors would stay home, thereby reducing the parish's expenses."[27]

The archbishop during this difficult era was Martin Dunin (1831–42). After Wolicki's death in 1829 Dunin emerged as the leading candidate for the post, and he enjoyed the full approbation of Prussian officials, who valued both his fluency in German and his aversion to conflict. "If nothing else," provincial governor Johann Baumann (1824–30) noted in a letter, "were Dunin to become archbishop the *ecclesia militans* would cease and the Catholic cultus would become more useful than it was under the previous archbishop."[28] During the first years of his tenure, Dunin did in fact strike a conciliatory tone in his dealings with the state. The new course in Prussian policy eventually disabused him of his willingness to compromise. Starting in 1837 he offered resistance on a number of fronts. When the state first floated the idea of creating a new seminary in Breslau for students from the grand duchy, Dunin initially acquiesced. Later he withdrew his support, rendering the project a dead letter. The archbishop also rejected Flottwell's proposal for eliminating St. Mary Magdalene's *collegiat* status, noting in a letter: "As archbishop I cannot offer a helping hand as one Catholic institution after the other disappears."[29] His boldest move, however, was to follow the archbishop of Cologne into what became known as the Kölner Wirren (Cologne controversy).

The Kölner Wirren concerned marriages between Catholics and Protestants. The Vatican long had instructed priests to consecrate mixed marriages only after both parties agreed to raise any children they might have as Catholics. But it had been the practice of clergy in Prussia to quietly adhere to state law, which as of 1803 required that children of mixed marriages be raised in the confession of the father. Renewed pressure from the Vatican prompted the recently appointed archbishop of Cologne, Clemens August von Droste-Vischering, to reverse course, and in 1836 he instructed priests in his archdiocese to follow the Vatican's instructions. After fruitless efforts to pressure him to back down, Berlin ordered the archbishop's arrest. Prussia's strong-arm tactics raised a furor throughout Catholic Europe. In the eyes of one German church historian, "There is hardly an event since the end of the Reformation in the sixteenth century that moved Germany more passionately and divided it more deeply." [30]

Historical treatments of the Kölner Wirren usually mention in passing, if at all, that a second archbishop followed Droste-Vischering's lead. Dunin sent out a pastoral letter to priests in his archdiocese in 1838, ordering them to follow official church teaching regarding mixed marriages. Berlin eventually ordered his arrest as well, interning him in Kolberg (Kołobrzeg), a town on the Baltic coast. Dunin's arrest raised the stakes in the church-state conflict considerably, ratcheting up the indignation of Catholic Europe and stirring latent antagonisms within the grand duchy.

While Dunin languished in Kolberg, his supporters in the grand duchy used various means to dramatize his cause and heighten pressure for his release. Taking cues from archdiocesan officials, parish priests ceased ringing church bells, draped their altars in black cloth, and led masses devoid of music. An eerie silence befell a society accustomed to orienting itself around the audible rhythms of its religion. More disturbing still, at least from the government's perspective, was what *was* being heard in Catholic churches. Priests were leading their parishes in fervent prayers for the archbishop's release. In some churches a subversive hymn made the rounds, the sixth stanza of which included a provocative plea to God to "topple the wicked enemy, break the chains of slavery, and return the treasure robbed by force." [31] Sensing grave danger in these developments, Flottwell attempted to stop the protests. On 5 November 1839 he informed the clergy throughout the province that he regarded their actions as illegal and ordered them to cease immediately. When this warning failed to have an effect, he stepped up the pressure, authorizing provincial authorities to seize the property of noncompliant priests.

By the end of December 1839 most overt acts of protest had ended, but the original cause of the problem—Dunin's defiance and imprisonment—remained unresolved. When King Friedrich Wilhelm III died in 1840, his son moved to mend fences with his Catholic subjects. While careful not to accept blame for the controversy, the new king released both archbishops. In 1841 he created a Catholic division within the Ministry of Religious Affairs (Kultusministerium), and he loosened press restrictions, allowing church institutions to publish freely documents of a religious nature. [32] His grandest gesture was the 1842 decision to fund the completion of the Catholic cathedral in Cologne. The thaw penetrated all the way down to Poznań, where government officials showed a renewed willingness to compromise. They finally saw Dunin's way, for instance, on securing the resources needed to preserve St. Mary Magdalene's *collegiat* status. The only condition for this assistance was the church's public recognition that the parish's endowment had fallen on hard times due to fire and war and that the state's assistance was to be understood as an act of liberality.[33] Sensing the need to restore its battered reputation, the state sought as much good press as possible from its actions.

Dunin was eager to respond in kind to such gestures. Adverse to conflict by nature, he likely never imagined the extraordinary proportions his act of protest would assume. Upon securing his liberty he sought to regain the state's trust.[34] His sentiments, however, did not correspond with those of many Polish nationalist leaders and Catholic officials, who had little desire for reconciliation with the state. Flush with a sense of victory in the mixed-marriage controversy, they were emboldened to press for further concessions.

Lay Sentiments

A small portion of the Polish-Lithuanian Commonwealth's Catholic population—particularly those among the intellectual elite—long had remained aloof from the religion in which they were raised. Few, however, chose to broadcast such sentiments too loudly. While some skeptics appreciated Catholicism's usefulness as a buttress of the social order, others feared punitive repercussions. The church's power was difficult to circumvent and intimidated even its most passionate critics. After 1793, when much of the church's authority was being dismantled, it still remained potent. In granting the church official recognition, the Prussian state assumed responsibility for defending it from slander and safeguarding its role in society, rendering the institution practically unavoidable for those born within its confines. It continued to supervise many critical passages of life, including birth registration, education, marriage, and burial.

While impossible to quantify, it appears that a growing number of Poznanians adopted skeptical dispositions toward the teachings of the Catholic Church over the first half of the nineteenth century. The Napoleonic era contributed to this trend. Economic pressures impinged upon the church's ability to minister effectively to followers. At the same time the Duchy of Warsaw was flooded with influences from France, where more cynical attitudes toward the church enjoyed common currency. Another factor at work was the influence of secular educational institutions, particularly German universities. Increasing numbers of promising Catholic youths from the Poznań area—Karol Marcinkowski among them—enjoyed the privilege of higher education in places like Frankfurt/Oder, Berlin, Bonn, and Leipzig, only to return home rich in knowledge and poor in piety. During their studies they found themselves immersed in climates that tended to celebrate human reason and dismiss the Catholic Church as an irrational relic from a dimmer era. It became both acceptable and common among the Catholic-born intelligentsia in Poznań to hold critical perspectives on religion.

If skepticism was common among the educated ranks of the Catholic-born population, it was by no means universal. Ample illustration of this comes from Marceli Motty's memoir. At one point Motty describes the church as "something entirely foreign" to educated members of his generation.[35] Yet in reminiscing on the many Poznanians he had come to know in his life, Motty offers literally dozens of examples that contradict this same assertion. He notes, for instance, how for years Jósef Kalasanty Jakubowski (1788–1877), a talented botanist and gymnasium professor, dedicated his free time to the carving of an image of the Black Madonna of Częstochowa into a large oaken disc, a work of art that eventually was offered to the church and displayed in the Poznań Cathedral.[36] Sharing Jakubowski's devotion to the Black Madonna was Władysław Niegolewski (1819–1885), who earned a law degree at the University of Bonn before returning to Poznań in 1845 to launch a long, successful career in politics. According to Motty, Niegolewski's "republican tendencies and his German academic training did not upset the religious piety instilled in him at home. He demonstrated this not only in his final hours but over the entire course of his life, giving to the church its due honor. During trying and anxious moments he sought comfort and insight in prayer, and he carried with him a small portrait of the most holy Virgin of Częstochowa wherever he went."[37] Motty also describes Stefan Raabski (1778–1847), a university graduate who served as an assessor in the provincial government and as editor of the Polish edition of the *Zeitung des Großherzogtums* (Grand Duchy gazette). The most enduring impressions Raabski made upon Motty included his "marked affinity for the priesthood" and his "strong, distinctive bass voice," which would fill the Parish Church when he sang with the choir.[38] Of a similar mold was Alfred Bentkowski (1813–1850), a medical doctor who enjoyed a flourishing practice in Poznań before joining the priesthood in the 1840s.[39]

As these examples suggest, higher education was hardly antithetical to religious faith within Poznań's Catholic population. Meanwhile, the church continued to enjoy the patronage of many of the area's most prominent nobles, including Edward Raczyński and Dezydery Chłapowski. And among the peasants, small farmers, craftspeople, merchants, and urban underclass who formed the bulk of the Catholic population, there is no evidence of any significant slackening of devotion at this time. In short, despite an increase in the number of disenchanted intellectuals, it is clear that the Catholic Church continued to command the allegiance of the large majority of those born in Catholic households.

If anything, there was, during this era, renewed intellectual vigor within the faith unseen for a long time. A dynamic social and economic climate and the city's increasingly direct exposure to the pulse of Western Europe—conditions that helped stimulate Poznań's cultural scene in the 1840s—also enlivened religious discourse. Karol Libelt, the city's premier philosophical mind, is one example. Whereas Marcinkowski, Motty, and many other well-educated, liberal-minded Poznanians found their intellectual and political values at odds with the religion in which they had been raised, Libelt sought to reconcile the two. In his scholarship Libelt advocated democratic government and the emancipation of the broad social stratum still struggling under feudal strictures, but he identified these goals as steps toward the realization of God's order on earth. He saw religion as both an internal experience and a means of forming the spirit of a nation.[40]

At the other end of the political spectrum, conservatives maintained their traditional alliance with religion. One of the leading conservative Catholic minds in Poznań in the late 1840s was Jan Koźmian. As he was coming of age intellectually in Warsaw in the late 1820s, Koźmian adopted the liberal, areligious mentality common in his milieu. But in the 1830s, while living among the Polish expatriate community in France, he gravitated back to the church. By 1845, the year he moved to Poznań, he was a committed ultramontanist. Ultramontanism, a movement gathering momentum throughout Catholic Europe at this time, emphasized the need for solidarity within the church and promoted the central leadership of the pope. Conservative Catholics in Poznań embraced the movement in growing numbers, and they found in Koźmian their most effective spokesman. Koźmian served as editor of the *Przeglądem Poznańskim* (Poznanian review), an influential press organ of the Catholic right.[41]

Most Catholics in the Poznań area not only continued to practice their religion, they remained passionately identified with it. Testifying to this passion were the extraordinary efforts the Prussian government took to avoid antagonizing the religious sensibilities of lay Catholics. In the South Prussian era government measures to curtail the wealth and power of Catholic officials did not pose an immediate danger of outraging the laity. Most Catholics shared in some measure the government's conviction that the prepartition church was too rich and powerful. Paradoxically, anticlerical sentiment and religious piety coexisted in the hearts of many Catholics in the Polish territories at this time. But lay Catholic disgruntlement with their leaders went only so far, and from the start the government recognized the volatile nature of Great Poland's new status, in which a Protestant elite governed a largely Catholic population. During the 1793 invasion, for instance, Prussia tiptoed around the Paulist monastery in Częstochowa, home of the Black Madonna, guaranteeing the monks ownership and control of the sacred icon.

Handling Częstochowa proved easy in comparison to a much larger challenge: harmonizing a region dominated by Catholicism with a state that maintained an official policy of parity between Catholicism, Lutheranism, and Calvinism while cultivating a special relationship with the latter two. Throughout the South Prussian era, the government took steps toward achieving its preferred confessional balance. In the interest of keeping the peace, however, it stopped far short of many of its goals, particularly at points that carried a symbolic charge for Catholics. The attempted secularization of the St. Joseph's Church and Cloister in Poznań is one case in point. The discalced Carmelite cloister had been in decline for some time, and by the 1790s the sizable complex housed only five monks. On 5 July 1801 the government announced a plan to secularize the cloister, transforming its physical plant and gardens into an army garrison and turning the church over to the Reformed community. The secularization plan—and in particular the decision to turn St. Joseph's into a Protestant church—touched a deep nerve within the Catholic community, and their anger quickly coalesced into mass protest. The monks organized a sit-in of sorts, staging around-the-clock worship in the church. A cobbler named Heyderowski emerged as a lay leader of the protest, delivering charismatic appeals to large crowds and organizing petitions to Catholic and government authorities. At the same time, miracles purportedly occurred. A statue of Mary in the church was said to have wept tears, and it was claimed that a portable statue of Joseph could not be moved. Alarmed by the unrest, the Prussian army stormed the church on August 12, forcing the protesters out of the building. Sensing the danger of their course, the government scrapped the most controversial part of the plan. The cloister gave way to a garrison, but the church remained unused for the next two years. Only in the aftermath of the 1803 fire, which gutted much of the inner city and consumed the populace with more pressing concerns, did the government quietly follow through with its original intention.

Government policy during the South Prussian era ensured that Catholicism's dominant position in the public space and time of the city remained intact, and it spared the state from any serious religious discontent in the province. That early harmony was strained during the Napoleonic wars. In an effort to justify the tremendous sacrifices required of war, government and church officials in the Duchy of Warsaw underscored the religious dimension of the conflict. The largely Catholic armies of the duchy and France, they noted, were engaged in battle with Protestant Prussia and Orthodox Russia. Prussian leaders teased out the same theme from a Protestant perspective in their own propaganda. This inflation of the war into an ultimate struggle between religious truth and falsehood made the Poznań area's eventual reabsorption into Prussia all the more difficult.

In 1815, as Poznanians began piecing their lives back together after many grim years and a final, disastrous defeat, the mood in Berlin was buoyant. Prussia's participation in the Belle Alliance and its overthrow of Napoleon's empire took on monumental proportions in Prussian hearts, where it would remain a singular moment of triumph for decades to come. The pious King Friedrich Wilhelm III was quick to spy God's hand in the victory, and he decided his entire realm should give thanks. He presented Catholic officials with detailed plans for a memorial ceremony on 4 July 1816, including the songs, Bible verses, and symbolic acts to be employed. According to his announcement, "The purpose of this celebration is not to stimulate hurtful feelings, but rather to comfort through the hope of eternal life that Christianity affirms, and to quicken in all hearts a feeling of love for the fatherland." [42] Police commissioner Johann Baumann (1815–24) anticipated a very different reaction in the Grand Duchy of Poznań and tried to dissuade Berlin from having such ceremonies staged there. He reminded Berlin that the province's residents had fought for the opposite side and had hoped for a very different outcome. The ceremony, he feared, would make "a bad impression." [43] Baumann's reservations point to the yawning emotional gulf between most of the province's inhabitants and their new king regarding recent events. His objections were ignored, however, and Berlin went on to inaugurate three national holidays related to the victorious campaign, which were to be celebrated in all Christian churches.[44]

Lay Catholic alienation from the Prussian state grew more intense in the 1820s and 1830s. The progressive withering of Catholic institutions provided one source of tension. Catholic officials, stripped of many of their earlier prerogatives and much of their income, no longer aroused the same degree of resentment once so common among the laity. On the contrary, lay Catholics now rushed to the defense of their spiritual leaders. Each successive secularization of Poznań's dwindling cloisters, for instance, aroused an emotional wave of public protest. Eager to close the last of the cloisters, Flottwell assured officials in Berlin in 1832 that such a move "would no longer cause the kind of sensation that has accompanied previous secularizations in this province."[45] He was wrong.

A parallel development equally disturbing to Catholics was the steady growth of the Protestant population and their increasing prominence in economic and social life. Knowing of the king's deep piety and his active support for Protestant communities in the region, many Catholics reached the conclusion that it was the state's policy to promote the Protestant faiths at the expense of Catholicism. Some government actions gave credence to this view. Many of the province's Protestant communities limped along with scanty financial means and no hope of funding a church on their own. Meanwhile, from the government's perspective, the region boasted an abundance of underused Catholic churches. Notoriously thrifty, the state reached an obvious solution: transferring control of Catholic churches to Protestants. The execution of such transfers provoked outrage among Catholics, eventually causing the government to halt the policy. As Altenstein explained in a letter to Flottwell: "The Catholic rural resident is particularly passionate about the formal details of his religion. The transfer of Catholic churches to Protestant communities has demonstrated this clearly."[46]

The measures Flottwell took to undermine the influence of the Catholic clergy on its constituency had, if anything, just the opposite effect. These measures depleted the Catholic public's trust in the state still further and heightened the stature of the clergy. Catholics went from feeling disadvantaged to openly persecuted on religious grounds. The imprisonment of Archbishop Dunin proved to be the decisive turning point. Government officials noted widespread rumors among Catholics contending that Dunin's arrest was part of a concerted effort to suppress Catholicism and promote the

Protestant confessions.[47] The clergy's skillful manipulation of the crisis made Dunin into a martyr for true Catholic doctrine. The Catholic population's extreme state of agitation caused alarm not only in Prussia but as well in neighboring Austria and Russia, where government ministers saw the potential for another Polish uprising. When overwhelming domestic and international pressure eventually forced the state to back down, Catholic Poznań erupted in jubilation. Archbishop Dunin returned to a hero's welcome in the city on 5 August 1840. Similar joy accompanied Flottwell's dismissal from his post.

In this same period relations between Catholics and non-Catholics deteriorated notably. Early in the Prussian era, Catholics and Protestants in Poznań managed to live together in relative peace. Aside from Catholic opposition to the transfer of St. Joseph's Church, there were no major disturbances over religious issues. An important factor behind this harmony was the Protestant tendency to defer to Catholic hegemony. This began to change as the century wore on. As the Protestant community expanded and its political clout rose, its members found the confidence to magnify their public profile. The state supported this impulse and sought to realize greater religious parity in the city. Catholics reacted strongly against these efforts.

Not surprisingly, the mixed-marriage controversy did nothing to foster trust between Catholics and Protestants. Previously marriages between Catholics and Protestants in Poznań had not been uncommon.[48] Dunin's order for priests to adhere more closely to canon law on matters of marriage and child rearing complicated such unions considerably. Couples planning to enter mixed marriages encountered priests unwilling to perform the sacrament, requiring first the conversion of the non-Catholic partner or a commitment to raise children in the Catholic Church. Consequently, conversions between Christian faiths skyrocketed, often embittering the families involved. Catholics grew especially hostile toward Protestants during Dunin's imprisonment, causing Protestants to fear for their security.[49]

As Catholic-Protestant relations soured, Catholic relations with the Jewish community went from bad to worse. At the turn of the nineteenth century, the Catholic majority still harbored a deep distrust of the Jews and rigorously opposed modest Prussian attempts to improve the Jews' legal and economic lot. This distrust was fueled by a combination of economic insecurity, religious prejudice, and superstition. A year after the 1803 fire, for instance, Poznań's German Catholic community requested permission from the archbishop to hold a special service in the Most Sacred Blood of Jesus Chapel to thank God that part of the city had been "miraculously sheltered" from the flames.[50]

Their choice of site was deliberate. The Jews, it was widely believed, caused calamities such as fires. The chapel, built to commemorate the Catholic triumph over the alleged Jewish sacrilege of 1399, offered a supernatural bulwark against this evil.

Catholic-Jewish relations entered a new phase after the 1833 legislation facilitating Jewish naturalization. As Jews moved beyond the ghetto and the restricted economic zones once accorded them, many embraced the German language and culture with zeal. This process sparked feelings of betrayal among many Polish Catholics. The Catholic historical understanding of Poland usually emphasized the state's tradition of tolerating religious minorities, discreetly ignoring the catalogue of abuses so deeply etched in the collective memory of Polish Jews. The fact that Jews were now allying themselves with things German struck many Poles as the pinnacle of ingratitude.[51] Another factor at play was the growing willingness of Poznań's Jews to assert their rights, a process that adversely affected many Catholic institutions financially. Jews began to challenge the legitimacy of the massive debt that was crushing their community. Payments on much of this debt went to Catholic institutions, and as Jews had some debts overturned and tied others up in lengthy litigation, the payments dried up. This was one reason why the endowment of St. Mary Magdalene's Parish ran into trouble in the 1830s.[52]

Anti-Jewish sentiment reached a new high in the early 1840s. The dark legend of the host desecration in 1399 was dusted off once again to provide a focus for Catholic animus during the annual Corpus Christi procession in 1843. The monks at the Corpus Christi Church crafted a small platform adorned with three wooden figures representing the Jewish elders who supposedly committed the 1399 offense, and during the procession "carriers lifted [the figures] up and down in order to stir up the crowd's animosity."[53]

In 1844 Johann Eichhorn, the Prussian minister of religious affairs (1840–48), mailed a circular to Christian leaders throughout the grand duchy, informing them of the heightened antipathy for the Jews among Christians. He urged them "to correct misguided religious feeling and its tendency toward un-Christian hate through teaching and admonition."[54] Vicar Gaierowicz, general administrator of the Poznań archdiocese, differed with this strategy. "Do not tempt the wolf out of the forest without a very good reason," he warned Eichhorn; to preach tolerance toward the Jews would likely only aggravate the problem. Like many educated Christians, Gaierowicz shared the opinion that the Jews had "an inborn slyness" and deserved their bad reputations.[55]

Catholicism and Nationalism

Having stood for centuries at the heart of Poland's political and cultural life, the Catholic Church accumulated an extensive heritage of traditions and monuments associated with the state. This heritage was largely off-limits to the reform party in the late eighteenth century as it sought to generate a genuine sense of political unity in the commonwealth. Inspired by Enlightenment-era thought, most adherents of the reform effort had little use for the traditional social mores and worldview long championed by the church. By contrast, the conservative opposition eagerly cloaked their movements with a Catholic mantle. They claimed to be defenders of the faith and of God's preferred order on earth.

After the partitions, as the political order of the commonwealth faded into obsolescence, Poland's Catholic heritage grew increasingly flexible and its adherents more receptive to the political values of the revolutionary era. Napoleon represented an important watershed in this process. He and his allies in the Duchy of Warsaw employed the familiar authority of the church to advance their innovative political agenda. When a version of the Napoleonic Code was introduced on 1 May 1808 as the new law of the land, for instance, government officials orchestrated an elaborate church ceremony in which the law book was carried up to the altar with great pomp and raised aloft, at which point all were encouraged to cheer, "Long live Napoleon!"[56]

In their enthusiasm for independence, most residents of the duchy responded positively to the political innovations the emperor introduced. The Napoleonic Code weakened some of the formidable legal barriers that formerly had compartmentalized society in the region. The mental barriers that supported this compartmentalization tottered as well. Napoleon's populist political style, combined with the immense military struggle in which he engaged the duchy's residents, ignited unprecedented levels of solidarity. Although there were conservative Catholics like Archbishop Raczyński, who feared Napoleon's innovations were weakening the social and moral order, many others were gripped by Napoleon's call to resist tyranny and social injustice. They found such concepts compelling and began to reconcile them with their religious faith.

After 1815, many committed Catholics retained the political and cultural values they had developed in the previous era. One of the most influential members of their ranks was the future archbishop of Poznań-Gniezno, Teofil Wolicki (1768–1829). Born to a moderately wealthy noble family, Wolicki studied law and theology before finding a position within Poznań's clerical hierarchy. Distinguished by an expansive mind and natural leadership ability, he became a trusted adviser to Archbishop Raczyński. In the 1820s he emerged as one of the most respected Polish leaders in Poznań. Wolicki's political and cultural orientation stood in sharp contrast to Raczyński's and pointed to a significant generational shift within the Catholic elite of the area. Coming of age well before the French Revolution, Raczyński believed wholeheartedly in the foundational theses of ancien régime politics: the divine right of royalty to power and the divinely ordained social hierarchy in which each fulfilled the responsibilities of his or her station in life. Molded within a powerful noble family and elite schools, Raczyński shared with Prussia's ruling elite the high culture of Europe's nobility, a factor that facilitated his positive relations with the Prussian state. While Wolicki was also reared in this noble culture, he came of age during the era of the French Revolution and its volatile aftermath. He was a student in Paris during the early 1790s, an experience that profoundly affected his political perspectives. When Napoleon created the Duchy of Warsaw, Wolicki dedicated himself to the new state and its policies, serving in its National Education Ministry. At the same time he demonstrated a strong commitment to the Polish language and cultural identity, reflecting the growing appreciation among educated Europeans for their national cultures over and above the Francocentric high culture of the old guard.

Wolicki recognized Prussia's systematic efforts to Germanize its Polish population, and he did what he could to stymie the process. He publicly protested the increasing presence of German in the gymnasium. His efforts convinced Provincial Governor Baumann that Wolicki was detrimental to the state's priorities. Referring to the state's intention to Germanize the grand duchy, he noted, "Men in positions of high honor cannot stand aloof from this process. Wolicki hardly belongs to the ranks of such men."[57] Altenstein shared the same view, noting in a letter to the king that Wolicki "stirred up emotions that are not altogether desirable, especially for achieving the assimilation of the Polish element into the German."[58]

Wolicki combined his nationalist sentiments with an abiding attachment to the legacy of the Catholic Church in Poland. He vigorously defended local Catholic traditions and institutions against a state eager to mold the church in a fashion more amenable to the state's aims. One example is the reorganization of the Gniezno Archdiocese, the oldest and most important church bureaucracy on Polish soil at the time. In the old commonwealth, the archbishop of Gniezno was recognized not only as the supreme leader of the church in

Poland but also as interrex and first senator. These political associations made Prussian officials uncomfortable, and after 1815 they sought to eliminate the archdiocese altogether. Wolicki helped rally clerical opposition to the plan. The two sides eventually reached a compromise in which the Gniezno and Poznań archdioceses maintained separate bureaucracies but were placed under a common archbishop based in Poznań. Wolicki subsequently struggled to salvage as much as possible of the prestige and traditions of the old Gniezno archbishopric for its new incarnation, the Archbishopric of Poznań-Gniezno.[59]

Wolicki viewed Poland's national and religious history as inseparable, and he sought to instill this conviction among his constituency. His most ambitious effort in this regard was the drive to erect a grandiose monument to Mieszko I and Bolesław the Brave, two of Poland's earliest rulers, who were buried in Poznań's cathedral. In a widely published appeal for donations, Wolicki emphasized the national and religious significance of the two rulers: "You know from historical accounts of our nation that the earthly remains of Mieszko I and the corpse of Bolesław the Brave were placed in Poznań's cathedral. It is no secret to you that the first enlightened the lands of the western Slavs through the introduction of the holy Christian religion, and that the second expanded the borders of the state in every direction and, by assuming the title of king, laid the cornerstone of the Polish monarchy and made Poland famous throughout the world."[60] Wolicki planned to interweave these two themes in the material form of the monument. He explored various designs and raised a considerable sum of money before his death in 1829. Wolicki's plans were eventually realized through the efforts of his supporters within the Polish aristocracy, chief among them being Edward Raczyński. The project, known colloquially as the Golden Chapel, entailed the redesign of a chapel in Poznań's cathedral. One of the finest monuments built on Polish soil in the nineteenth century, the Golden Chapel gave material expression to the emerging nationalist consciousness among the city's Catholic elite.

The space of the chapel represents both a world and a worldview. Its gilded ceiling swells into a hemisphere, a symbol of the dome of heaven. Below, a range of images refer to important events, institutions, and figures from Polish history. Certainly Mieszko and Bolesław figure prominently. Situated in a niche along one wall, their bronze statues generate the greatest visual gravity in the space, and their achievements are described in the two historical paintings hanging in the chapel. But ultimately the rulers are subsumed into a larger ensemble. They are portrayed as the founders of something greater than their own lives: the Polish nation. God's providential hand operated in

6. The Golden Chapel, detail. In a niche along the northern wall of the chapel stand statues of Mieszko I and Bolesław the Brave. Above is the painting *Mieszko I Breaking the Idols*. Photograph by Robert E. Alvis.

Polish history through their leadership, guiding the Poles to their own unique, divinely ordained destiny.

The heavenly and terrestrial spheres of the chapel are tightly interlocked. In the painting *Mieszko I Breaking the Idols,* the image of the Black Madonna adorns a prominent banner carried by the duke's entourage. For centuries the Catholic Church in Poland has cultivated the notion that Poland occupies a special place in the Virgin Mary's heart and enjoys her protection, and the image of the Black Madonna has long served as an icon of that relationship. The Golden Chapel appeals to this tradition, suggesting that Mary exercised her influence on behalf of the Poles already in Mieszko's day.

7. The Golden Chapel, ceiling. Photograph by Robert E. Alvis.

Painted in the center of the golden dome is an image of God the Father, raising a hand in benediction of the individuals and undertakings below. He is ringed by twenty saints associated with Polish history, individuals who excelled spiritually while on earth and who now serve as heavenly envoys for the petitions of subsequent generations. The second historical painting completes the chain of intercession. The work references the encounter between Bolesław and the Holy Roman Emperor Otto III in Gniezno in the year 1000, depicting the two rulers praying at the tomb of St. Adalbert, the tenth-century bishop of Prague who oversaw Mieszko's conversion. In juxtaposing the human petitioner, heavenly intercessors, and God, the Golden Chapel illustrates Poland's position in the interconnected layers of the Catholic universe.

Mieszko I Breaking the Idols reiterates the connection between heaven and the Polish people in a powerful, narrative manner. The work depicts Mieszko's introduction of Christianity to the pagan tribe over which he ruled. Luminous astride his horse in the center of the image, he leads a parade of clerics through a cluster of submissive Slavs, their idols scattered before him on the ground. The image of breaking idols draws obvious parallels to the Old Testament and Moses' efforts to lead the Israelites away from their idolatrous ways and toward the proper worship of Yahweh. It establishes Mieszko as a new Moses spreading true religious teachings to a new chosen people, the Poles.

Wolicki and Edward Raczyński were by no means alone in identifying the Catholic Church as the cornerstone of a more conservative nationalist vision. This view was shared by many among the nobility, especially women. Already in 1806 Justus von Gruner, reporting to the Prussian government from French-occupied Poznań, singled out "fanatical women" as the "primary insurgents and true ringleaders" of anti-Prussian activity.[61] Flottwell made similar observations during the mixed-marriage controversy, noting the religious element behind the rebellious actions of some Polish women: "The clergy's [ill disposition toward the state] has a powerful influence over the Polish nobility's wives, who have a strong tendency toward religious fanaticism and, most regrettably, transmit the same to their families. Recent events in Poznań provide evidence of their exalted mission. A large number of Polish ladies put on widow's weeds immediately after the incarceration of Archbishop Dunin, and they removed them upon the death of the most blessed Royal Majesty, leaving no doubt about their sentiments and perspectives."[62]

Klaudyna Potocka (née Działyńska) was but one example of many women in Poznań who simultaneously maintained strong nationalist and devout Catholic sentiments. Born in 1801 to one of the wealthiest and most powerful noble families in the region, the young Działyńska spent her childhood in the rarefied atmosphere of her family's palaces, surrounded by servants and a French governess. Yet much of her early life was also shaped by war. Napoleon's army occupied the region by the time she was five, and for the next nine years she was confronted regularly with that era's great international struggles, whether through her father, who served in the Duchy of Warsaw's government, the regular passage of troops, or her family's own flight from the eventual Russian advance on the region. Działyńska was caught up at an early age by the struggle for Polish independence, and according to a biographer she developed an abiding interest in Polish history and culture. She was also a pious Catholic, and these two dimensions of her social identity fused together integrally. Illustrative of this fusion is her description of a ceremony on

Poznań's market square in 1815 when the Prussians, having reoccupied the city, replaced the Polish eagle on the town hall with the Prussian eagle: "Through our tears we witnessed the removal—like Christ from the cross— of our white eagle, in order to lay him in the tomb. . . . We believe that, just as Christ rose from the dead, so too will our eagle some day stir from the grave and spread his wings over a free fatherland."[63]

Klaudyna Potocka held no official position of authority, but like other leading ladies she exercised considerable influence over the sentiments of many Poznanians. Their sphere of activity was not the bureaucratic office but rather the home, the salon, and the ballroom. As mothers, women like Potocka instilled in their children an abiding love for their Polish heritage and the Catholic Church. As wives, they influenced the management of vast noble fortunes, channeling these resources toward causes both patriotic and pious. As social facilitators they helped shape opinion, cement alliances, and bolster resolve. Many were inclined to more direct action. Upon learning of the November Uprising in 1830, Potocka herself crossed the border to the Congress Kingdom to help support the insurgency.

Adherents of this brand of religiously charged nationalism found considerable theoretical support for their views from some leading intellectuals and cultural figures throughout the Polish-speaking world. Most prominent among them was Adam Mickiewicz (1798–1855), one of Poland's most famous poets. Mickiewicz came of age in the Congress Kingdom, and his early works created a sensation in the 1820s. Credited with introducing Romanticism to Polish literature, Mickiewicz built upon foreign literary influences such as Schiller and Goethe to create a novel Polish idiom that differed markedly from the rational orientation of Polish Classicism, the literary establishment at the time. Mickiewicz's works introduced a new set of interests and values to Polish audiences. He explored the mystical, the unseen, and the irrational. More importantly, he displayed a keen, celebratory interest in Polish history and traditions, including the customs and tales of the Polish peasantry. His poetry struck deep chords within a new generation of Polish elites, who tended to be ardently liberal and nationalist, inclined toward revolutionary political action, and impatient with what they viewed as the complacency of their elders.[64]

Polish Romanticism rapidly established itself within the literary mainstream, and Mickiewicz evolved from being the darling of the liberal avantgarde to a poet of widespread renown. At the same time, his own thought evolved. After moving to Paris in 1831, Mickiewicz became a practicing

Catholic, and his works from the 1830s and 1840s struck a more religious tone, emphasizing the Catholic character of Polish history and culture. He also became the leading proponent of Polish messianism. The term "messianism" refers to systems of thought in nineteenth-century Europe that combined the venerable Judeo-Christian tradition of millennial expectation with the contemporary vogue of nationalism. Like millenarians of all persuasions, messianist thinkers anticipated the dawning of an ideal era of harmony and progress, only in their view the catalyst of this shift would not be a person but a nation. In his literary works and lectures Mickiewicz posited that the crucifixion of Jesus Christ was but the first phase of the salvation process. In addition, there would occur a collective redemption effected by the martyrdom of a Christ-like nation, namely Poland. In patiently bearing a series of humiliations, Poland was paving the way for a new and improved world order.[65]

The millennial scenario described by Mickiewicz contradicted the official teachings of the Catholic Church, and as a result a number of his works were placed on the church's index of forbidden books. Despite these doctrinal differences, Mickiewicz and another influential Polish messianist, Andrzej Towiański, remained devout Catholics and encouraged their many disciples to follow their example. During his visit to Paris in 1842, Marceli Motty became acquainted with Mickiewicz's and Towiański's circle, and he notes in his memoir that they distinguished themselves by their "piety and frequent visits to church."[66]

Polish messianism represented one way in which many Poles reconciled nationalist perspectives with their Catholic affiliation. A more orthodox route was taken by Feliks Kozłowski (1803–1872), a conservative Catholic intellectual. Kozłowski was disturbed by contemporary trends within Polish philosophy and in particular the efforts of Bronisław Trentowski to create a Polish "national philosophy." In his book *The Beginnings of Christian Philosophy*, Kozłowski attacked Trentowski's efforts, claiming that Catholicism represented the true national philosophy of the Polish people, for it was the only philosophy embraced by the broad majority of Poles. Kozłowski's argument illustrates how thoroughly nationalism had redefined the general terms of debate among Polish intellectuals, as well as how conservative Catholics began refashioning nationalist notions to accommodate their religious views.[67]

Polish Catholic nationalism initially was an ideology of the more tradition-minded elite. As public expressions of this ideology multiplied, it made inroads into the consciousness of the broader Polish population. Tracking such a process is difficult, as the poorly educated general public tended to leave few enduring records of their perspectives. But some clues suggest that Poles of humble origins were increasingly inclined to identify as one nation and to see the Catholic faith as an important element of that bond. Prussian police reports of disturbances in the Poznań area during the November Uprising offer some fascinating examples. It was noted, for instance, that a rumor had been circulating throughout the countryside that the uprising would spread to the grand duchy on Good Friday, 1831. From this one can deduce that the Polish peasantry were keenly aware of the struggle for Polish independence unfolding in the neighboring Congress Kingdom. The fact that the uprising was to spread on Good Friday, a day heavy with religious significance, favors the conclusion that the peasantry were inclined to recognize the hand of God behind the uprising and, as Catholics, to identify with its cause.

Such a conclusion is strengthened when one considers a couple purported miracles that occurred around this time. In the small town of Jarocin, not far from Poznań, religious fervor swelled with the news that a devotional painting of the Virgin Mary in a private room of a young woman had shed tears of blood. The county councillor *(Landrat)* quickly dismissed the phenomenon, claiming that the woman had unknowingly splashed the painting with water, which, as it rolled down the dusty surface, turned brown. His explanation did not prevent a flood of pilgrims to the image or the popular conclusion that Mary was shedding tears over the fate of Poland.[68] A similar sensation washed over Poznań when it was reported that one of the crosses atop the Parish Church was seen to have turned toward Warsaw. Other reports soon followed, and the consensus emerged among less sophisticated residents that the struggle for Polish independence would be successful.[69]

During the November Uprising, ethnic Poles were not the only sector of Poznań's population to feel sympathy for the insurgents in the Congress Kingdom. Along with numerous German liberals who supported the cause on political grounds, there were also German Catholics who felt connected to the uprising on religious grounds. Carl Friedrich Kufal was one such person. Kufal was born to German Protestant parents in Kolberg. As a young adult he converted to Catholicism after reading an influential book. He later moved to Poznań in order to train for the priesthood. When the November Uprising broke out, he tried to cross the border into the Congress Kingdom. Kufal was arrested, and during his interrogation he explained to horrified Prussian authorities that his purpose had been to fight for his "coreligionists."[70]

At the time of Kufal's arrest in 1831, German and Polish Catholics enjoyed warm relations, signaled by harmonious communal worship and high rates of intermarriage. German Catholics long had adapted themselves to the customs and leadership of the dominant Polish Catholic population. As time progressed, however, these relations grew increasingly strained. Polish Catholics were developing a strong interest in their national heritage, and nationalist sentiments found an ever higher profile in their religious life. The same process began to occur within the German Catholic community, encouraged in large part by the Prussian state and by Catholic immigrants from other parts of Germany. As German Catholics in Poznań expressed their national distinctiveness, tensions emerged both within their community and between it and the larger Polish Catholic population.

In the early 1830s Flottwell launched a drive to organize Poznań's large German Catholic community into one ethnically based parish. Up to that time they had been worshiping among Polish majorities in the area's six parishes or in the St. Anne's Brotherhood, an impoverished organization of German Catholics with no permanent priest or place of worship that organized religious services and sacraments conducted in German. Flottwell considered the existing situation a recipe for Polonization:

> If good-intentioned Catholics of German extraction in Prussia continue to be limited to German preaching from time to time in this or that church, as the archdiocesan authorities have decided, to have their confession heard by a priest from a different parish, and to send their children to religious instruction, it is inevitable that they will be compelled to have their children learn Polish in order that they may fulfill their religious obligations. And there is no mistaking how, among the lower classes, growing accustomed to the Polish language leads to the alienation from German customs and culture and the adoption of a Polish mentality.[71]

Flottwell convinced the Prussian king to turn over St. Anthony's Church (formerly operated by the recently secularized Franciscan monastery) to the St. Anne's Brotherhood and to create an endowment to fund a permanent German-speaking priest for the organization. Large numbers of German Catholics flocked to the brotherhood, drawn by the beautiful church and the opportunity to practice their religion primarily in German.

Not long after its reorganization, the St. Anne's Brotherhood became the center of a heated controversy. In 1839 Father Franz Pawelke from Silesia was appointed to lead the community, and he launched a series of bold liturgical and decorative reforms that transformed the worship experience at St.

8. St. Anthony's Church, interior. Photograph by Andrea Hoelscher.

Anthony's. Pawelke's efforts sharply divided the brotherhood. In November 1840, around a hundred members formally complained to the archbishop. They accused Pawelke of the following: substituting their old songbook, which consisted of German translations of Polish hymns, with a new one containing some Lutheran hymns; placing a board near the altar listing the hymns to be sung during mass (a practice they regarded as Lutheran); delivering sermons that sounded so Lutheran that even Lutherans themselves could not tell the difference; and finally, stripping the church of its statuary and funerary monuments and whitewashing over its frescos, leaving a restrained white interior much like the Lutheran Cross Church. From all the evidence they concluded that Pawelke was a closet Lutheran, and they begged the archbishop to remove him and to reintroduce "purely Catholic customs" to their worship.[72]

Pawelke vigorously defended his efforts, noting that the new songbook and the use of a song board were commonly employed in other German-speaking Catholic regions.[73] Many members of the brotherhood jumped to his defense, claiming that Pawelke had elevated the quality of worship.[74] The dispute continued for many months before archdiocesan authorities ultimately settled it by transferring Pawelke out of the city.[75]

The conflict within the St. Anne's Brotherhood suggests an emerging cultural fissure within the German Catholic community in Poznań. Many of its members had been raised on a Catholicism molded within a Polish cultural context. This background shaped their liturgical expectations and affections, and they reacted negatively to foreign innovations. Pawelke was undoubtedly correct in claiming that some of his changes accorded with approved Catholic practice in other German-speaking regions. But to locally born Catholics, these changes appeared strange and disturbingly similar to Lutheran practice.

On the other hand, Pawelke found some of his strongest supporters from the growing number of German Catholic immigrants to the Poznań region. As German Catholics arrived, they encountered Catholic parishes dominated by different customs and the Polish language. One such person was Vincent Bittmann, a newcomer from Silesia, who delivered an impassioned defense of Pawelke. He explained that when he moved to the area he had difficulty understanding Polish priests, and his experiences at church were so unrewarding that his faith began to slacken. Then he had the opportunity to hear Pawelke preach. "Just as a spark ignites gunpowder, his sermons stirred my inner spirit," Bittmann claimed.[76] Pawelke's German-language preaching, his use of beloved German hymns, and his employment of familiar devices such as the song board created a welcoming atmosphere for people like Bittmann.

Pawelke divided not only his own congregation but the larger Catholic community as well. During the conflict the first clear signs of tension emerged between German and Polish Catholics. Pawelke's detractors noted that "hatred and mistrust against the German Catholic community have arisen among Poles, for they argue that the German Catholic church is half Lutheran."[77] Pawelke himself admitted to the problem: "The resentment and hatred [Polish Catholics] have secretly harbored for a long time emerged because it pains them that this church has been transferred to the German-speaking Catholics and that . . . the main mass is no longer conducted in Polish."[78]

A Time of Troubles

By releasing Archbishop Dunin and introducing a number of liberal gestures, Friedrich Wilhelm IV hoped to inaugurate a new era of harmony in the strife-torn Grand Duchy of Poznań. Quite the opposite occurred. Polish nationalists exploited these new freedoms to advance their cause. Their campaign was energized by growing support among lay and ordained Catholics. The 1840s unfolded as one of the most troubled decades in the history of the province.

However unintentionally, Dunin emerged as a hero for both Polish nationalists and Catholics, a martyr figure around whom less choate sentiments of national and religious persecution could coalesce. In the process Berlin's worst fears began coming to pass: the nationalist cause of a small Polish elite and the religious sentiments of the vast Polish majority began dovetailing to an unprecedented degree. After the mixed-marriage controversy, the political struggle of Polish nationalists adopted an increasingly Catholic character. Having previously rejected the church as backward and reactionary, many liberal Polish nationalists came to appreciate the church's virtues, including its powerful sway over a broad swath of the Polish population. One such liberal was the philosopher Bronisław Trentowski. In his work he criticized the church as a medieval artifact out of step with contemporary culture. Yet he conceded that for Poles, stripped of their independence and so many of their cultural institutions, the church constituted one of the last and most important repositories of living Polish tradition.[79] At the same time, some leading Catholics who had earlier felt alienated by the secular tone of the nationalist movement began to recognize an essential connection between the defense of the church and defense of the Polish nationality. Their ranks included the agricultural modernizer Dezydery Chłapowski.[80]

A telling example of this alliance came during the funeral of Karol Marcinkowski in 1846. The event, orchestrated by Polish nationalist leaders to broaden sympathy for their cause, attracted huge crowds eager to honor the good doctor. Marcinkowski had drifted away from the church during his student years in Berlin and never returned. On his deathbed he apparently refused to take Holy Communion and explicitly declined a Catholic funeral. "Despite this," explained provincial governor Maurice Beurmann in exasperation, "on the day of his funeral the archbishop appeared at the head of the entire clergy in clerical robes and joined the funeral procession."[81] Beurmann reacted so strongly to this because it foreshadowed his own worst fears. As he had explained two years earlier: "Two levers command unparalleled power to move the local population: nationality and religion. The first exercises its influence over the nobility, and the second over the common people. A combining of the two, through which religious interests also come to oppose the government's intentions, will spell trouble."[82]

Heinrich Wuttke recognized the same ominous signs. In 1846 he noted: "Three or four years ago a rapprochement or alliance occurred between the Poznań-area nobility and various clerics. Its exact nature remained unknown at the time and is still unclear, but it has been betrayed by its effects. Many noble men and women widely known to be irreligious suddenly demonstrated great piety. Our disenchanted world no longer quite believes in the sudden illumination of the Holy Spirit."[83]

The troubled relations between confessions, Catholic antipathy toward the state, and the increasing influence of the Polish nationalist movement all underlined the gravity of the election of a successor to Archbishop Dunin, who died in December of 1842.[84] In the end Leon Przyłuski was tapped for the post. Berlin was generally well disposed toward Przyłuski, recognizing him as tolerant, moderate, and open to suggestion. He spoke excellent German and was known as a cultured, if not worldly, man—important credentials for the many ceremonial roles of the office. Interestingly, Przyłuski also enjoyed the support of many nationalist-minded Polish nobles. Trapped between two diametrically opposed constituencies, Przyłuski managed for a time to cultivate both. This feat grew more difficult as religious and political tensions within the grand duchy mounted. After assuming office, the archbishop gravitated more and more toward the nationalist camp. On 5 December 1846 Beurmann complained to Eichhorn that "the efforts of Przyłuski clearly support Polish tendencies. Examples of this are as many as his tenure in office is short."[85]

Just days before Przyłuski's election, a religious and political movement known as Deutschkatholizismus (German Catholicism) began to coalesce. Eventually it provided a fresh affront to the already inflamed sensitivities of much of the grand duchy's Catholic population. One of the initiators of the movement was Jan Czerski, a renegade Catholic priest. Born to Polish parents in Werlubien on the northwestern edge of the province, Czerski was educated in schools in Bromberg (Bydgoszcz) and Konitz, which were dominated by German Protestants, and his experiences there seem to have shaped his theological views. He first made waves in 1839 when, as vicar at the Poznań Cathedral, he publicly demanded fundamental reforms within the Catholic Church, calling for an end to clerical celibacy, papal authority, and condemnation of mixed marriages. In addition he advocated greater lay access to the Bible, saying the Mass in vernacular languages, and offering the laity both the bread and the wine at Holy Communion, drawing many of his arguments from Protestant sources. Needless to say, Catholic officials in Poznań were less than receptive to Czerski's demands. They promptly transferred him to the village of Wiry deep in the countryside, where his ideas were unlikely to garner much attention.[86]

After a subsequent transfer to the town of Schneidemühle (Piłe) in the northwestern edge of the province, Czerski resumed his public call for reforms early in 1844. Church authorities suspended him from office, and he responded by convincing a small band of supporters to break away from the church on 19 October 1844 and to form a separate religious community. In this predominantly German and Protestant region, Czerski's demand for German-language masses, greater access to the Bible, and Holy Communion offered in both forms found considerable support. His call for an end to the ban on mixed marriages likewise resonated in a town where roughly one out of every three marriages was mixed.[87]

Czerski's movement likely would have had only local significance were it not for another suspended priest, Johannes Ronge, living in the obscure town of Laurahütte in Silesia. In an open letter to the bishop of Trier published in a liberal Leipzig newspaper, Ronge attacked him for promoting an August 1844 pilgrimage to Trier to behold a garment identified as the seamless robe of Christ, an event that attracted more than five hundred thousand of the faithful. He called for an end to such "superstitious" practices and the ultramontane culture in which they thrived, and he defended the freedom of the German nation on matters of faith in contradistinction to ultimate papal authority. He also articulated many of the reform demands being made by Czerski. Ronge's letter caused a sensation throughout Central Europe. Before long the protests of the two priests came to be perceived as one movement. Ronge's skillful promotion won supporters in many corners, and by early 1847 the movement had amassed around seventy thousand members.[88] It attracted diverse followers, including Protestants who saw the movement as the completion of the Reformation; Catholics who shared the same disgruntlement as Czerski and Ronge; and nationalist-minded Germans who longed for a solution to a nation divided by confession. Writing to Czerski's Schneidemühle community, a group of Catholic supporters from Hildesheim articulated this nationalist dimension: "Your message is spreading like a powerful wave in ever greater circles throughout the German lands and has touched the hearts of more attentive German brothers, whose enthusiasm knows no bounds. We, too, were convinced early on that the glorious goal of spiritual unity of all German believers would be more quickly reached the sooner men of strength and bravery rallied to the cause of pure Christian teachings."[89]

In the grand duchy, church leaders moved to crush Czerski's group and were dumbfounded to find the Prussian government—normally zealous in its prosecution of dissent—unwilling to cooperate.[90] Minister Arnim-Boitzenburg justified the state's inaction by claiming not to want to lend the movement any weight by repressing it.[91] But clearly many government bureaucrats quietly sympathized with Czerski and Ronge. As representatives of the movement spread their message, Protestant congregations lent support and the use of their churches. Organized groups of adherents sprang up across the province, eventually establishing themselves in Poznań as well.

The movement provoked an explosive reaction from a great many Catholics, who viewed it as a blatant attack on the church and who suspected the government of complicity. When Czerski arranged an impromptu service in the town of Swarzędz (Schwersenz) just outside of Poznań in May 1845, Police Commissioner Julius Minutoli called in the Prussian army to help keep the peace. He informed Berlin that "had the residents of Poznań learned earlier of Czerski's visit, they would have gathered in large numbers, and planned attempts to disturb the peace would have been unavoidable."[92] Two months later Poznań's Lutheran community allowed Czerski to preach in their church. In a show of force, Archbishop Przyłuski organized a large public procession in the center of town on the same morning. Disturbed by the massive throng of agitated Catholics, the police attempted unsuccessfully to clear the market square. Ultimately a cavalry regiment had to be called in.[93]

Yet another example of the emotions aroused by Deutschkatholizismus was the sad fate of Robert Raabski, the son of the pious assessor with the strong voice we learned of earlier in this chapter. Raabski was studying medicine in Breslau when the movement surged across Germany. He engaged in a dispute with Chamski, an enthusiastic proponent of the new teaching, which ultimately led to a duel. Raabski sustained a bullet in the chest, which left him in chronic pain and hastened his death.[94]

The nationalist accent surrounding Deutschkatholizismus did much to expand the discussion on nationalism and its connection to religion. The movement's vigorous expansion was both a party to and product of a flurry of pamphletry and editorial debate in which religion and nation figured prominently. The greatest testimony to the movement's popular reach are the dozens of grassroots communities that sprang up across Germany. In Poznań the intense opposition of church leaders and most Catholic laity assured that the city's deutschkatholische community remained relatively small. The group peaked in 1846 at 552 members, the large majority being of German extraction.[95] Its very presence, however, ensured that German and Polish Catholics alike considered anew the national dimension to their religious commitments.

If Deutschkatholizismus eroded still further the trust of Catholics in the state, the failed 1846 uprising damaged the government's hopes of ever winning the loyalty of the church. Although only two priests in the Poznań-Gniezno archdiocese were ever found to have been connected to the plot, the state's suspicions ran wild. A group of seminarians, drinking tea and playing cards in the apartment of a colleague in the town center on the night of the uprising, noticed considerable police activity and decided not to risk venturing back to the Lubrański Academy until morning. The police recorded their absence and subjected them to interrogation before determining their innocence.[96] By July 1846 Beurmann drew the grim conclusion that "the large majority of the Catholic clergy in this province is disinclined to support the government."[97]

An event in the winter of 1847 further demonstrated the raw animosities dividing Prussian officials and Polish nationalists, as well as the extent to which the Polish nationalist movement and the Catholic Church now marched in step. In January Anton Babiński, an emissary from the Polish Democratic Society, killed a police officer who had tried to apprehend him. Babiński was soon caught, interrogated, and executed in Poznań on February 1. Incensed by the police's action, several leading Catholic women, including Isabella Kurnatowska, Rosalie Kierska, and Tekla Dobrzyńska, organized elaborate memorial services in which Catholic identity and the nationalist struggle were interwoven. On 8 January 1847 Professor Iding from the Lubrański Academy and Father Kamiński from St. Martin's Church led "a large throng of women dressed in black, followed by a row of young girls in white dresses, who sang a patriotic song and carried a crucifix (supposedly kissed by Babiński before his death) ringed with a laurel or oleander wreath, which was passed around and kissed." A second service took place at St. Martin's on January 12. En route to the church, "a part of the crowd passed the nearby Canon Square (Canonenplatz), where they prayed at the spot of the execution." A third service, planned for March 3, was scheduled to include a procession to the Chwaliszewo Bridge, where insurgents had clashed with police in the failed 1846 uprising.[98]

The elaborately staged public mourning of Babiński dramatized the tense atmosphere in Poznań on the eve of 1848. Police Commissioner Minutoli could barely restrain his rage in assessing the ceremonies: "[The idea of holding memorial services] was enthusiastically embraced by the Polish ladies. They conveniently ignored that Anton Babiński was a common assassin. They forgot that Gendarme Komorkiewicz was a Pole and a Catholic who died honorably fulfilling his duty and is much more deserving of their prayers. They relished the opportunity to publicly mock the rule of law, to agitate the Polish population, to stimulate hatred and bitterness against the Germans, and to flaunt their patriotic sensibilities and hopes before the eyes of government officials."[99] Where Prussian officials saw a cold-blooded killer engaged in a crime against the state, many of the city's Polish Catholics recognized a martyr who had died for a noble cause. The discrepancies between the perceptions of the two sides could hardly have been greater.

4

Protestant Poznań

During the first half of the nineteenth century, despite decades of impressive growth, Poznań's Protestant community never reached the size of the Catholic population. By 1846 the number of Protestants had reached 11,431—more than a fivefold increase over estimates in 1793—but this amounted to just over 30 percent of the total population.[1] Their presence was even slighter in the public life of the city. Although many Protestants excelled in their economic endeavors, they made only modest contributions to Poznań's cultural scene and public discourse. There were very few Protestant counterparts to people like Raczyński, Libelt, and Dunin, prominent figures who provided leadership to the city's Catholics. The main exceptions were government and military leaders from other parts of Prussia, and they often were only temporary residents. One result of this low profile is a sparse archival record. In the first half of the nineteenth century Poznań's Protestants produced relatively few documents from which one can piece together the Protestant population's activities and attitudes. Not surprisingly, the scholarly literature on the community is also thin. With little to work with, historians usually have glossed over the subject with brief surveys of major events. From the limited resources that do exist, it is nevertheless possible to draw conclusions regarding the relationship between the Protestant faiths and nationalism.

Allegiance to Protestantism was an important factor leading many of the city's Germans to develop a pronounced sense of attachment to the German nation. Between 1793 and 1848, the Protestant sphere of influence, whether at church, school, or public events, increasingly was shaped by forces from other parts of German-speaking Central Europe, forces often openly sympathetic to nationalist discourse and the creation of a unified German state. Protestant Poznanians were encouraged to embrace this kind of thinking in terms that resonated with their core spiritual beliefs.

At the same time, their faith played a leading role in weakening the bonds they once shared with their Catholic neighbors. Protestantism in the Poznań region expanded notably in terms of adherents, infrastructure, and political influence. This growth alarmed Catholics, and it emboldened a Protestant community long accustomed to deferring to the Catholic majority. Protestant growth helped undermine the old compromises upon which Protestant-Catholic cohabitation had been built. Interconfessional relations deteriorated into bitter conflict. These conflicts led many Protestants to adjust their boundaries of belonging. Shaking from their feet the dust gathered during their long sojourn in Poland, they grew more inclined to identify with German Protestants in Central Europe.

Reinventing Protestantism

One of the leading forces of change affecting Poznań's Protestant community during the first half of the nineteenth century was the Prussian government. The Protestant congregations of Great Poland arose in a predominantly Catholic state with a weak central government. In the best of times they were benignly neglected, allowed to conduct their affairs with little interference. At other times they had to endure harassment without recourse to a state willing and able to defend their interests. In Prussia the situation was entirely different. Here the organs of government were strong, and the government's power extended deep into the realm's Protestant churches, where the Prussian king served as the highest ranking bishop. Indeed, the monarchy had come to rely heavily upon the Protestant churches to inculcate values conducive to political stability. After the partitions, Prussia sought to establish this same relationship with the Protestant churches of Great Poland. In the process it transformed these institutions dramatically.

To better understand the state's impact, it is helpful to recall some basic contours of Protestant life in Prussia. Prussia emerged as an early advocate of religious toleration, and Calvinists, Lutherans, and Catholics all enjoyed the freedom to exercise their religious commitments. At the same time the state maintained a special relationship with the Reformed and Lutheran bodies in the kingdom, known as the state churches *(Landeskirchen)*. Prussian kings enjoyed broad authority over the state churches, and during the seventeenth and eighteenth centuries this authority was used to merge church officials into the bureaucratic mechanisms of an increasingly absolutist state. In effect, the Protestant clergy became government officials, and every aspect of their official lives, from their clerical training to their mode of dress, became subject to state regulation. As representatives of the state, Protestant pastors were expected to encourage the population to work hard, obey authorities, and revere the king, their divinely anointed ruler.

Ironically, just as Prussia's kings were exerting a normative influence over the state churches, the Protestant community was fracturing over questions of theology, piety, and style. The orthodox establishment encountered stubborn challenges from two very different fronts: the Enlightenment and pietism. The former, with its high esteem for human reason and its quest for universal truths, appealed to many educated Prussians, including a substantial portion of the Protestant elite. "Enlightened" Protestants tended to eschew the seemingly irrational, metaphysical claims of Christianity and immoderate expressions of piety, emphasizing instead their religion's ethical dimension and its salubrious influence on the social order. Such attitudes attracted accusations of religious laxity and even atheism from orthodox clerics, but enlightened Protestantism thrived, especially during the long reign of the rationalist fellow traveler Friedrich II (1740–86).[2] Concurrently, an assortment of Protestant voices referred to collectively as pietists pressed for religious change of a very different nature. Leaders under this banner accused the orthodox establishment of empty formalism while criticizing adherents of the Enlightenment for their arid intellectualism. They called instead for a more heartfelt piety focused on the core Christian concepts of sin and grace. To provide Protestants with a more satisfying spirituality and to reform the state churches in the process, pietists formed small groups across Prussia for Bible reading and informal worship.

Politically speaking, Protestant leaders of all persuasions tended to be unflinching in their support of the status quo. While some may have been ideologically opposed to absolutism, few dared risk the harsh punishments administered to dissenters.[3] Yet this general commitment to the throne-altar axis began showing signs of strain after 1789. The French Revolution blazed a bold path from Enlightenment-era theory to concrete political action. The Enlightenment's emphasis on the worth of every rational individual translated into a much broader basis of political enfranchisement than previously exercised. Its suspicion of irrationality resulted in the dismantling of the old social hierarchy and the notion of innate distinctions between castes. Recognizing the affinity between the Revolution and their values, Enlightenment supporters in Prussia tended to sympathize with the reforms unfolding in Paris. Despite the radical excesses of the Jacobins, many leading Prussian intellectuals saw the hand of the Zeitgeist propelling the Revolution forward, and they pressed for a similar transformation on Prussian soil.[4]

Just as the French Revolution galvanized many rationalist-minded Prussians to demand social and political change, it also inspired a strong conservative reaction among those committed to the ancien régime. The conservative camp included the powerful bloc of landed gentry (Junker) in the eastern provinces of the kingdom, the orthodox clergy, and a class of lay and ordained Protestants known as the neopietists. The neopietists shared many of the same characteristics as their pietist forebears. They were distinguished by their sharp antipathy toward revolution and rationalism—causes they associated with social and moral degradation—and their commitment actively to combat the manifestation of either. Their ranks included Ludwig Nicolovius (1767–1839), who for decades steered the course of the Prussian Ministry of Religious Affairs. He systematically promoted the careers of clergy and church bureaucrats sympathetic to his views. Both the conservative reaction in general and the neopietist movement in particular enjoyed the support of Prussia's kings.[5]

After taking control of Great Poland, Prussian officials instinctively viewed the Lutheran and Reformed congregations there as an important base of support. As practicing Christians (the large majority of Prussian officials were Protestant), they looked in the same direction for religious fellowship. In both respects they were initially disappointed. The Protestant congregations of Great Poland, unlike their Prussian counterparts, were largely autonomous entities with no tradition of submission to centralized agencies, and they were especially wary of governmental interference. They were also few in number, financially weak, and institutionally poor. Such weakness limited their ability to exert the sort of influence encouraged by the state. Furthermore, the local congregations differed in terms of liturgical life and theological orientation. Prussian officials complained that the local congregations expected excessive financial contributions from their members.[6] Newcomers were also apt to view the native Protestant population as unsophisticated and superstitious. Especially galling was the local Protestant tendency to mimic Catholic practices, most notably in the celebration of holidays with no basis in Protestant theology.

Using their own conventions and convictions as models, Prussian officials set about "reforming" Protestant practice in the region. They dissolved the region's Protestant consistories and created new structures to govern Protestant life. The task of drafting a new constitution for the Reformed community was assigned to an official named Woyoll in Breslau, and his efforts honored the government's wish for control over religious matters. As he explained in a letter to his superior, Karl von Hoym, Reformed church and school affairs would be removed from the arbitrary decisions of local Protestants and placed "under the unmediated guardianship and supervision of the state."[7] In 1795 the state created the South Prussian Consistory, a provincial council composed of Lutheran and Reformed members and designed to manage Protestant affairs. The consistory was answerable to authorities in Berlin.

The state also took steps to remedy the financial and institutional weakness of Protestant congregations in the region. It established two funds to provide annual stipends to help meet their operating costs.[8] Poznań's Cross Congregation received 200 thaler per year from the Lutheran fund. When it requested additional aid to finance the completion of its church in 1801, the king personally allotted 2,948 thaler for the task.[9]

Regarding differences in religious practice, initially the state was slow to push for change. Aware of the sensitivity surrounding such matters, in some instances government officials decided to ignore conventions they regarded as inappropriate, lest they ignite the ire of native Protestants. A prime example was Protestant observance of Catholic holidays. Astute observers in Berlin recognized that many Protestants were deeply attached to the holidays and would resent their elimination. One government minister even alerted the king to the practical benefits of such practices. It promoted harmony between Protestants and Catholics and helped maintain public order. "Were such [religious observances] to disappear," he noted, "the average Protestant might be given over completely to drunkenness" on these days.[10] The king agreed to allow the practice to continue, insisting only on modest conditions. If Protestants chose to hold a religious service on a Catholic holiday, they were required to focus exclusively on themes that accorded with Protestant doctrine. Those Protestants who chose not to celebrate Catholic holidays were to remain indoors, thus avoiding unnecessary provocation of the Catholic faithful.[11]

In the troubled aftermath of Prussia's defeat in 1806, the king conceded to the demands of reformers to revamp the government in the interest of creating a more rationalized chain of command. After 1815 these reforms were applied to the Poznań region. Lutheran and Reformed affairs were placed under the control of the Protestant Consistory (Evangelische Konsistorium) in Poznań. The consistory operated in turn under the direct supervision of the provincial governor.[12] Through these changes the central government once again assumed control over Protestant life in the grand duchy.[13] It used this control to bring the congregations into ever greater conformity with its ideal: disciplined Protestant churches capable of inculcating conservative values.

Operating through officials in the Protestant Consistory, the state established new standards of practice for Protestants and kept watch for signs of resistance or backsliding. It required candidates for pastorates first to pass a ministerial examination. It dictated to pastors how they were to dress, counseled them on how to preach, and issued specific instructions on how to manage everything from financial records to rituals. In 1818, for instance, a Berlin official alerted the consistory that Protestant congregations in the grand duchy were not adhering to Prussian standards for confirmation, a ritual whereby Protestant adolescents formally acknowledge the teachings of their confession. Apparently the region's Protestants were confirming children who were too young and lacked the requisite training, and the ceremonies they held were too short on order and solemnity.[14] The consistory dutifully distributed guidelines throughout the province concerning confirmation. Its officials periodically visited the region's Protestant congregations to ensure that on this and other matters the grand duchy was adhering to Prussian models.

The imposition of new standards like the ministerial examination had a significant long-term impact on the Protestant community. Its most influential members, pastors, now had to receive the requisite training at German universities. Protestant pastors operating in the grand duchy first passed through the heart of the German intellectual world, where they forged important relationships and were exposed to new currents of thought. They would later transmit these perspectives to their flocks back home.

The state also took great care in the appointment of Protestant officials. It recognized that its goals for the Protestant churches could only be fulfilled by candidates who sympathized with its priorities. This concern was clearly in evidence in October 1846 when the Poznań-based Fifth Army Corps began its search for a new chief pastor *(Oberprediger)*. With tensions still high from that year's failed uprising, General-Lieutenant Colomb noted the sensitivity of the post: "Under the highly unusual circumstances at work in this city and military region, the temperament of the chief pastor of the army corps is of particular importance. If he measures up to this challenging situation, he could exercise a welcome influence. If he does not, he would make matters worse."[15] Once in office, Protestant officials never lacked for direction from the government. They were carefully supervised, and if they failed to comply they risked being dismissed from their posts.[16]

Alongside its efforts to regulate the Protestant churches, the state continued to offer generous financial assistance to individual congregations. It hoped that stable congregations and a network of new churches would bolster the influence of the Protestant faith. Between 1817 and 1830, the state helped fund the building of nineteen new Lutheran churches in the grand duchy.[17] In the city of Poznań the state's largesse manifested itself in the erection of Peter's Church (Petrikirche) just south of the old city, built for the Reformed community through a twenty-thousand-thaler gift from Friedrich Wilhelm III.

After 1815 the state was more inclined than before to put the Protestant churches to political use, demanding pastors to make symbolic gestures and statements in line with the state's priorities. In 1816, for instance, authorities in Berlin informed provincial governor Zerboni di Sposetti (1815–24) of several new national holidays connected to the recent victory over France. In their Sunday sermons pastors were "to recall [these holidays] solemnly and joyously to mind and in so doing to reignite faith and patriotism within the Christian congregations."[18] In December 1830, just days after the November Uprising broke out in Warsaw, Altenstein instructed the Protestant Consistory in Poznań to order the clergy to promote loyalty among their flocks. The consistory dispatched a letter that distilled the essence of the state's expectations. Pastors, it noted, are obliged to warn their flocks "against the un-Christian and

9. Peter's Church. Courtesy of the Muzeum Narodowe w Poznaniu.

corrupting spirit of disorder and opposition to law and divinely ordained authority" and to promote "civic peace, a quiet Christian life, and loyal obedience to law and state."[19]

By far the most audacious action the state took in refashioning the Protestant churches had little to do with ulterior political calculations. It was the king's effort to unite the Lutheran and Reformed Churches of Prussia into a single entity. From the very start of his reign, the pious Friedrich Wilhelm III hoped that such a union would dismantle confessional divisions, which he felt obscured the essential cohesiveness of the Christian message. This step, in his words, "measures up to the great goals of Christianity; it corresponds to the earliest intentions of the reformers; it lies in the spirit of Protestantism; it stirs churchly sensibility; it encourages domestic piety; it bears much promise for the betterment of churches and schools, which have often stagnated on account of confessional differences."[20] In 1808 he approved the merger of the highest administrative bodies of both churches into a common Cultus Division (Kultusabteilung), later known as the Ministry of Religious Affairs. On 31 October 1817, the three-hundredth anniversary of the posting of Luther's ninety-five theses, the king attended a religious service jointly administered by Lutheran and Reformed clergy. He publicly expressed his wish that the ceremony would serve as a model for Protestants throughout the kingdom.

News of the union concept was greeted with great enthusiasm. The actual creation of a joint Protestant Church proved much more difficult, however, owing to numerous differences in theological emphasis, liturgical practice, and styles of piety. The king only complicated matters by drafting a new joint order of liturgy, known as the *Agende,* in 1822. In the years prior to its publication, Friedrich Wilhelm III had grown fascinated by Christian liturgy and, in particular, the earliest liturgical forms of the Lutheran Church. Drawing upon countless hours of personal research, he drafted the *Agende* on his own, believing that it accorded best with practices authorized by Martin Luther himself. Furthermore, he thought it would facilitate Protestant union and spark a larger process of Christian renewal. So convinced of the document's eminence and utility, he could not comprehend the resistance it aroused among many Protestants. Soon his officials were applying enormous pressure on hesitating congregations to "willingly" accept the *Agende.*[21] The *Agende* eventually was accepted, however reluctantly, by most Lutheran and Reformed congregations in the grand duchy, but the strong-arm tactics of the government stimulated widespread resentment. Ironically, one of the casualties of the *Agende* was the very thing it was intended to promote: Protestant unity. The favorable disposition toward union, once so in evidence, evaporated over the course of the 1820s. After years of fruitless struggle, the king eventually consented to a watered-down version of union that allowed congregations greater freedom to retain practices particular to their confession. This compromise proposal was widely embraced, but it failed to achieve the degree of fusion the king originally sought.[22]

Although the planned union ran aground, in the main the Prussian state achieved the goals it had set for reinventing the nature of Protestantism in the Poznań region. It gradually dismantled the old structures and traditions native to Great Poland, replacing them with models common to Prussia. At the same time it encouraged a remarkable expansion of both churches in terms of infrastructure and population. Through its active participation in church affairs, the state ensured that influential pastorships and administrative positions were filled with loyal Prussians who could be counted on to act in accord with the state's priorities. Once disdainfully dismissed by Prussian officials, the Protestant congregations in Poznań gradually developed into model institutions. An 1842 inspection of the Cross Congregation by officials of the Protestant Consistory yielded only praises. According to the official report, the choir music was "good," the liturgy and organ music were "excellent," and the preaching of Pastor Fischer was "beyond reproach."[23]

Conformity and Dissonance

The state's efforts to transform the Lutheran and Reformed churches of Great Poland elicited a variety of responses from local Protestants. Initially there was considerable resistance. Many were suspicious of the government's intentions. Others remained deeply committed to local traditions and resented the imposition of new standards of practice. In the end, though, few dared openly to defy Prussia's designs. Their own weakness and the government's powers of persuasion proved overwhelming. This compliance had important ramifications. Protestants in the Poznań region found themselves within a sphere of influence increasingly in tune with the religious culture of Prussia and Protestant Germany. As they fulfilled their religious obligations, they were encouraged to disengage from their long association with Poland and to reimagine themselves belonging to a community with a very different legacy and mission in the world.

When the Prussian army entered Poznań in 1793, Protestants reacted with the same mixture of fear and passive resignation displayed by the rest of the city's population. Although their experiences during the reign of Stanisław August had been quite positive, they were too well schooled in disappointment to let their optimism take wing. This invasion, like the many before it in Poznań's unhappy eighteenth century, would unfold according to God's inscrutable will. Theirs was not to question, but rather to cooperate with the authorities that be and hope for the best.

Although Protestants shared confessional bonds with Prussia's ruling house and a majority of its population, they remained suspicious of the state and its motives. Its foreign policy toward the Polish-Lithuanian Commonwealth contributed greatly to Prussia's poor reputation. Most Protestants could recall the hardships they had endured on account of Prussia's attempts to undermine the commonwealth's economy. This helps explain why Friedrich Bielefeld, a prominent Lutheran in Poznań, feigned ignorance of German when initially approached by the Prussian invaders.[24] It also illuminates the reaction of the Lutheran congregation in 1794 when Field Pastor Wegner from the Prussian army asked if his soldiers could worship in the Cross Church between eight and nine A.M. every other Sunday. The congregation warily consented. Fearful that the state would lay claim to the edifice the congregation had struggled so hard to build, it prepared an agreement stating unambiguously that the congregation surrendered none of its rights to the church.[25]

It was not long, though, before this early suspicion gave way to the perception that the government was sympathetic to local Protestant interests. Protestant Germans benefited more from Prussian rule than any other segment of the native population. Their cultural and religious commitments earned them the state's trust and availed them privileged access to the reins of local power. Their congregations began enjoying the state's generous patronage. Also, the fact that native Protestants shared the same language and faith as the large majority of incoming Prussian bureaucrats and soldiers facilitated the building of friendships and alliances. One indication of just how much closer relations between local Protestants and Prussian newcomers had grown came in August of 1815, not long after Prussia regained control of Poznań. The field pastor of the local army corps once again requested access to the Cross Church, only this time he planned to have his troops worship alongside the congregation. In contrast to the tone of their earlier response, local Lutheran leaders now noted that they would "very happily" open their church to the soldiers.[26]

Although it did not take long for local Protestants to warm to the new political order, their resistance to the state's efforts to intervene in church affairs was more enduring. Among Reformed Protestants, sensitive issues included the retention of their synodal system and the episcopal ordination of church elders.[27] Another local tradition was the honoring of holidays associated with the Virgin Mary, a practice Prussian officials regarded as inappropriate. In the journal maintained by Poznań's Cross Congregation, the author notes in an entry from 1815 that on December 8 of that year, "on the day of Mary's Assumption," the congregation would formally open a search for a new pastor.[28] Several months later the author reported that on 25 March 1816, "on the day of Mary's Annunciation," the congregation would vote for one of the several pastor candidates they had interviewed. Such references suggest the enduring centrality of Mary in the sacred calendar of local Lutherans. Not only were Marian holidays celebrated throughout the province, they also remained important points of temporal orientation for the community. The fact that two critical steps in the process of selecting a new pastor fell on such holidays may have been more than mere coincidence. It seems entirely likely that leaders of the Cross Congregation were hoping for Mary's beneficent influence over such a serious endeavor.

The Protestant defense of their local traditions met with some success as Prussian officials either conceded or chose discreetly to ignore practices they found unbecoming. Such victories grew rarer with time. With few institutional resources and shaky finances, local Protestants were in no position to mount sustained resistance to Prussian demands. Meanwhile, a closer alignment with the vibrant Protestant churches of Prussia proved highly attractive, especially for a new generation of Poznań-area Protestants, for whom Poland was more of an abstract idea than a concrete reality.

As inexorably as the passing of time, the old Protestant leadership gradually departed the scene. Andreas Ackermann, who had helped craft the Warsaw Tractate in 1768 and led the Lutheran congregation through the arduous task of church building, finally passed away on 20 August 1811 at the age of ninety-five. He was followed two years later by Helling, an early manufacturer who had served as chief Lutheran elder since the 1790s. In 1816 Pastor Stechebahr died after thirty-seven years of service both to the Cross congregation and to the administration of Protestants throughout the province.[29] They were replaced by a new group of leaders, many of whom hailed from other parts of the kingdom, ardently identified with Prussia, and had little affection for local customs. They included Christian Fischer, who served as pastor for the Cross Congregation from 1816 to 1848. Fischer was born and raised in Silesia and studied at the University of Halle, Prussia's largest theological center. Major Carl von Bünting emerged as one of the most prominent Protestant lay leaders in Poznań. Originally from Pomerania, the pious Bünting first came to Poznań in 1819 as a member of the Fifth Army Corps and remained until his death in 1860. During that time he played a leading role in the local chapter of the Bible Society (Bibelgesellschaft) as well as the Gustav Adolf Union (Gustav-Adolf-Verein), an organization designed to promote the expansion of the Protestant faith.[30] Berlin-born Friedrich Cranz first came to Poznań in 1841 to serve as chief pastor of the Fifth Army Corps. He later became general superintendent of the grand duchy, the highest post in the provincial church bureaucracy.[31]

Over time the Protestant churches of the Poznań region developed into vehicles for identification with the Prussian state and its policies. One temporary obstacle was the king's attempt to unify the Lutheran and Reformed confessions. At first Poznań's Protestants responded warmly to the initiative. Leaders planned a joint Protestant service in the Cross Church on 1 November 1817, and enthusiasm was widespread. An entry in the Lutheran journal a week before the event noted that the college of elders "wishes unanimously to celebrate this holiday in the most festive manner . . . and hopes that the unification of the two local Protestant confessions will be realized. . . . There is not a single member of either confession who does not share this same wish."[32] Not long after this service, the Lutheran college of elders began deliberations over practical matters related to the proposed union. It was here that difficulties emerged. Many of Poznań's Lutherans felt their congregation was already too big for its facilities, and the thought of making room for Reformed Protestants struck them as too great a burden.[33] More disturbing still was the 1822 *Agende*. Although the king's liturgical order gradually found its way into most Protestant congregations, the tactics used to promote it undermined Protestant receptivity to union, stimulating instead a renewed appreciation for the distinctive characteristics of the Lutheran and Reformed confessions. For a considerable minority of Protestants, the *Agende* represented just the latest in a series of troubling moves testing their commitment to the Protestant state churches. The grounds of their discontent included excessive governmental interference in congregational affairs, the watering down of traditional practices, and the influence of rationalist theology.

Some Protestants in the grand duchy demonstrated their dissatisfaction by fulfilling their religious needs outside of the state churches. The first signs of this tendency appeared in the early 1820s. The Protestant Consistory reported to Berlin about the existence of small groups of Protestants in Poznań and the town of Pinne who were gathering in private homes for devotional meetings *(Erbauungsstunden)*.[34] Worries grew over the following decade as the number of such groups mushroomed and their messages, in some cases, grew divisive in tone. In 1834 the Protestant Consistory prepared a report on the various ultraecclesial organizations in operation. They ranged from small groups looking for additional spiritual uplift to more extreme varieties that rejected state-sanctioned churches and schools altogether.[35]

These more extreme groups eventually aligned themselves with a movement known as the Old Lutherans (Alt-Lutheraner). The Old Lutherans were a group of some thirty pastors and their congregations based mainly in Silesia, who as of 1830 were led by Johann Gottfried Scheibel (1783–1843), a pastor and professor of theology at the University of Breslau. The movement resisted the *Agende* and insisted upon a greater degree of congregational autonomy than the Prussian state was willing to accept. Later they sought to break off from the state church and form a separate religious organization. The Old Lutheran movement captured the imagination of a handful of disaffected pastors and missionaries in Poznań and elsewhere in the grand duchy.[36]

The government eventually cracked down on the Old Lutheran communities in Silesia, fearing that liberals were attempting to exploit the issue for their own advantage.[37] The military broke up their services, jailed pastors, fined participants, and confiscated property.[38] The state never took such a hard line against Old Lutherans in the grand duchy, perhaps on account of their relative weakness. An Old Lutheran congregation continued to operate in Poznań up through the end of the 1840s, although it remained rather small. In 1847 it was led by Pastor Phillip Jacob Oster and included 260 members.[39]

The Old Lutheran movement was not the only revolt against the authority of the state churches at this time. In the early 1840s a movement known as the Friends of Light (Lichtfreunde) gained considerable prominence. Led by a group of rationalist clergy mainly in Saxony, the Friends of Light called for greater freedom in matters of theological expression. Their challenge to the authority of the state and its conservative politics endeared them to liberals across Germany, and when the state took punitive action the Friends of Light were apotheosized as martyrs in the liberal press. Before long their ranks expanded to include many lay members, and their platform took on an increasingly political dimension.[40] In the grand duchy, however, these movements never had much impact. Their goals fired the imagination of random individuals, but no organized clusters emerged to champion their causes.[41]

While it is important to consider dissenting voices in the Protestant population, one conclusion such an exercise underscores is just how successful the state churches were in retaining the confidence of their members. At its peak in the early 1830s, the Old Lutherans in Poznań amounted to a very small percentage of the total Protestant population, and adherents of the Friends of Light were fewer still.

Within the state churches, Protestants were more and more likely to encounter messages that resonated with the state's own religious and political visions. Exercising its privileges of patronage, the state took great pains to ensure that only loyal-minded individuals would rise to positions of influence. Its efforts were richly rewarded. The city's Protestant pulpits rang out with enthusiastic endorsements of the Prussian king and his restoration politics. Speaking at the ceremony honoring the cornerstone laying of the new Peter's Church, General Superintendent Freymark led the crowd in the following prayer: "Dear God! You are both sun and shield and keep the pious free from want. Sustain, protect, and bless our king, who piously and graciously extended his paternal hand for this project. Bless him richly! O bless him, bless him and his entire precious house!"[42] In applying to become pastor of Poznań's garrison congregation, a cleric named Seegemund echoed a similar political orientation:

> The office of Protestant pastor in the Prussian army seems to me all the more important the more it dawns on me how in the army rests the main power and defense of the state. But the inner strength of the army, that which constitutes and leads it, is moral power. And this power, if it is to have a solid foundation and to last into the future, must be steeped more and more in the spirit of Christian witness and piety. To help ensure that the spirit of true, living Christianity increasingly becomes synonymous with the spirit of the Prussian army—that appears to me to be one of the most worthy and fruitful tasks of a servant of the Gospel and a loyalist to king and fatherland. May I nurture devotion to Prussia and, above all, heartfelt faith in Christ.[43]

Just as Poznań's Lutheran and Reformed congregations served as channels of conservative political education, they also helped inculcate Poznanians with a Prussian social identity. It was in this arena more than any other that the city's Protestants came into regular contact with the many newcomers from other Prussian provinces. Their mutual faith served as an immediate and powerful basis for cooperation and a means of overcoming cultural differences. The fact that the large majority of the Prussian military and bureaucratic establishment in Poznań were Protestant enabled the native Protestant community to identify more readily with them and to welcome their leadership. This close bond was greatly in evidence during the celebration of the Cross Congregation's fiftieth anniversary (1836) and the cornerstone laying of Peter's Church. Provincial government and military leaders were amply present, both as honored guests and as integral members of both congregations.

The Nationalization of Protestant Consciousness

The state was largely successful at remaking the Protestant churches of Great Poland in its preferred image. As a result Protestants were integrated into institutional structures that stretched across the Prussian Kingdom and, in many respects, into other Protestant German states. The political ramifications of this development were quite significant. The Protestant world encompassed many perspectives, not all of which corresponded with the priorities of the Prussian regime. Of particular interest for our purposes was the substantial interface between Protestantism and German nationalism. Many leading nationalist theorists and concepts had deep roots in the Protestant faith. This sympathetic bond facilitated the adoption of nationalist forms of identity among German Protestants. As Protestants from Great Poland entered into closer communication with the German Protestant world, many experienced similar processes. They were exposed to notions of German unity developed within Protestant contexts, notions that harmonized with many of their basic religious impulses. Their religious commitments encouraged Protestants in Poznań to imagine themselves as part of the German nation.

It would be a mistake to assume that there existed a discrete, clearly defined ideology embraced by all nationalist Germans. On the contrary, many strains of nationalism were in circulation. What they shared was a belief in a powerful force that united the German people and justified the creation of a German nation-state. At issue was the precise nature of that force and who exactly it encompassed.

One common typology used in the study of nationalist ideologies is the distinction between political and ethnic nationalisms. The former, most commonly associated with France and the United States, has as its unifying core the commitment to the political values and system of government of a given state. In a case where political nationalism is operative, membership within the nation is open to almost everyone, regardless of ethnic background, who lives within its boundaries and respects its political values. Such a concept was hardly practical for Europe's German-speaking population, which was scattered across dozens of different states. Instead, it was the notion of an underlying cultural unity that gradually won adherents. The most obvious source of this unity was the German language. But theorists of German national identity were quick to expand the notion of German culture to include a wide variety of tendencies and cultural expressions. They were also prone to speak of this common culture in metaphysical terms, describing it as a spiritual power that inhabits the German soul, compelling Germans to express themselves in culturally specific ways and in keeping with their divinely ordained destiny.

From the start, such ideas had to account for preexisting forms of culture that also made metaphysical claims about the social identity of humankind: namely, the Christian churches. Another unavoidable issue was the deep-seated ambivalence and significant cultural differences separating Protestant and Catholic Germans. In their efforts to craft persuasive cultural definitions of the German people, nationalist theorists had to grapple with some fundamental questions. Was German culture essentially Christian, or was Christianity a foreign import that had altered, or even corrupted, the original German character? And if German culture was essentially Christian, was it Christian in general or was it specifically Catholic or Protestant? It is not my purpose to chart the complex responses to these questions.[44] It is relevant to note, however, that most of the Germans who struggled with these issues were from Protestant northern Germany, and the responses they formulated quite often reflected Protestant perspectives.[45]

With Great Poland's absorption into Prussia, Poznanians were exposed to the intellectual currents running through the kingdom, whether through acquaintance with Prussian newcomers, availability of Prussian books and periodicals, or greater access to Prussian schools and universities. These currents included nationalist notions that, when developed by fellow Protestants, had the potential to resonate powerfully within the Lutheran and Reformed communities. Many of the early theorists of German national identity hailed from Protestant backgrounds, and their religious roots often had an enduring impact on their thought. Herder, for instance, was a Protestant minister, and one of his most important intellectual influences was the pietist Johann Georg Hamann. It was Hamann's fascination with language that laid much of the foundation for Herder's thought. Hamann drew parallels between language and biblical references to the Logos. Speech, in his view, was divine in origin and expressed the very nature of the human soul.[46] Herder retained much of the spiritual weight Hamann attached to language as well as many of the metaphysical assumptions acquired in his Protestant upbringing. God remained at the summit of his worldview, and his attribution of significance to nations rested mainly on their status as conduits of God's continuous revelation.[47]

The real breakthrough in terms of the appeal of nationalist ideas, their often pronounced Protestant character, and their warm reception among Protestants in Poznań came during the Napoleonic era. Prussia's humiliating defeat at the hands of the French army in 1806 inaugurated a painful era in which the kingdom, stripped of over half of its former territory, was obligated to pay huge indemnities to Napoleon. These payments, which over the first two years alone exceeded Prussia's prewar annual revenue by some sixteen times, nearly bankrupted the state and forced it to wring as much wealth as it could from its remaining subjects.[48] With the army decimated and the economy in shambles, many Prussians resigned themselves to a difficult, uncertain future. But among a growing portion of the cultural elite, the recent turn of events inspired active resistance. The preexisting impulse to promote the German language and culture over foreign imports found a new immediacy with France's military domination of Central Europe. German intellectuals of various persuasions sought to rouse the public's indignation over the current state of affairs and stimulate pride in their German heritage.

Some of the most powerful messages within this drive originated in the Protestant sphere and were designed for Protestant audiences. The French invasion ignited the patriotic ardor of numerous Protestant ministers, including the celebrated theologian Friedrich Schleiermacher, and they took to delivering passionate sermons that painted the conflict with France in terms of a holy war. A common element within this thinking was the equation of Napoleon with the devil. The French emperor's callous treatment of religion, his disregard for once-sacrosanct traditions, and the audacity of his geopolitical ambitions conjured up such associations even among rationalist thinkers, who long had dismissed the Prince of Darkness as so much superstition.[49] A related perspective portrayed the conflict with France as a new chapter in the clash between Catholicism and Protestantism. In his 1806 work *Teutschland und Preußen,* Karl Gottlieb Brettschneider was the first to articulate what would become a popular theme. He linked the essential purpose of Germany with the cause of the Reformation and urged Protestant Germans to resist foreign and Catholic domination and to help complete the work started by Luther.[50]

At first Friedrich Wilhelm III and his government tried to rein in such efforts, fearing that they could stimulate the political ambitions of the broader population and antagonize the French.[51] After Napoleon's disastrous Russian campaign in 1812, however, the military landscape shifted considerably. The czar's army now went on the offensive, and Napoleon's position in Central Europe appeared vulnerable for the first time. Sensing opportunity, the Prussian king allied his state with Russia. To rally popular support for the upcoming conflict, the Prussian and Russian governments conducted massive propaganda campaigns. Through a flood of pamphlets, broadsides, and cartoons, Germans were encouraged to believe that God was actively engaged on the side of Prussia and Russia against a diabolic enemy.[52] Meanwhile, the Prussian state enlisted the help of religious leaders to reinforce its narrative of holy war. Ludwig Nicolovius charged the clergy with an important task: "It remains the work of the clergy all across the fatherland to uphold the belief that no sacrifice for the common good is too great and to give themselves willingly and completely to this cause. Your office as caretakers of the soul is to let the spirit conquer the flesh. Strive now to ensure that each person lives not for himself but for the fatherland. Encourage all to join in and contribute the gifts they have enjoyed from God, to seal and maintain a holy covenant with the fatherland, so that God will once again bless it richly."[53]

The state's propaganda drive generated widespread enthusiasm both within Prussia and beyond its borders. Among those who responded to the call were Protestants in Poznań. With the Russian army's occupation of the Duchy of Warsaw in 1813, the political fate of the Poznań region was very much in limbo. But for the city's Protestant community, the future they preferred was clear. They were stirred by the narratives emerging from Prussia, whether they were accounts of God's active hand in the fight against France or glorious descriptions of the special mission of the German people to advance the cause of the Reformation. Motivated in part by religious convictions, they began to imagine themselves as integral parts of a larger social identity that stretched across Protestant Germany. They not only imagined, but acted. Protestant congregations in Poznań and the surrounding region held collections for the Prussian army, gathering 24,129 thaler—an impressive sum considering the difficult economic times. In addition, around 450 men volunteered to fight in the Prussian army.[54]

For all of the enthusiasm and spirit of sacrifice generated during the struggle against Napoleon, the satisfaction of ultimate victory was remarkably short-lived. Many had hoped that they were fighting not just to check Napoleon but also on behalf of a new European order. The idea of a strong, united Germany seemed well within reach, as did the liberal dream of a fairer social order grounded upon human equality, constitutional government, and the decentralization of power. Those who entertained such dreams were bound to be disappointed by the political reorganization that actually took place. At the Congress of Vienna in 1815, the Prussian king joined his counterparts from Austria and Russia in a concerted effort to turn the political clock back to the status quo ante. Calls for progressive political reforms were ignored as monarchical rule was reasserted across Central and Eastern Europe.

Among Poznań's German community, reactions to the king's restoration politics varied. Those who had been culturally Polonized or were avowed liberals tended to gravitate toward the cause of Polish independence, which at this time was inherently revolutionary and closely associated with core liberal principles such as constitutional government and the right of nations to self-determination. But for those who had responded to distinctly Protestant versions of the German nationalist call, the new political landscape was much more ambiguous. A resurrected Poland was unattractive because such a state likely would have a pronouncedly Catholic character. And yet the new Prussian state fell far short of the lofty ideals generated during the revolutionary period.

The remainder of Friedrich Wilhelm III's reign was not an encouraging time for German nationalists. In 1819 Prussia and the other leading German-speaking states jointly approved the Carlsbad Decrees, a cluster of legal provisions designed to extinguish the lingering embers of liberal and nationalist ardor. Nationalist student organizations known as *Burschenschaften* were banned, university professors were placed under greater scrutiny, and censorship was tightened. Public expressions of support for liberal reform and German unification became politically dangerous acts, imperiling careers and inviting the possibility of police harassment. In the face of such dangers, nationalist agendas remained alive, but they were manifested in subtler forms.

The nationalist passions recently displayed by Protestant Germans in Poznań subsided in tandem, but they did not disappear. In fact they were nourished in a variety of ways over the following decades and developed a much more solid foundation. During this period Poznanians were exposed ever more directly to the pulse of Prussia's political and intellectual life, and there were voices and ideas that exerted particular influence over the city's Protestant Germans. In this new context, many among their ranks found a renewed sense of German national identity, and their religion helped facilitate such conclusions.

As his reign wore on, the king grew more and more conservative on religious matters. He never sought to silence the liberal rationalist wing within the Protestant churches, but he tended to support conservative thinkers and projects.[55] Nevertheless, Prussia remained the center of innovative theological thought in the Protestant world at this time. At its leading universities theologians and their students engaged in novel research, subjecting Christianity to new questions and rigorous analytical methods. Conservative critics condemned this rational approach for rendering banal the mystery of faith and weakening the bonds of religion altogether.[56] But to supporters, such innovation belonged to a larger ethos of progressive Protestantism. As they saw it, Protestantism was a living tradition that had to adapt to the demands of the Zeitgeist in order to survive and remain relevant. This same openness to change spilled over into the political and social spheres, where liberal Protestants added momentum to the reform agendas of the day. In their eyes Protestant Germany had the potential to play a progressive role in the world, ushering in a more just society and political system. This kind of thinking was very much in keeping with many of the nationalist visions articulated in the Napoleonic era.

Liberal Protestant culture found a warm reception in the Poznań region after 1815. At this time works by rationalist pastors filled the libraries of many Poznań-area congregations, and sermons clearly reflected this influence.[57] The rationalist and erudite tone of the region's pastors was one factor that provoked General Superintendent Freymark, himself a moderate rationalist, to issue a circular urging the clergy not to forget the needs of the less sophisticated laity.[58] Just as they had embraced the religiosity of Prussia's liberal Protestant culture, Poznań-area clerics undoubtedly were influenced by its political leanings as well. Liberal Protestant leaders like Schleiermacher presented an attractive ideal of a progressive society bound together by national bonds and a glorious mission. Through an appeal to their religious sensibilities, Protestants in the grand duchy were led to identify with this lofty endeavor.

Alongside this positive appeal came a negative one—disdain for Catholicism—that encouraged Protestants to end their loyalty to Catholic-dominated Poland in favor of a more attractive German alternative. Integral to the idea of progressive Protestantism was its self-definition vis-à-vis an antithetical other, namely, Roman Catholicism. Lutheran and Calvinist apologists routinely contrasted their churches with a caricature of the Catholic Church that protrayed it as steeped in superstition and dominated by corrupt prelates. Such polemics were especially keen in the German states, where the struggle for dominance between Protestantism and Catholicism led to decades of bloody conflict.

The antagonistic edge that long had characterized Protestant-Catholic relations in Central Europe dulled somewhat during the Enlightenment. In an intellectual climate that emphasized the general and the practical within religion over minute doctrinal distinctions, representatives from both camps adopted more charitable evaluations of the other faith. This measure of ecumenical harmony declined once again after 1815. At work was a process known as reconfessionalization, in which Christians, be they Lutheran, Calvinist, or Catholic, found a renewed appreciation for the distinguishing characteristics of their particular churches. One factor behind this change in Protestant Prussia was the imposition of the king's *Agende*. Ironically, the policy rekindled affection for the confessional differences it sought to overcome. Meanwhile, the revised geopolitical situation in Central Europe after 1815 contributed to growing uneasiness between Protestants and Catholics. The Napoleonic era undercut Austria's former dominance over the German-speaking world while enhancing Prussia's strength. Conflict between these two roughly equal powers appeared inevitable were Germany to overcome its political, cultural, and religious schizophrenia. Would Germany's future be determined primarily by Protestant Prussia, or by Catholic Austria? The question helped reignite the deep-seated mistrust between religious camps.

As the Poznań region was integrated into Prussia, the widespread antipathy Prussian Protestants felt toward Catholicism influenced local perspectives. Relations between Protestants and Catholics in the old Polish-Lithuanian Commonwealth had not been free of enmity, but the dynamic between the two parties had differed considerably from that existing between their counterparts in Prussia. For one, Poland's Protestants always had formed a vulnerable minority. Dependent upon the goodwill of their Catholic neighbors, they could ill afford to antagonize them through public expressions of contempt for Catholicism. Furthermore, a substantial majority of the commonwealth's most respected citizens, from its writers, artists, and scholars to its patrons and power brokers, were Catholic. Protestants thus had little reason to view the culture of Catholicism as hopelessly backward compared to their own. That all changed with the Prussian takeover. In this new context it was Catholic Poland that now fared poorly in comparison with Protestant Prussia, be it in terms of technology, economic strength, or military prowess. With the influx of the mainly Protestant military and bureaucratic elite, not to mention Protestant publications, came Prussian attitudes toward Catholicism that were dim, if not vitriolic.

One prominent voice in this regard was that of Heinrich Wuttke, who in a series of widely disseminated newspaper articles warned against the Polish national movement, which he viewed as all the more dangerous for its deeply

Catholic character. In a typical passage from his writings he summoned up the image of Catholic intolerance: "Do we wish to have in Brandenburg and Pomerania, in Silesia and Prussia the same influences as the Rheinland has experienced from Belgium? Would not Poland be ten times as bad as Belgium, a swarm of clerics, a nest of Jesuits? Do we wish to subject ourselves to the work of the Jesuits?"[59] Such ideas were infectious. Under this influence Great Poland's native Protestant community gradually shed its deference to the Catholic majority, coming instead to perceive Catholics mainly in negative terms. The most important turning point in the process was the mixed-marriage controversy. While Catholics reacted angrily to the jailing of two of their archbishops, Protestants had a very different response. The controversy seemed to ratify Protestant suspicions that Catholics were ultimately loyal not to Prussia but to Rome. Heightened antipathy toward Catholicism played a significant role in the development of nationalist consciousness among native Protestant Germans. It alienated them from their historic connections with Poland and encouraged them to imagine themselves as integral members of a progressive, Protestant Germany.

It should be noted that this tendency to identify increasingly with the Protestant culture of parts of Germany and less with the mainly Catholic environment of Great Poland appeared almost exclusively among Protestant Germans in Poznań. Among the few Protestant Poles in the region, linguistic and cultural bonds facilitated the building of sympathetic relationships with the Polish Catholic majority despite confessional differences, and it tempered the appeal of outside models from Germany. One prominent embodiment of this alternative sensibility was Jan Wilhelm Cassius (1787–1848), a scholar and pastor descended from Czech Protestants who had immigrated to Poland back in the seventeenth century. Cassius studied philology and theology in Heidelberg before returning to Poznań to serve as a pastor and gymnasium professor. Despite his Protestant faith and his firsthand knowledge of Germany, Cassius emerged as a passionate defender of the Polish language and culture in which he was raised. His active cultivation of these sentiments among his students led to his dismissal from the gymnasium in 1824. In 1841 Cassius joined a number of other Poles in publishing a scathing rebuttal to Flottwell's *Denkschrift* of that same year, in which the former provincial governor had enumerated the fruits of his Germanization policy in the grand duchy.[60]

With Friedrich Wilhelm III's death in 1840, a new energy influenced the vectors of Protestant and nationalist identity in Prussia. While the deceased king had vigorously opposed German nationalism, his son and successor had a much different orientation on the matter. Friedrich Wilhelm IV had come of age in the nationalist era and was drawn deeply to the idea of German unity. Yet in the divided cultural climate of his day, as the Enlightenment and Revolution inspired the cultural and political backlash known as Romanticism, the new king's temperament accorded decidedly with the latter. This romantic orientation had a profound impact on his approach to the nationalist question. Through a series of public gestures he began to articulate a conservative nationalist vision for the German-speaking states of Central Europe. He fantasized about recreating a new version of the Holy Roman Empire, a state where inhabitants would be united by their common German heritage and commitment to Christianity, and where everyone would fit within a traditional social hierarchy.[61]

Not surprisingly, nothing ever came of the king's airy vision. It was, however, significant that nationalist notions had become acceptable at the highest levels of the Prussian government and that cultivation of such notions had become a matter of government policy. To give just one example, in 1843 Minister Eichhorn ordered Freymark—and presumably all general superintendents throughout the kingdom—to instruct the "German congregations" under his authority to observe the millennial anniversary of the Treaty of Verdun, which he identified as the beginning of German political independence. He explained:

> The contract signed . . . at Verdun in the year 843, which placed the German-speaking tribes under the authority of King Louis the German, awakened within them the full awareness of their national bond, and all of the seeds of a rich and powerful national life that lay hidden within them were given space and nourishment with which to grow. Over the course of ten centuries and innumerable fortunes and misfortunes, everything great and noble about the German people has become manifest, spreading their fame throughout the nations of the earth and earning them a place in history. All of this found its origin . . . in the event through which the Germans achieved political independence.

Eichhorn went on to connect this anniversary with Christian piety: "The German temperament cannot contemplate such lofty matters without meekly acknowledging the hand of God, the orderer and controller of all things, and raising up a sacrifice of pious gratitude for the preservation of national unity and independence."[62]

There is no surviving record of how Poznań's Protestant community honored the anniversary of the Treaty of Verdun, but the fact that the celebration was ordered at all is quite remarkable. Protestants were encouraged to identify with a people and an event buried a thousand years in the past, supposedly connected to them by the unbreakable thread of nationhood. They were summoned to locate themselves within the stream of a sacred history, a dramatic tale of the trial and triumph of their divinely guided nation. Once again, religion served as the primary medium for the message.

Not long into Friedrich Wilhelm IV's reign, the Polish national movement began reaching new levels of intensity. In the face of this mounting threat, government officials sought to strengthen the cultural autonomy of the region's German population. Interestingly, they identified Protestant churches as an infrastructure critical to this process. Early in 1846 Eichhorn contacted the Protestant Consistory in Poznań regarding the "crisis" of Protestantism in the grand duchy. The government long had been concerned about the shortage of Protestant schools and churches there, particularly in the eastern, largely Catholic portion of the province. Eichhorn ordered consistory officials to conduct a detailed study of the problem, including a precise accounting of financial and infrastructural needs.[63] Their eventual report was not encouraging. They called for a massive investment, including the creation of ninety-three new church systems. "We have become convinced," they added, "that only in this way can a rich seed be strewn here for the spread and activation of *German*, respectively *Protestant,* culture. . . . Political considerations reinforce this same conclusion, in particular the recent history of the Polish movements, which have been nurtured by the Catholic clergy. Without a doubt, these considerations demand us to take steps *to encourage and consolidate the German element* here."[64]

The cultural climate of Protestant Germany and the policies of the Prussian government under Friedrich Wilhelm IV ensured that the native German Protestant population in Poznań developed an increasingly passionate sense of national identity. That commitment would most clearly manifest itself during the 1848 revolution. But there were signs of it already in the early 1840s. In 1840, for instance, various Protestant congregations throughout the grand duchy requested permission from the Protestant Consistory to celebrate 15 May 1840, the twenty-fifth anniversary of the resumption of Prussian rule over the region.[65] Eschewing their former ambivalence, Protestants were now proud to be a part of Prussia and, by consequence, the German world. The fact that they should choose to celebrate this day in church is highly suggestive.

Another telling sign was the Protestant response to Deutschkatholizismus in 1845. Deutschkatholizismus excited Protestant nationalists across Germany. The reforms advocated by its leading personalities, Czerski and Ronge, were in keeping with Protestant innovations centuries before. If the movement gained wide support among Catholics, it had the potential to complete the Protestant Reformation and, in Karl Gottlieb Brettschneider's words, "to finally free Germany from the long-burning fire of church division."[66] Such an outcome accorded with the fondest wishes of many nationalist Protestants, who understood the propagation of their faith as the essential mission of the German nation. Many Protestants in Poznań interpreted the matter in similar terms. A local bureaucrat named Eck recorded a long "historical account" of the early months of the Deutschkatholizismus movement in the Cross Congregation's church journal. He wrote: "Everything has its cause. The cause of the Reformation in 1517 was the indulgence affair. . . . The cause of Ronge's and Czerski's current reformation is the 18 August 1844 display of a garment that was declared to be the seamless robe of Christ by Bishop Arnoldi of Trier. . . . The man who has made an object of veneration out of this manufactured garment, the man who has manipulated the religious feelings of the simple minded, tricked the poor, hungry folk out of their money and property, and exposed the German nation to the ridicule of other nations, this man is a German bishop."[67] Eck equated the significance of Deutschkatholizismus with that of the Protestant Reformation, and he viewed both through the lens of German nationalism. Bishop Arnoldi's actions were roughly analogous to the medieval marketing of indulgences, and the perpetuation of both forms of corruption on German soil were embarrassments to the nation. Czerski and Ronge, by contrast, had the potential to redeem the nation much as Martin Luther had done by spreading the light associated with the Protestant Reformation. Judging from his entry, the Cross Congregation was awed by the opportunity to participate in this great historical event. Eck detailed how the community enthusiastically opened the doors of their church to Czerski on 29 July 1845. Afterward, church leaders were careful to place a copy of his sermon in their archive.

Protestantism's Place in the City

In the final decades of the Polish-Lithuanian Commonwealth, Protestant Poznanians lived under improved but still somewhat precarious circumstances. They had won important safeguards through the 1768 Warsaw Tractate, but the government lacked the means to enforce the law. Therefore, they continued to rely on their time-tested strategy of deference to the Catholic majority. Prussian rule altered the Protestant-Catholic dynamic in the city in many important respects. Protestants won expanded legal protections and an array of unofficial privileges, all of which were guaranteed by a powerful state. Their old fears melted away, as did the need to accommodate Catholic sensitivities. With time they began challenging once sacrosanct boundaries and conventions, encouraged in part by an influx of Protestant newcomers and government officials eager to enhance the prestige of the Protestant churches. One result was the deterioration of Protestant-Catholic relations to a degree not seen for generations. This bad blood provided Protestants ample reason to sever any emotional attachments to their largely Polish-Catholic environment and to identify first and foremost with Protestant Germany.

After seizing control of the Poznań region in 1793, Prussia moved to establish there the same laws and governing structures common to other parts of the kingdom. Protestants suddenly found their status greatly enhanced. No longer merely tolerated, they were placed on equal footing with the province's Catholic population. What is more, they could look forward to sympathetic treatment from the German-speaking Protestants appointed to the courts, municipal offices, and provincial government. Prussia's sizable military presence in Poznań offered welcome reassurance that the new laws would be rigorously enforced.

Protestants took advantage of their improved legal status to address long-standing grievances against the Catholic Church that they previously had had to ignore. One such grievance was the tax *(Stolgebühr)* Protestants had to pay to Catholic clergy every time they celebrated a baptism, wedding, or funeral in a Protestant church.[68] Whenever the Cross Congregation buried someone in their cemetery north of town, for instance, they had to pay a priest at the St. Adalbert Church, in whose parish boundaries the cemetery lay. More remarkable was the demand of Poznań's Reformed community, whose members insisted that the Catholic Church reimburse them for the destruction of the Bohemian Brethren's church complex nearly two centuries in the past. In a 1799 letter the congregation's pastor and elders explained their position to the king: "We . . . simply are demanding modest reparations from that confession that destroyed our local church and parish complex and possesses the property to this day. In this case Catholics cannot raise objections if we request a replacement from among their extraneous holdings, for in 1616 a group of students and commoners, whipped into a frenzy through repeated public sermons by Catholic priests, and in particular the Jesuits, razed two Reformed churches . . . to the ground, along with eight dwellings and their facilities."[69] The fact that the Reformed congregation dared make such a request reveals much about the way Protestant attitudes regarding their place in the city were changing. They displayed a growing willingness to assert their rights and to participate actively in Poznań's public sphere.

This gradual shift in consciousness is clearly illustrated through the comparison of two conflicts within the Cross Congregation, both of which, interestingly enough, occurred over dead bodies. In February 1795, not long after Prussia gained control of Poznań, the wife of Post Director Keyser, one of the most distinguished Lutherans in the city, passed away. Her funeral drew the church elders and a large portion of the congregation, all eager to pay their respects to the highly esteemed lady. Unfortunately, the solemn event turned out rather badly. For reasons unknown, Elder Böhme began behaving shabbily toward his colleagues. When reprimanded by Elder Heintze, Böhme lashed out, and the argument between the two men nearly came to blows. Alarmed by so heated an exchange between elders, a clash that threatened to divide the entire congregation, Pastor Stechebar summoned his flock to an emergency meeting in the church. There, before the watchful eyes of most of the city's Lutherans, he coaxed Böhme into apologizing to Heintze. Heintze accepted the apology, "whereby all of the citizens and church elders present were harmoniously united with satisfaction and solidarity and the whole matter was forgotten."[70]

What is instructive about this incident is the manner in which it was resolved. In keeping with the defensive orientation of a beleaguered minority, the Lutherans placed a high premium on maintaining group solidarity and solving their problems quietly among themselves. They rigorously avoided letting congregational matters spill over into the wider and potentially hostile public sphere. This posture was remarkably absent in a similar conflict that rocked the community some twenty years later. In August 1817 a Lutheran named Wildenheim took his own life. Both Lutheran canon law and Prussian state law *(Allgemeine Landesrecht)* specified that suicides should be deprived of the normal honors accompanying a funeral. But in the case of Wildenheim, the elders decided to make an exception. They allowed his body to be placed on the congregation's standard bier, covered with its pall, and carried by the congregation's new hearse. During the ceremony they also had the church bell rung. This break with protocol enraged a portion of the Lutheran community. Led by a tailor named Lutz, a carpenter named Gortz, and a glove maker named Geisler, this group demanded that the "desecrated" pall, bier, and hearse be replaced and that the church elders be relieved of their authority. What was so unusual about their protest was its exceedingly public nature. The group published their cause openly in the city and dragged police and city director Czarnowski, a Polish Catholic, into the fray. Ahlgreen, one of the elders under fire, displayed a similar willingness to air the congregation's dirty laundry. In a letter to Czarnowski he requested that the city protect church leaders from unruly members of the congregation. The traditional Lutheran impulse toward understatement and insularity was nowhere to be seen. In recounting the course of the conflict, the Lutheran chronicler described the matter as "so well known" and an "embarrassment for the congregation."[71]

The newfound assertiveness of Poznań's Protestants was matched by their growing numerical and symbolic presence. Their share of the city's total population rose from around 15 percent in 1793 to over 30 percent in 1846, and this pattern was repeated across much of the province. The grand duchy's Protestant congregations were ill equipped to handle the expanded demands placed upon their facilities. To remedy the situation, Friedrich Wilhelm III offered financial support to the dozens of communities seeking to expand their churches or build new structures. As a result, the towers of new or enlarged Protestant churches began reaching into the sky all across the province.[72]

In Poznań the Lutheran and Reformed faiths made inroads into a landscape long dominated by the Catholic Church. The king offered the Reformed community—known as Peter's Congregation as of 1831—the exceedingly generous sum of twenty thousand thaler for the building of a new church. They eventually chose a plot on a prominent corner just south of the old city. The building they commissioned was not very successful aesthetically. Its unadorned brick façade was distinguished by two square towers, rising upward with little variation in brickwork or change in dimension to lend a degree of visual interest. Its interior was similarly spare. Before long the new church was derisively referred to as the *"Hosenkirche"* (pants church) because of its resemblance to a pair of upside-down trousers.[73] Regardless of style, the congregation was satisfied finally to have a permanent home that could accommodate their burgeoning ranks. Between 1793 and 1848 its membership had grown roughly tenfold.[74]

Poznań's Cross Congregation also experienced growing pains. No longer able to accommodate all of its members, Lutheran officials realized that a second congregation was required. They eventually made this move in the 1850s.[75] In the meantime they took great pride in the accomplishments of their congregation, a sentiment they no longer tried to hide. In 1836 they marked the fiftieth anniversary of their church's dedication by sponsoring a large celebration. The rising profile of Poznań's Protestants even promised to touch the marginalized Old Lutheran congregation. In the 1840s its legal right to exist was affirmed and in 1846 the central government in Berlin seriously considered transferring a former Catholic church to the congregation. The government eventually backed away from the plan, fearing a negative Catholic reaction.[76]

Brimming with newfound confidence, Poznań's Protestants dared not only to demonstrate their presence but also to press against the boundaries of their own confessions and evangelize openly to outsiders: Catholics, Jews, and the unchurched. They were inspired to do so, in part, through their growing contact with Protestant northern Germany. As we have seen, one of the influential ideas that shaped this part of the world during the Napoleonic wars was the notion that Germany, the birthplace of the Reformation, had a world-historical mission to complete the work initiated by Luther. This idea continued to resonate long after 1815 in a variety of movements designed to accomplish the goal. Many Protestants in the Poznań region gravitated to these movements. In 1817, for instance, a group in Poznań formed a local chapter of the Bible Society, which disseminated Bibles and sponsored the activity of Protestant preachers in the region.[77] In 1822 a local chapter of the Jewish Mission Society (Verein zur Beförderung des Christentums unter den Israeliten) was created. In an early pamphlet it noted, "Many among [the Israelites] have felt the need to improve their faith and find that their religion is no longer satisfying. But lulled into slumber by ancient prejudices and fanatical hopes, they lack the strength to celebrate openly the better way that lies before them and to convert."[78] The society sought to lead Jews to this better way, convincing them that Jesus Christ was the Messiah for whom the Jews had been waiting. Despite investing large sums of money and decades of hard work, the group enjoyed remarkably little success.[79]

This expansionist spirit was by no means limited to the province. Many Protestants trained their attention on international developments, such as the work of Protestant missionaries among "heathens" around the world. In Poznań a bureaucrat named Barschall led a group of Protestants who met to discuss the global missionary effort.[80] In the nearby town of Pinne, a wealthy Protestant noble named Karl von Rappard founded the Missionary Aid Society (Missionshilfsverein) in 1832 to support such activity abroad.[81] Protestants also responded favorably to Friedrich Wilhelm IV's 1841 move, in partnership with England, to found a Protestant bishopric in Jerusalem in order to promote the faith in the Middle East.[82] In 1843 Eichhorn informed the kingdom's Protestant clergy that on January 21 of that year they were to lead their congregations in celebration of this achievement as a means of expressing their "unity with the Protestant Church in its entirety" and their support for "the future of the Orient." Protestants in the grand duchy honored the holiday enthusiastically. Some suggested that it be celebrated every year.[83]

The rising profile of Protestants in the Poznań region and their willingness to challenge their place as a submissive minority was a leading factor behind a dominant trend during this time: a vicious cycle of recrimination that poisoned Protestant-Catholic relations. Poznanian Catholics had gradually concluded that under the Prussian scepter they were being exposed to religious persecution (see chapter 3). Protestantism's rising stature seemed to confirm their darkest suspicions, and some Catholics reacted badly. This, in turn, reinforced the negative Catholic stereotypes held by many Protestants. Catholicism was widely viewed by its Protestant detractors as a hopelessly backward religion that trapped its adherents in superstition and intolerance. Such views provided them all the more reason to champion the Protestant cause.

Protestant-Catholic conflict raged most intensely when the state turned over Catholic churches for Protestant use. The 1801 incident in Poznań over the St. Joseph's church building (described in chapter 3) was an early example of a pattern that recurred time and again throughout the province. When Protestants in the town of Gołańcz (Gollantsch) were granted use of the church at the former Bernardine monastery in 1833, local Catholics sought to prevent the transfer and assaulted a Protestant pastor in the process. The incident prompted the state once again to curtail such exchanges, as it had in the 1820s, but the temptation remained strong to satisfy Protestant infrastructural needs so affordably.[84]

Another front in the emerging Protestant-Catholic conflict was the alleged effort of zealots on either side to seek converts from the other confession. Prussian law guaranteed to the three officially recognized churches of the realm protection against proselytism. Despite this, judging by numerous complaints from around the province, interconfessional proselytism appears to have been on the rise in the decades after 1815. At the very least, Catholics and Protestants developed acute sensitivities to such activities. In 1824, for instance, the Sisters of Mercy, who not long before had started a hospital in the city, fell under suspicion after several Protestants in their care converted to Catholicism. Provincial Governor Sposetti presented the matter to Archbishop Gorzeński in a letter: "Recently several Protestant patients at the hospital of the Sisters of Mercy have converted to the Catholic faith, and it is widely believed that both the sisters themselves and the Catholic priest stationed there are guilty of proselytism. Although this charge has not been officially substantiated, it has caused a sensation among the local Protestant population, which has harmed the reputation of the hospital."[85] In 1829 Father Koperski, a Catholic priest based in the town of Mirosław, complained to the provincial government that Gerlach and Hartmann, two preachers associated with the Jewish Mission Society, were disseminating anti-Catholic literature and trying to convert Catholics with whom they came in contact.[86] The issue grew so heated that in 1830 the government implemented stringent new rules governing conversion between Christian confessions. Individuals were still able to convert according to the dictates of their conscience, but greater efforts were taken to ensure that such decisions were made freely, without pressure from outside sources. The priests and pastors involved on both sides of conversion cases were required to report to the Protestant Consistory in Poznań regarding the motivations of the convert. The consistory, in turn, was responsible for providing Berlin detailed annual reports on the matter.[87]

One excellent measure of evolving Protestant attitudes toward their sense of place in the Poznań region, as well as the interconfessional acrimony that resulted, is reflected in their perception of time, in particular in their celebration of religious holidays. Many Protestant communities in the old Polish-Lithuanian Commonwealth had come to internalize the Catholic calendar as their own. In neighboring Prussia such interconfessional blending was prohibited. The state took great pains to ensure that the calendar of one confession did not impinge upon that of another. Every Christian citizen of Prussia was obliged to observe only those holidays pertaining to his or her own confession, while respecting the right of other confessions to their own holidays.

After initially ignoring this discrepancy, the state began cajoling Protestants in the province to adhere to the general Prussian model. Gradually they did so, but the change hardly facilitated harmony between confessions. As relations between Protestants and Catholics deteriorated over the 1820s and 1830s, the issue of religious holidays emerged as a flash point of conflict. Government authorities began to receive numerous complaints from representatives of both sides regarding alleged violations of the sanctity of their holidays. Protestant pastors, once inclined to lead their flocks in worship on Catholic holidays, were emboldened to protest when their Catholic neighbors failed properly to respect Protestant holidays. Likewise, Catholic priests kept a vigilant watch over their own religious feasts, sensitive to every Protestant violation of the requisite decorum. One priest, incensed by the growing Protestant willingness to conduct business affairs on Catholic holidays, condemned the behavior as "a new type of proselytism." Tensions between confessions peaked in the years during and immediately after the mixed-marriage controversy. For those Protestants and Catholics eager to display their disdain for each other, religious holidays provided the perfect occasion.

The large number of violations eventually prompted the police commissioner to take unprecedented action. In 1842 he called together seven leading Protestants and seven leading Catholics and ordered them to work out a compromise that both sides could abide. Their deliberations resulted in the following plan: all Christians, regardless of confession, would be obliged to respect eighteen different holidays. Some of the holidays, like Easter, were recognized by all Christian parties; the majority of holidays were exclusively Catholic; and two were exclusively Protestant. All Christians were to cease public activity on the mornings of these holidays while religious services took place.[88] Judging from the numerous complaints the government continued to receive, the compromise plan failed to command widespread observance.[89]

A further illustration of the changing sense of place among Protestants occurred during the funeral of Archbishop Dunin on 1 and 2 January 1843. At the passing of so prominent a leader, it was understood that the highest officials of the military, the city and provincial government, and the other Christian confessions should attend the funeral and pay their respects. As General Superintendent Freymark of the Protestant Consistory noted in a letter to Minister Eichhorn in Berlin, such gestures from Protestant leaders were particularly critical if interreligious peace was to be restored.[90] Freymark was thus deeply chagrined by the fact that the three pastors of the Cross Congregation, Fischer, Friedrich, and Schoenborn, declined the invitation and provided no explanation to Catholic officials. Their actions, in fact, were intended to display their explicit disrespect for the deceased archbishop. As the three men explained to Freymark in an emotional letter, they felt "too deeply injured by the actions of the Catholic Church over the previous few years" to attend the funeral. In particular, they cited Dunin's leadership style, which they characterized as "hostile to Protestantism." They also noted the behavior of the local Catholic clergy during Friedrich Wilhelm IV's visit to Poznań in the summer of 1842, which, as they saw it, was a blatant attempt "to hurt the feelings of every friend of the fatherland."[91] The sentiments of Fischer, Friedrich, and Schoenborn undoubtedly mirrored those of a large portion of their congregation. As Protestants they were no longer willing to play a subservient role to the Catholic Church. As loyal Prussians and proud Germans they could no longer stand idly by as nationalist Poles challenged Prussia's claim to the region. These two bases of identity, religious and national, had become tightly bound and mutually reinforcing.

5

A Revolutionary Spring

Johann Erich Biester's description of Poznań in the early 1790s offers many valuable insights. It is one of a small number of firsthand accounts of the city by German outsiders before the dissolution of the Polish-Lithuanian Commonwealth. It is also an unwitting eulogy to the end of an era. At the time of his visit, Poznań remained remarkably faithful to age-old patterns of thought and practice. The city was like an ancient, well-used palimpsest upon which each new generation left a record of its experiences without erasing completely the imprints of those who came before. Its material form still adhered in large measure to plans drafted in the thirteenth century, while accommodating expressions of later tastes and conventions. Its complex network of legal boundaries read like an archive of Polish history.

This heritage was on the verge of eclipse. When Prussia seized control of Poznań, it sought to impose its own history, urban traditions, and style of governing upon the city. Poznań was to serve as capital to a new Prussian province and thus had to be refashioned in a manner consistent with Prussian law and precedents. Prussian efforts coincided with complex forces of modernization that in their own ways dramatically remolded the form of the city and the activity that took place there.

A comparison of Biester's impressions to the Poznań of 1848 illustrates clearly just how much the city evolved over the half century in question. The transformation penetrated beyond the brick-and-mortar forms of the city, affecting as well its economic systems and social and political structures, and the cultural impulses of its inhabitants. While still tied to its venerable urban template, by many measures the latter-day Poznań was an entirely different entity. In this chapter we take stock of the basic outlines of this new city. Such an exercise illuminates the nature of the revolution that erupted there in March

1848 and, more importantly, the fusion of religious and nationalist sentiment that caused the conflict to burn so brightly.

A City Transformed

Were Biester able to visit Poznań in 1848, he likely would have been astounded by how much the city had changed. To be sure, many hallmarks of its venerable urban core were still there, but the larger context in which they had once functioned had been altered nearly beyond recognition. What was once a typical medieval town had dissolved into a much larger and more modern entity. Poznań's symbolic landscape evolved in tandem. In many respects, the Polish city Biester had once sought to understand now had become oddly familiar. In its latter incarnation streets and squares were labeled in German and often after famous Prussians, and buildings were designed in a clearly Prussian manner. The same governmental, legal, and military institutions found throughout his native kingdom were now prominent fixtures here as well.

After assuming control in 1793, Prussian officials immediately took steps to assert their authority over the space of the city, replacing the Polish eagle atop the town hall with its Prussian counterpart. They commandeered the most prestigious locales in town, housing the organs of government in the elegant buildings of the former Jesuit college and the castle. Not long thereafter the king appointed Friedrich Gilly, a leading Berlin architect and urban planner, to draft plans for an ambitious expansion of Poznań in keeping with existent Prussian models. Gilly's eventual design called for the development of a large area just west of the old city. Dubbed Friedrich Wilhelm City, the development resonated with contemporary urban practices in Berlin and other European centers. Its open design—in pointed contrast to medieval towns like old Poznań—called for wide, rectilinear streets and no defensive walls. Its signal features included Wilhelm Square, a large, open, rectangular space. A major north-south axis was planned just east of the square. Named Wilhelm Street, it took the form of a tree-lined boulevard reminiscent of Berlin's famous Unter-den-Linden Street. Along the southern side of the square ran an east-west axis called Berlin Street, in reference to the cardinal geographical point around which the new city was to find its orientation.

Gilly's plan provided a framework for the city's development for decades to come. The state sponsored a series of public works, including a large theater at the western end of Wilhelm Square. Meanwhile, the old city began losing im-

10. Wilhelm Street and the Raczyński Library, circa 1833. The classical building in the center of the image is the Raczyński Library. The tree-lined boulevard to the right is Wilhelm Street. The open space to the left is the eastern end of Wilhelm Square. Courtesy of the Muzeum Narodowe w Poznaniu.

portant elements of its former character. An 1803 fire laid waste to 276 buildings in the northern and eastern sections of the old city. In the 1790s the state initiated the gradual dismantling of the city's defensive walls. It also applied official German names to the city's streets in an attempt to standardize a facet of everyday life where German, Polish, and Latin variants once had coexisted.[1]

Upon regaining control of Poznań in 1815, the state began writing a new chapter in the city's urban development. On the revised map of Europe, Prussia's border with the Russian Empire lay much closer to Berlin than it once did. In preparation for potential hostilities, Prussia decided to fortify a number of towns near the border. Poznań emerged as the focus of one of the largest military building projects of the nineteenth century. In a dramatic about-face from the open urban design developed by Gilly, a new corps of architects drafted an audacious plan to encircle the old city and the new Friedrich Wilhelm City with a system of walls and forts, accompanied by a sprawling, state-of-the-art citadel just north of town.[2] The refortification program represented a marked departure from the city's morphological history. Poznań had once been a walled town, but these defenses were entirely self-

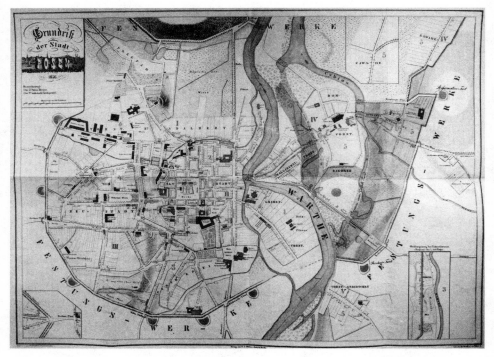

Map 3. Poznań, 1856. The old city center's tight grid of streets is still readily discernible. Extending to the west and south are the avenues and squares of the new city. The whole ensemble is ringed by massive fortifications. Courtesy of the Raczyński Library.

referential, designed to protect it from outside aggression. The new defenses were built to meet the defensive needs of the entire Prussian state. They signaled the city's increasing integration into that much larger entity.

Through its engagement with the space of Poznań, the state intended to mold not just the city but its residents as well. In placing the names of Prussian heroes on the new squares and streets, it encouraged Poznanians to participate in Prussia's collective memory. As it imposed its language, traditions, and governing style, the state hoped they would become second nature to a new generation of loyal Prussians.

That hope largely became a reality within Poznań's German community. Many expressed enthusiasm for the Prussian initiatives. In an 1803 edition of the short-lived *Südpreußische Monatsschrift* (South Prussian monthly), an anonymous German resident penned a poem in praise of the town. The poem noted with approval the building "of many houses large and small,/ Solid and handsome in long straight rows," undoubtedly a reference to the flurry of con-

11. View of Poznań from the south, circa 1838. This image suggests the massive scale of the citadel on Winiary Hill and how it came to dominate the cityscape. Courtesy of the Muzeum Narodowe w Poznaniu.

struction taking place in the new Friedrich Wilhelm City. It also painted an attractive picture of Wilhelm Street, where "chestnut and poplar trees bloom" and where those on a promenade could find sustenance from the "punch, cake, ice cream, music and beer" on offer. The poem concluded on a proud note: "O! If you could only join us,/ You certainly would find here a small Berlin."[3]

There were some exceptions, of course. German liberals who had crossed into Poland to support the November Uprising clearly disagreed with Prussia's geopolitical vision for the region. But in the main Germans welcomed the state's investment in their city and were pleased by the rapid growth, the broad avenues, and the stately new buildings. It is safe to assume that the new face of Poznań, in conjunction with the worldview transmitted in state-sponsored school curricula and newspapers, played an important role in colonizing their spatial imaginations. Like the city itself, German Poznanians were oriented increasingly westward, toward Berlin and the rest of Germany.

Many aspects of the new Poznań thus would have been familiar to Prussian visitors like Biester. But there were still some jarring disjunctions. The Polish language remained prevalent on the streets, and in that language many residents were articulating ambitions for the city that were sharply at odds with the state's vision. The Polish community clung with growing intensity to the notion that Poznań belonged to Poland, not Prussia, and it sought to express that relationship in a variety of ways.

Many Poles found Poznań under Prussian rule to be evolving into an unfamiliar and alienating place. Visiting in 1821, the celebrated writer Julian Ursyn Niemcewicz expressed the feeling well: "Since the Prussians assumed control of this city, everything has taken on a fresh, foreign shape. The double walls have been razed, the deep moats filled in, the temples of the Lord put to worldly uses. There are newly laid streets in the middle of which—as in Berlin—are planted four rows of trees. It all might be pretty, but it is not ours."[4] Many Poles felt not only alienated but dispossessed of what was rightfully theirs. Such sentiments emerged as German immigrants began to alter the demographic composition of the city and as the economic profile of the German and Jewish bourgeoisie grew more prominent. As one Pole despaired in an 1843 issue of the *Orędownik Naukowy,* "Everywhere foreigners are composing the center and pulse of economic life, and increasingly they are pushing our own out of the heart of the cities and into squat huts in the suburbs."[5]

Pockets of Polish opposition to the government's spatial politics gradually took shape. As the state launched the massive expansion of Poznań, disgruntled Poles developed their own colloquial lexicon for the project. Rather than using Friedrich Wilhelm City, the development's official name, they called the area "the upper city" *(górne miasto),* in reference to its higher elevation. And instead of Wilhelm Square, they referred to "theater square" *(plac teatralny).*[6] Their purpose was to avoid that which the state encouraged them to do: acknowledge Prussian history as their own.

In the late 1830s Polish leaders adopted a novel tack in their struggle over the space of Poznań. Karol Marcinkowski and his allies in the Organic Work Movement had determined that the goal of Polish independence could best be reached by building a strong Polish middle class capable of excelling in all fields of endeavor. They decided to construct a space in the heart of Poznań that could nurture this sort of social change. The space was the Bazar, an imposing building erected on New (Neu) Street near Wilhelm Square. The Bazar included under one roof a hotel, a ballroom, and space for well over a dozen cafés, restaurants, and shops. The purpose was to provide budding Polish merchants and entrepreneurs with a venue for their ventures in a city dominated by their German and Jewish counterparts. The Bazar was also designed to accommodate Polish organizations and social events.

A far more audacious move was the 1842 drive to build a monument to General Jan Dąbrowski (1755–1818), a renowned Polish military hero who served on behalf of the Kościuszko Uprising and the Duchy of Warsaw. A Polish committee petitioned the state for permission to erect a statue of the general at the east end of Wilhelm Square. The statue would portray Dąbrowski either standing alone or on horseback, and the text on the pedestal would read: "From the nation in gratitude for service to country." The seditious subtext to this proposition was not lost on provincial officials. They relayed the petition to Berlin along with their own admonitions. Government President *(Regierungs-Präsident)* Maurice Beurmann reminded the king that in 1806 Dąbrowski was among the first to betray his sworn allegiance to the Prussian king and side with Napoleon. To now honor such a man would go against "the present order of things" and "would be a clear demonstration against the current government."[7] Provincial Governor Arnim-Boitzenburg focused his criticism on the proposed inscription on the pedestal. As he understood the text, the word "country" referred to Poland. The entire project was thus another example of the larger effort "to ignore recent changes and to portray the Polish Empire as still in existence, thereby maintaining the notions of its unity and indivisibility."[8] Following their advice, the king rejected the petition.

Accompanying the evolving spatial horizons of Poznanians in this era was the emergence of novel conceptions of time. It is generally conceded that in the modern era a revolution took place in terms of how Westerners interpret the passage of time.[9] This development, often referred to as historicism, was predicated on the gradual discrediting of faith-based, premodern historiography. The Bible and other religious resources once provided the foundational elements of historical thought in the West, including a metanarrative (creation, sin, and redemption) and hermeneutical strategies that emphasized God's regular intervention in human affairs and that encouraged the collapsing of the sacred past and the mundane present into cycles of prefiguration and fulfillment. The Poznań that Biester encountered, for instance, was still a place where Catholics saw the Virgin Mary's benevolent engagement on their behalf and where Protestants equated their circumstances with those of the ancient Israelites.

Over the course of the eighteenth and nineteenth centuries European intellectuals abandoned premodern historiography in favor of a more "scientific" approach, viewing the past as a vast collection of discrete events that un-folded across time in ever new patterns of cause and effect. The new science of history developed into a matter of research and lively debate, taking its place alongside theology, law, and language as an independent field of inquiry at universities. It also found its way into the curricula of the ballooning net-work of elementary and secondary schools. In this way it shaped the temporal perspectives of ordinary Europeans, once wed to the rhythms of the agricul-tural cycle and the liturgical year.

The emergence of the modern approach to history coincided with the de-velopment of nationalism, and the two made compatible bedfellows. With the waning influence of religious narratives, the way was clear for new devices to frame the historical record into meaningful patterns, and the concept of na-tion presented itself as an attractive candidate. The past emerged as a critical tool for understanding the grand dimensions of national character. The his-torical record, whether logged in chronicles or buried in the dirt, frozen in stone monuments or as liquid as the oral traditions of the peasantry, contained valuable clues to the nature of a nation's ancestors, a nature that surely still flowed through the veins of present representatives.

In Poznań the historicism-nationalism symbiosis played itself out in inter-esting ways. History emerged as a popular topic, as illustrated by the increasing impetus to celebrate anniversaries, to memorialize fallen heroes, and to write interpretive narratives about the past. As this interest developed, however, a stubborn point of contention arose regarding the status of Poznań in light of its history. How should the historical record inform the contemporary under-standing of this place and its destiny?

For nationalist-minded Poles, the answer was clear. Poznań was the site of centuries of Polish history and, most significantly, the residence of Poland's earliest kings. In their minds this heritage bound the city inseparably to the Polish nation. Indeed, based on this same logic, more precocious nationalists claimed for Poland much of the Prussian provinces of Silesia and Pomerania. Because Poles had settled there before the Germans, and because pockets of ethnic Poles still lived there, these regions belonged in a future Polish state. Re-garding the contemporary situation, Polish nationalists grounded some of their harshest criticisms of Prussia's Germanization policy on historical argu-ments. In their open letter to Flottwell, a group of Poznanian Poles con-demned his efforts as being against history: "What unjust, arbitrary attacks still remain in your campaign to speed the development of history? Will you turn this development over to the passage of time and the quiet control of history, or will you bend it violently through harsh measures?"[10]

As Poles developed their interpretation of the present city based on its past, Germans reached their own, quite different interpretations. Once again intellectuals in other parts of Germany provided the models that would influence the thinking of the local German population. Alternative readings of the historical record arrived already with the first waves of Prussian administrators in 1793. Official Prussian sources justified the partitions on account of centuries of Polish misrule. Poland's rulers had ceded all rights to the former commonwealth through their poor stewardship. The imposition of Prussian discipline over a region once rife with lawlessness and oppression was the fortuitous end that justified the unpleasant means. Eventually a second theme appeared: an appreciation for the achievements of the ethnic German minority that had lived in the region for centuries. This impulse was clearly in evidence in 1834 when Karl Friedrich Schinkel, the famous Prussian architect, visited Poznań. One of the structures that most impressed him was the Church of the Virgin Mary near the cathedral, which despite its decrepit condition was still recognizable to him as an esteemed example of "pure German architecture." He recommended the building be restored. Flottwell enthusiastically embraced the proposal, seeing an opportunity to augment German claims to the grand duchy.[11]

Another champion of German history in the region was Heinrich Wuttke. Based in Leipzig, Wuttke helped found the Union for the Defense of German Interests in the Eastern Borderlands (Verein zur Wahrung der deutschen Sache in den östlichen Grenzländern). Through a series of passionate editorials in German newspapers, he sought to convince his readers that the natural boundaries of the German nation stretched deep into the east, encompassing all of the grand duchy.[12] He highlighted the fact that Germans had settled in Great Poland as early as the thirteenth century. Challenging the claims of Polish nationalists, Wuttke argued that the area was not essentially Polish but rather an ethnic borderland. For this reason Prussia had "as least as much of a natural right" to the region as did Poland.[13] Wuttke also contended that the German presence in Great Poland was part of a larger pattern of German eastward expansion. He interpreted this as an integral part of the flow of history that his contemporaries should not attempt to stop.

The evolution of Poznań's spatial and temporal profile was conditioned in no small measure by the changing demands of state and international politics.

The city Biester once visited had living roots extending deep into the Middle Ages. An amended version of the thirteenth-century Magdeburg Law still defined the communal responsibilities of Poznanians in the city center and their relationship to the state. In the immediate vicinity, at least eight other townships maintained separate regulations of their own. The special rights of the Jews, the nobility, and the Catholic Church were enshrined in laws of similar antiquity. Taken together, the legal arrangements governing the area were exceedingly complex, comprised of many competing claims to authority and riddled with idiosyncratic privileges.

This arcane political culture disintegrated under the combined pressures of Prussian rule and the far-reaching influence of the French Revolution. The Prussian government was at once absolutist and highly bureaucratic, and after gaining possession of Great Poland it monopolized authority and rationalized the mechanisms of control. In 1796 it claimed ownership of the Catholic Church's property and restricted the authority that institution used to wield over large swaths of the region. It also eliminated many of the separate jurisdictions exercised by the townships and villages immediately surrounding Poznań proper, merging them into a single urban entity.[14] Through a series of legislative acts it broke down the unique legal status that distinguished Jews from their Christian neighbors. After the 1803 fire destroyed much of the Jewish Quarter, the state made it easier for Jews to settle in other parts of the city. In 1824 it submitted all Jewish children to the same school curricula and standards required of their Christian counterparts. The 1833 law regarding Jewish naturalization availed to qualified Jews nearly all of the freedoms guaranteed to Christian citizens of the kingdom.[15]

In short, Prussia collapsed Poznań's maze of separate jurisdictions and corporate loopholes into a comprehensive structure with a clear chain of command leading straight to Berlin. The city developed into a more rationalized space in which almost all of its residents, regardless of ancient privileges and boundaries, were subjected to the same standards, standards that usually exercised sway across the entire kingdom. The state also asserted its presence in the city by stationing there a sizable military force and a raft of bureaucrats. It announced new developments in its policies through press organs like the *Amtsblatt der Königlichen Regierung zu Posen* (Official gazette of the royal government in Poznań). For a population accustomed to parochial legal arrangements and weak central government, these changes forced them to reassess their group identities. The old boundaries that used to shape their experiences—Śródka, Grobla, the Jewish Quarter—grew porous and inconsequential. Collective arrangements that once defined the course of life—noble, Protestant, serf—lost much of their power.

Still larger factors were at work in the erosion of older boundaries of belonging, including dramatic improvements in transportation and communication. Wolfgang Schivelbusch has written persuasively about the transformative impact of the railroad in the middle decades of the nineteenth century. Mechanized travel dramatically shortened the time required to travel from place to place, in effect causing the world to shrink. Such change rendered the products and experiences of once-distant locales much more accessible, affecting the relationship between humans and their environment.[16] In Poznań the railroad first arrived in 1848. Long before its advent, however, Poznanians had been experiencing the revolutionary shifts Schivelbusch associates with the steam engine.

To fully appreciate the advances made during the first half century of Prussian rule, it is important to recall how isolated Poznań was back when Biester made his visit. Its main artery, the Warta River, was clogged with silt, making passage difficult for larger vessels. Roads linking the city with other centers were relatively few in number and poorly maintained. This underdeveloped infrastructure dampened the flow of traffic to and from the city, reinforcing its provincial demeanor.

The Prussian state and the demands of an expanding economy gradually nudged Poznań out of its isolation. In the 1790s the state expended large sums to improve the Warta as a channel linking the region with neighboring provinces to the west.[17] Subsequent improvements contributed to a fourfold increase in water traffic in and out of Poznań between 1819 and 1846. After 1815 the state began paving the main arteries running between the city and other Prussian centers such as Berlin and Breslau. On these roads traveled more sophisticated coaches with large, metal-rimmed wheels and wider gauges. Such improvements allowed for a smoother ride, greater speed, larger loads, and more reliability. The trip between Poznań and Berlin, once a torturous two-day odyssey, was shortened to just twenty-six hours. The state also developed regular postal routes for the transportation of both mail and people between Poznań and other towns. Traffic increased markedly. By 1848 thousands of people were traveling between Poznań and Berlin every year. To accommodate surging demand, dozens of privately owned courier services sprang up.[18]

As a result, the horizons of ordinary Poznanians expanded notably. Long-distance travel, once the purview of the few, evolved into a more democratic experience. More common still was the encounter with travelers. Poznań welcomed growing numbers of outsiders either passing through or settling down for an extended stay. They brought with them firsthand accounts of distant lands. Their testimonies helped flesh out the swelling body of knowledge garnered in school, in newspapers, and other sources. For Poznanians the wider world was becoming less an abstract concept and more a living, comprehensible reality. At the same time they cultivated an expanding network of personal contacts with this wider world in the form of correspondence and participation in far-flung associations.

This new spatial consciousness and the infrastructure upon which it was built had important consequences for the emergence of nationalism. It enabled large numbers of Poznanians to see beyond their immediate environment and to feel intimately connected to a sprawling collectivity. The activities of Polish nationalist groups illustrate well the newfound possibilities in a shrinking Europe. Recall that Poland was absorbed into three powerful states intent on preventing its reestablishment, and that many among the Polish elite were scattered across Western Europe. Despite great distances and many international borders, nationalist-minded Poles plotted together with alacrity. Organizations like the Hotel Lambert and the Polish Democratic Society coordinated their efforts across all three partitions, often under the direction of leaders based in cities hundreds of miles away.

The accomplishments of German nationalists were no less remarkable. Here the main challenge lay in the fragmentation of the German-speaking population into dozens of independent states of varying size and character. Despite hostility from the established powers in these states, nationalists managed to place the question of political unification high on Central Europe's agenda. They disseminated their views through dozens of periodicals and voluntary associations. Germans in the grand duchy were gradually inculcated with this new spatial consciousness.

So as the Prussian state imposed its style of governance and social vision from above, demands for political change bubbled up from below. The principles of human equality and expanded political enfranchisement found ever wider acceptance among the petty nobility, the bourgeoisie, and the lower classes. Gaining credence was the notion that Poznanians were part of one great people who had a moral right to one state attentive to the popular will. But contentious questions remained. What were the most essential bonds within a nation? And to which nation-state should the Poznań region belong? By 1848 Polish and German Poznanians were reaching divergent conclusions.

Earlier tendencies to elevate liberal principles of human equality over ethnic criteria, once so in evidence in the 1820s, had given way to more effusive celebrations within each camp of their distinctive national characteristics.

The 1848 Revolution in the Grand Duchy of Poznań

The perspectives and allegiances Poznanians had developed over the first half of the nineteenth century would find decisive expression in the crucible that was 1848. During the early months of that year, governments from Paris to Vienna toppled with stunning ease, shaken by spontaneous nationalist movements and the demands for political and social change. King Friedrich Wilhelm IV's government collapsed as well, and in Prussia's moment of weakness the Polish community in the grand duchy launched a daring bid for independence. As the enthusiasm of the Poles took wing, it was matched by sentiments of similar intensity among the German population, although their driving purpose was to bind the region to the united German state that seemed to be in the offing. The ensuing struggle demonstrated the extent to which nationalist identities had triumphed, superseding the multitude of distinct collectivities and parochial worldviews that once coexisted in the city. It also revealed the central place of religion in these new identities.

The discontent that flared up so violently during the 1848 revolution had been mounting for years. Having summoned the genie of German nationalism to assist in its war with Napoleonic France, the Prussian government labored with great difficulty to put it back in the bottle. It faced this challenge again in the early 1830s after revolutions in Belgium, France, Greece, and the Congress Kingdom of Poland revived the dream of a German nation-state. By the late 1840s another period of crisis seemed imminent. Nationalist enthusiasms had soared to new heights, stimulated in part by a loosening of restrictions on publication and popular association early in Friedrich Wilhelm IV's tenure. An additional factor was the widespread frustration with Prussia's traditional political order. The bourgeoisie, which had been growing steadily in both size and confidence, chafed under its limited political influence. The situation was much more dire for the lower classes. Prussia's economy failed to create sufficient opportunities for the booming population, forcing large numbers to work for pitifully low wages. Their economic insecurity was only aggravated by a series of poor harvests that caused the cost of living to rise. All across the state, the desire for change was palpable.

France provided the spark that touched off the unrest. Dogged by a powerful wave of opposition to his unpopular rule, on February 24 King Louis Philippe abdicated and fled to England, leaving the reins of power in the hands of a coalition of reform-minded moderates and liberals. This turn of events electrified opposition movements across the continent, and they immediately raised the pressure on their respective governments. On March 13 Austria's archconservative chancellor, Prince Metternich, was forced to step down, and the royal family fled Vienna soon thereafter. Surrounded by a large, angry crowd and fearing the same fate, Friedrich Wilhelm IV made a series of extraordinary concessions. On March 18 he came out in support of a constitution for Prussia and the creation of a united Germany. The next day he appeared on the balcony of the royal palace to face the thousands of Berliners gathered there, and at their insistence he paid homage to the corpses of citizens killed by the military in recent street clashes. On March 21 he agreed to take part in a parade through the city following the black, red, and gold flag that had come to symbolize the cause of German unification. One of his closest advisers, Friedrich Wilhelm von Rauch, traveled alongside the king that day and burned with shame as the aura of the Prussian monarchy was reduced through such vulgar associations. "I cannot describe the impression that this ride made on me," he noted. "It seemed to me as if everything had gone mad."[19]

The atmosphere in Poznań had been highly charged in the weeks preceding the Berlin revolution. Many nobles from the surrounding region had gathered in Poznań in order to obtain late-breaking reports from around the continent. When the courier arrived early on March 20 with news of the recent events in Berlin, the city crackled with activity. By ten o'clock almost everyone had heard, with the reports growing more exaggerated with each retelling.[20] The Polish response was amazingly swift. Before long, women had hung dozens of red and white Polish flags from the windows of the Bazar and many private residences, and thousands of Poles filled the streets.

In his memoir Marceli Motty recalls his impressions of that memorable day: "The streets were choked with people like on a major holiday; without a trace of the police or army and with the government either in hiding or maintaining a very low profile. . . . Here in the market square teemed men and women and people of all ages. Seeing their faces and hearing their voices, one would have thought it was Poznań in the sixteenth or seventeenth centuries, for on this day just about every person and every word in circulation was Polish. The Germans and Jews were sitting at home, not sure of what to make of our intentions."[21] Motty's comments capture how the initial breakdown of royal power in Berlin ignited the hopes of a broad cross section of the Polish population, unnerved most Germans and Jews, and paralyzed local Prussian authorities. His description also suggests how the events of that day displayed in dramatic, palpable fashion what was at stake for the city. For Motty and other Poles, the fluttering Polish flags and the chorus of Polish voices in the streets allowed them to imagine themselves back in time to a preferred Poznań that was proudly and indisputably Polish, an idealized past that could serve as a model for the future. For Germans and Germanized Jews, however, these same scenes likely brought less savory associations to mind. The temporary eclipse of the symbols of Prussian power and the presence of German culture underscored how fragile their privileged position in the city actually was.

Polish leaders from the various political factions gathered at the Bazar already on March 20 to plot strategy. They formed the National Committee to lead the effort. Designed to harmonize the wide variety of interests within Polish society, the committee's ranks combined wealthy nobles like Jędrzej Moraczewski and members of modest means like the artisan Paweł Andrzejewski. It included radical republicans like Ryszard Berwiński and Walenty Stefański and moderate liberals such as Gustaw Potworowski and Maciej Mielżyński.[22] It immediately swung into action, appealing for Poles to unite behind its leadership, mollifying the concerns of Germans and Jews, and pressing the Prussian government for concessions.

The confidence and audacity displayed by the National Committee in the opening days of the movement were striking. "We can be neither Prussians nor Germans," the committee declared, "so long as Polish blood courses through our veins, so long as we contain but a flicker of moral integrity, for the curse of shame clings to he who denies his people and betrays the holy cause of his fathers."[23] Their goal was no less than the restoration of Poland in its historic entirety, and recent events suggested that such hopes were entirely within reach. The collapse of the Prussian and Austrian governments had been so complete, and the enthusiasm for political reorganization based on nationalist principles so widespread, that a united Germany and a revived Poland seemed to be the will of history. The committee heard, for instance, how Karol Libelt, Ludwik Mierosławski, and the other Poles imprisoned in Berlin for plotting the failed 1846 uprising had been freed on March 20 by a large crowd of Berliners, brought to the royal palace, and honored as heroes of the nationalist cause. They heard as well that the king had formed a new liberal cabinet that included Heinrich Alexander von Arnim-Suckow as its foreign minister, a man who publicly had declared his support for the restoration of a

Polish state. The French foreign minister had expressed the same intention. The only major roadblock was the Russian czar, who thus far had weathered the revolutionary storm and condemned the idea of Polish independence. Indeed, a war between Russia and Prussia over the issue seemed likely. The National Committee began planning for such a conflict, calculating that Polish valor on the battlefield might guarantee the success of its cause.[24]

From the start, Catholicism factored heavily within the Polish movement. Support for the independence drive was strong among church officials. Three members of the National Committee (Jan Janiszewski, Antoni Fromholz, and Aleksy Prusinowski) were themselves priests, and priests throughout the province cooperated closely, reading the committee's pronouncements from the pulpit and providing logistical and moral support. The movement's most important church ally was Archbishop Przyłuski. Already on March 21 he led a delegation to Berlin in order to relay Polish expectations to the king, and over the weeks that followed he repeatedly intervened on behalf of the movement.

Przyłuski's actions stood in telling contrast to those of his predecessor, Archbishop Ignacy Raczyński. When faced with the Kościuszko Uprising of 1794, Raczyński had opposed it, choosing instead to defend the Prussian king's authority over the Poznań region as divinely ordained. That a church official of so high a rank should now openly support the cause of national self-determination suggests how dramatically the political landscape had changed, and how tangled together Polish and Catholic identity had become.

Catholicism's role in the 1848 revolution was not limited to the involvement of church officials. Polish leaders regularly struck Catholic themes in their calls for popular support, an approach that met with remarkable success. On March 21, Junker Ober-Conreuth, councillor of the county of Czarnków (Czarnikau) northwest of Poznań, alerted his superiors to an inflammatory poem circulating in the town of Lubasz that was distributed to Catholics on their way out of church after Mass. The poem presented in rhyming verse a view of recent revolutionary events in Europe. It noted an obscure convergence in the Catholic liturgical calendar that its author interpreted as proof of Poland's imminent independence:

> The Swiss have won—Italy is still aglow.
> And in the countryside various people are murmuring.
> St. Adalbert's feast day falls on Easter,
> Therefore war is certain to come.

Such prophecy has come down from heaven,
The Pole will soon drive the Prussian from the land.[25]

Credited with having brought Christianity to Poland, St. Adalbert long has ranked as one of the nation's most important patron saints. The fact that Easter Monday should fall on his feast day (April 23) readily conjured up ideas associated with Polish messianism. Was not this rare convergence a sign that Poland, the Christ among nations, would also rise from the dead? Many Polish Catholics thought so, and in the weeks leading up to Easter this complex of ideas was repeated over and over throughout the province. It was a powerful argument, one that reinforced the notion that Polish independence was a holy cause. In Lubasz, Ober-Conreuth noted, "although the Mass in the church had already ended, numerous Poles were so stimulated by the reading [of the poem] . . . that they apparently returned to the church and fell to their knees in prayer."[26]

The events of March 1848 provoked very different reactions among Germans living in the grand duchy. For the small contingent of Polonophile liberals who managed to weather the divisive atmosphere of the 1830s and 1840s, there was genuine enthusiasm for the idea of Polish independence. The large majority of Germans, however, were much more conflicted. Like the Poles, they had concluded that the grand duchy would break off from Prussia. Lest the revolutionary moment pass them by, German leaders in Poznań formed an association of their own, known as the German National Committee, in order to defend German interests in the event of political reorganization. Like its Polish counterpart, the German National Committee spanned a diverse membership. Its ranks included numerous bureaucrats, ranging from Assessor Crousaz, a liberal democrat eager for rapprochement with the Poles, and government councilor *(Regierungsrat)* Ernst Viebig, a native Poznanian and constitutional monarchist. Robert Hepke, a professor at Poznań's Catholic gymnasium, emerged as the committee's most effective publicist. Belonging as well were a number of business leaders and artisans, including an innkeeper named Kaatz and a banker named Mamroth, both of whom were Jews.[27]

The German National Committee's early official statements were highly sympathetic to the Polish cause. On March 22 the committee declared, "The hour has struck for the unshackling of the nations. From the Rhein to the Prosna rises just one call: freedom! The breath of God passes over the earth and carries the call from nation to nation, all uniting in him. Poland! Finally the day of freedom has also come to you, the day of atonement for the great crime in history."[28] In celebrating the idea of national self-determination and acknowledging the view, widespread among the Poles, that the partitions were a "great crime," the committee hoped to ingratiate itself with the Polish leadership. And bearing in mind the city's intoxicating atmosphere during the first days of the revolution, such grandiose talk of freedom and interethnic solidarity was perhaps sincere. It would soon become clear, however, that most Germans wanted no part of an independent Polish state. The mistrust between the two groups was too embedded to be brushed aside at once. Moreover, pressing economic concerns entered the equation. Many Germans in Poznań were on the Prussian government's payroll or had benefited handsomely from Prussian policies. Polish independence thus could undermine the financial well-being of many German families. By the end of the month, German communities across the grand duchy actively were seeking to have their immediate areas excluded from the province's uncertain destiny and joined to a future German state.

In contrast to the Polish movement, the German campaign did not rely heavily on the Protestant churches. The main reason for this was that the potential supporters of the campaign were not uniformly Protestant. The grand duchy's large Jewish population, which of late had been cooperating closely with Germans in local politics and in general was favorably disposed to a future as part of Germany, was a particularly important ally. Also, the substantial German Catholic population might be drawn in as well. Cultivating these relationships would be critical if they were to prevail over the Polish majority. Therefore, tying German aspirations to a specific confession had to be avoided. Nevertheless, religion was appealed to time and again throughout the German campaign. One of the earliest and most consistent strategies Germans used to discredit the Polish bid for independence was to portray it as radically Catholic. According to this reading, intolerant Catholic priests were among the leaders of the Polish effort, and if the Poles achieved their aims, members of other religious groups would be exposed to persecution. This argument resonated with Protestants and Jews alike, and it stood a chance of appealing to some within the German Catholic community.

The early days of the revolution in Poznań belonged to the Poles. The turmoil that had enveloped the Prussian central government and military deprived Prussian authorities in the grand duchy of their mandate to rule. The Polish National Committee quickly exploited the power vacuum. It took control of the town hall for use as its base of operations, thereby signaling its symbolic hegemony over the city. To extend its influence it organized a network of subordinate committees in towns and villages throughout the province and established a system of taxation to fund their operations.[29] It also created a press organ, the *Gazeta Polska* (Polish gazette), in order to influence perspectives and shape the public debate.[30]

The Polish National Committee ordered the creation of national guard units in every village and town, composed of all able-bodied Polish men between seventeen and fifty. Newly returned from Berlin, Ludwik Mierosławski was charged with organizing a substantial military force that could defend Polish interests in the grand duchy and perhaps even assist a Polish uprising in Russia. Before long he had assembled more than six thousand troops in makeshift camps in three towns, Września (Wreschen), Książ (Xions), and Pleszew (Pleschen). Another four thousand to five thousand troops had been gathered together in Środa Wielkopolski (Schroda) under the leadership of Augustyn Brzeżański. Smaller camps were later established elsewhere. A large percentage of these "soldiers" were poorly trained peasants, armed with little more than scythes and pitchforks.[30]

The Polish National Committee recognized that its success or failure hinged on its ability to win the support of the peasantry, a group that still formed the large majority of Polish society. On March 25 and April 1 the committee issued two formal appeals to this group, read mainly from church pulpits throughout the province, promising numerous benefits for all who joined in the fight for Polish independence. Volunteer soldiers could expect generous tax breaks, land, and benefits for their wives and children. More importantly, the committee assured its audience that a future Poland would be free of deep caste divisions: "From now on, all of the previous estate distinctions are to be lifted. There will be neither nobles nor peasants, rather only free citizens as sons of a Polish mother."[31] These appeals met with mixed results. While thousands of peasants did join the makeshift military units, many more passively stood by, unwilling to risk their lives and livelihoods. There were even instances in which groups of Polish peasants demonstrated their commitment to the Prussian Crown, which many still regarded with affection on account of land reform in the 1820s and other measures.[32] Cut off from most of the educational and cultural opportunities available to their urban compatriots, the Polish peasantry held on longer than other groups to premodern, parochial worldviews. They were hardly the most receptive audience to nationalist ideologies.

The extensive organizational efforts of the Poles alarmed Poznań's German community. The German National Committee immediately sought to join the Polish National Committee as a means of giving Germans a voice within the organization that, at the moment at least, seemed to control the grand duchy's fate. The Polish leadership, however, did not trust the motivations of their German neighbors and refused to include them in their deliberations. A March 28 order from Jędrzej Moraczewski to Ryszard Berwiński spelled out the Polish strategy in this regard: "One should make every effort not to alarm the Germans in order to avoid a strong reaction from their side. On the other hand it is necessary to maintain supremacy over them." [33]

Meanwhile, Polish-German relations were being tested by a wave of violence that engulfed the province. The breakdown of Prussian authority allowed long-simmering resentments to explode, resulting in a spate of robberies, assaults, and killings. In the eastern, southern, and central counties, where Poles formed a comfortable majority, symbols of state like the Prussian eagle were vandalized, Prussian officials were forced to flee, and ordinary Germans and Jews were exposed to various indignities. In the northern and western counties where Germans were numerous, just the opposite prevailed. Here Germans gathered into civilian guards and bullied Poles in their vicinity. Poles also lodged numerous complaints about excesses committed by Prussian troops.

The violence eroded the initial civility in relations between Polish and German leaders. In a carefully worded complaint from March 26, the German National Committee urged the Polish leadership to rein in the abuses committed against Germans and Jews: "There have been many cases in which armed groups of your people have threatened and violated the property and personal security of your German-speaking neighbors. Keep in mind that through such acts of infamous violence you stain the honor of your nation, and you undermine the sympathy for your cause among the nations of Germany and Europe." [34] The Polish National Committee formulated a pointed response. It observed that much greater acts of violence were occurring in German areas gripped by revolution, such as Baden, Hessen, Württemburg, and Vienna. In other words, the Germans were in no position to complain, especially considering that it was Germans who were responsible for partitioning Poland and oppressing the Poles for decades. The committee also insisted that the violence was the work of an unruly few. If Germans are to condemn all Poles for the misdeeds of a few, it noted, then "we would certainly be justified in pinning the blame for the bitterness and the shame of servitude of the last thirty-three years on those who, in working for the authorities, placed themselves above us and gave themselves up as tools for our humiliation." The committee leveled another stinging accusation against their German interlocutors: "You have no desire to rise to the idea of universal freedom, to divorce yourselves from the material benefits of domination. You would rather have servants than brothers." [35]

Rebuffed in its effort to work with the Polish leadership, the German National Committee focused more exclusively on German and Jewish interests. Instrumental to this shift was government councilor Eberhard Kolbe von Schreeb, a combative German nationalist who emerged overnight as a popular leader among Poznań's German and Jewish populations. An April 3 letter from the committee to Germans throughout the province reflected this new spirit. It declared, "The time has come in which we, too, must stand up for our German rights. Therefore we issue the urgent appeal: unite and work together in the awareness of German strength. Gather around us for the German cause, so that your wishes can be heard truly and fully. 'To each his own' shall be our motto." [36]

Poznań Germans were inspired in part by the self-defensive measures of the largely German counties in the north and east of the grand duchy. Here, almost from the start of the revolution, German communities began forming committees and paramilitary units to defend their interests and to prevent local Poles from organizing. Recognizing that there was strength in numbers, they displayed an uncharacteristic openness to their Jewish neighbors, welcoming them into their committees and counting them as Germans. By March 23 these committees began besieging Berlin with petitions to exclude their areas from the political reorganization being planned by the Poles and to incorporate them instead into a united Germany. [37]

An important element behind the swift organization of these communities was a Protestant faith shared by a large majority of Germans there and, in turn, a deeply rooted antipathy toward the Catholic Church. In the town of Meseritz, Director Kerst of the local *Realschule* led the German organizational effort, and in a letter to a friend he marveled over the passionate response it engendered: "Everyone is enthusiastic about our cause, and the villages are arming themselves completely. . . . The sentiment in the cities and towns is far exceeding our expectations. We have nothing to fear. . . . The reaction against the priests is fully underway." [38] His final offhand remark, equating the Polish drive for independence with priests, is telling. In his mind and undoubtedly in that of many supporters, for all its talk of freedom and international harmony the Polish movement was, to a large extent, an effort to restore the hegemony of the Catholic Church. And this was a cause well worth fighting against.

At the outset of the revolution, Prussian authorities in the grand duchy and throughout the kingdom appeared to be at the mercy of a mass movement aglow with nationalist fervor and hungry for political change. When Provincial Governor Beurmann declared the founding of the Polish National Committee to be illegal, his admonition was ignored. The Fifth Army Corps initially set up outposts in Poznań's squares and thoroughfares, but they soon retreated to the safety of the citadel. From there General-Lieutenant Colomb had posted throughout the town a public notice urging peace and quiet. These were ripped down and mocked.[39] A similar flouting of established authority was taking place in Berlin and other centers of nationalist ferment. But the king still had powerful cards to play, should he choose to oppose the course of events unfolding on the street. He enjoyed deep reservoirs of support among conservatives and in the central provinces of the kingdom such as Mecklemburg and Brandenburg. He also continued to command the loyalty of the army, which was clearly superior to the ragtag bands of scythe-wielding Polish peasants assembled in the grand duchy.

Discerning Friedrich Wilhelm IV's attitude toward the revolution and a coherent strategy behind his actions was a challenge for his closest advisers, and it remains a challenge for later historians as well. He was roundly criticized in his own time for being inconsistent, and this predilection seems to have been magnified by the pressures of state in so uncertain a moment. There is good reason to believe that the king's initial promises to work toward constitutional government and German unity were sincere. His romantic nature disposed him in particular to the latter, and he allowed his imagination free rein over how Germany's medieval legacy might be revised for the modern era. But the democratic nature of the revolutionary enterprise—the large demonstrations of the rude masses, the disregard of traditional hierarchies, the compromises required in parliamentary politics—proved far too taxing of his royal sensibilities. The king quickly tired of the processes unfolding in the new State Assembly in Berlin and the pan-German National Assembly in Frankfurt/Main and sought the sanctuary of the royal estate outside Potsdam. From here a small coterie of conservative advisers were better able to command his attention and dispose him toward a counterrevolutionary agenda.[40]

The king's vacillating attitude toward the revolution mirrored his approach to the Polish question. His first actions were very favorable toward Polish ambitions. On March 24 he ordered the formal reorganization of the grand duchy. He then appointed General-Major Wilhelm von Willisen, a figure sympathetic to the Polish cause, to oversee the process. In so doing he conformed to the designs of his new foreign minister, Arnim-Suckow, who was appealing to liberal Germans as a means of cementing Prussia's preeminence in pan-German affairs.[41] But by the beginning of April the king began moving in the opposite direction. Worried about a possible conflict with Russia over the matter, he quietly ordered Colomb to take tough measures to pacify the province.[42]

Willisen arrived in Poznań on April 5 and immediately went to work. His early actions disappointed the German community greatly. He did not address alleged Polish abuses against Germans, and in his statements on the reorganization of the province, he promised the Germans simply that they would be guaranteed "the rights that [their] language affords them"—in other words, they would be administered by German-speaking officials.[43] Meanwhile he conceded to the main demands of the Poles, including the formation of a national legal system and government, the appointment of a Polish governor, and the eventual creation of Polish military units. The only catch was that the Poles first had to disarm. In the eyes of the Prussian state, unsanctioned military units threatened the stability of the province. The Polish leadership was loathe to do this, as it mistrusted Prussia's intentions and feared losing one of its best sources of leverage. Finally, with Colomb's forces threatening to eliminate the Polish military camps by force, Willisen and the Polish leadership reached a compromise (the Jaroslawiec Convention) whereby the Poles were allowed to maintain four military camps and a reduced troop total of around three thousand until a final decision was reached on the region's defensive arrangements.

For all of his good intentions to satisfy the national ambitions of the duchy's Polish majority while respecting the rights of its German and Jewish minorities, Willisen's mission was hamstrung by the fierce resistance of local Germans and the widespread animus toward Polish independence among the conservative Prussian establishment. The groundwork he began laying incited passionate expressions of nationalist identity within German communities. Germans living in and around the town of Meseritz addressed him with the following complaint:

You mean to separate us, to cut us off forever, from our great fatherland Germany? You mean to deny us our highest hope of participating in the great future of our collective fatherland? You wish to subject us to a nation whose language and mores are foreign to us, and that has openly voiced its wish not to participate in Germany's future? General, we consider it our holiest obligation to explain to you loudly and clearly that we do not want to pass a single hour without that sacred honor: to belong to Prussia, which has become one with Germany, and its lofty royal house; to identify as Germans; to be governed by German officials; to serve under German commanders; and to follow no other flag but the German, in union with German brothers for a purely German cause.[44]

Willisen was dogged by a growing chorus of condemnations for having "betrayed the German cause."[45] The antagonism undermined his mandate and forced him to avoid German population centers such as Poznań. On April 20 he quietly slipped out of the grand duchy and returned to Berlin. Not long thereafter he was relieved of his duties.

Willisen's departure was just one of a number of setbacks that plagued the Polish movement during the month of April. More distressing was the expanding presence of the Prussian army in the region and its growing willingness to enforce order.[46] There were ample indications that the state was recovering from its earlier disorientation and would not tolerate the Polish paramilitary threat. Equally damaging was the waning support across Germany for Polish independence. In March, Polish leaders benefited enormously from the powerful mystique that had surrounded their cause in Germany ever since the failed November Uprising of 1830–31. Many Germans long had admired the Poles as valiant freedom fighters, waging an uphill battle against the reactionary regimes of Prussia, Russia, and Austria. The celebrated Prussian author Theodor Fontane, for instance, noted in a letter to a friend how as a child he had "wept when it was all up with Poland" toward the end of the November Uprising.[47] These romantic associations resurfaced again in 1848. But as the revolution in Germany matured, other, more negative stereotypes of the Poles gained credence.

A key reason for the deterioration of the Polish image was the effective publicity campaign conducted by conservative voices within Prussia's bureaucratic and military establishment and the German community of the grand duchy. The Polish cause, they argued, was not about liberty but oppression. It was being led by self-centered nobles eager to reestablish their hegemony and by intolerant Catholic clerics bent on stamping out all other religions besides their own. Colomb's April 11 manifesto is a good example. In it he painted a portrait of unhinged Polish ruffians who had systematically disgraced the symbols of the Prussian Crown, assailed its representatives, and plundered public resources and the private property of law-abiding Germans. Their ultimate aim was nothing more than "the return of the earlier hated situation under the influence of the nobility." A scheming Catholic clergy was responsible for much of the problem: "The clergy have been busy delivering fanatical polemics from the pulpits and from the feet of their altars, stirring up the people for war on behalf of the holy Catholic religion and against the Prussian government. They have been waving the standards that the bands of armed peasants are supposed to follow. In several places they have claimed that 'priests have been killed,' and 'they want to force the Poles to convert to Protestantism,' simply to enrage the agitated population in the countryside."[48]

Polish independence, which had seemed inevitable in mid-March, was drawn into doubt by mid-April. In the pan-German preliminary parliament *(Vorparlament)* assembled in Frankfurt, an April vote on the concept could not even generate a simple majority. Erstwhile German advocates of Polish independence now hesitated or retracted their support altogether. Their initial enthusiasm, born in the heady opening act of revolution, was being replaced by national self-interest. The Polish cause, many now reasoned, was not worth the spilling of German blood. A prominent spokesperson for this new orientation was the well-known democrat Wilhelm Jordan, who chastised his fellow Germans for "losing sight of the fatherland" with their cosmopolitan politics.[49] A similar conclusion had been reached in France, where the government reasoned that if an independent Poland meant war with Russia, the price was too high.[50]

Not only were Germans across Central Europe losing sympathy for the Polish cause, they were also being stirred by the fervid expressions of nationalist sentiment made by German communities in the grand duchy. Alongside their declarations of love for the fatherland, these communities beseeched the Prussian king, the Prussian State Assembly, and the National Assembly in Frankfurt that they, too, might be joined with Prussia, if not a future united Germany. The above quote from the Germans of Meseritz is a characteristic example of the florid feeling their letters and petitions contained. Their pleas met with a great deal of sympathy. Support mounted for the concept of partitioning the grand duchy between its predominantly Polish and predominantly German parts. The latter would be excluded from any plans to create an autonomous Polish political entity. On April 14 the king made it official, declaring in a cabinet order that of the grand duchy's twenty-four counties, ten in the north and west would not take part in the region's political reorganization.[51] On April 26 he pushed the line of demarcation deeper into the province. Now the Poles were left to work with just nine counties and parts of six others. Most notably, the city of Poznań was now classed with the German sector.

The decision to divide the grand duchy satisfied most, but not all, of the region's Germans. Once again, religion factored into the equation. Catholic Germans living in the proposed German sector were discomfited by the Protestant character of the local German committees and defensive organizations, especially the sharply anti-Catholic tone of many of their pronouncements. Catholic Germans were moved as well by appeals for solidarity made by Archbishop Przyłuski and other clergy. In a widely disseminated pastoral letter from April 21, Przyłuski warned Catholics living in the German sector that their interests might be threatened. Think carefully, he urged, "whether you are really indifferent about the bonds of your national unity, your heritage, and above all your religious affinity with the rest of this province. Think whether you really want to separate from the Grand Duchy of Poznań and join the German Union, in which your interests, particularly your religious concerns, might lose their meaning and defense."[52] Such appeals were highly effective. Nearly all of the German Catholic communities in the German sector prepared petitions of their own to the Prussian government, in which they asked to be reunited with the Polish portion of the grand duchy.[53]

Polish leaders decried the notion of dividing the grand duchy into Polish and German sectors. On an emotional level they felt that the division would remove a portion of territory that historically belonged to Poland. In practical terms they recognized that they would be left to work with a small, underdeveloped stretch of land that would be hardly tenable as an autonomous unit. Moreover, once cut off from Prussia, their share of the grand duchy would be vulnerable to Russian incursions. On April 17 the Polish National Committee issued a scathing response to the plan: "At the present moment, in the year 1848, the year of the freedom of the nations, we have received an official report that a new partition of Poland is in the works! . . . So long as the reestablishment of Poland in its entirety is not completed, we will regard every arbitrary division of our province as a new partition of Poland. We will protest against this before the nations of Europe, and we will deliver the initiators and executors of this plan unto judgment before the just and unwavering tribunal of the present and the afterworld."[54] Their response is instructive. As the committee accurately understood the situation, their only source of leverage by this time was public opinion. In the field they stood little chance against the reinvigorated Prussian army.

With their position growing weaker, the Polish leadership turned their attention to the upcoming elections for the Prussian State Assembly and the German National Assembly. The former body, which began operating on May

22, was designed to offer Prussians a voice in the process of creating a Prussian constitution. The latter body, consisting of representatives from the German-speaking states of Central Europe, was charged with the task of forging the framework for a united Germany. Polish leaders hoped to have a sizable contingent of sympathetic representatives elected to both assemblies, where they would be able to champion Polish issues in the legislative arena. On April 15 the Polish National Committee issued a circular through its subsidiary organs, urging Poles to vote and to support only Polish candidates. Archbishop Przyłuski followed this with a similar appeal to all Catholics on April 18.

As Polish leaders organized for elections, German leaders sought to strengthen their organizations and to prepare for a possible civil war. Some of the German paramilitary groups were armed by the Prussian army, and their capability grew rapidly. By late April there were roughly eight thousand armed German civilians in the Netz District to the north of Poznań and another six thousand or so around the towns of Meseritz and Neutomischel to the west.[55] In Poznań German and Jewish efforts proceeded apace. The charismatic Schreeb orchestrated large popular gatherings of Germans and Jews that met every third day to discuss the grand duchy's fate and demonstrate their solidarity. The German National Committee founded a press organ, the *Deutsche konstitutionelle Blatt* (German constitutional paper), to inform their constituency about the legal and social questions of the day and to prepare them for their responsibilities under a constitutional German state. A group known as the Constitutional Club was created for the same purpose. Sensing a shift in momentum in their favor, the committee drafted its boldest position to date on April 17, requesting that the central government include the city of Poznań in the German sector in the event of partition, and recommending that the state facilitate population transfers between the two sectors to prevent future German-Polish conflicts. Three days later it delivered a petition signed by thousands of residents from the city and surrounding countryside, requesting the area's "immediate unification with Germany."[56]

As the German movement in Poznań gained strength, it effectively wrested control of the city from the Poles. Karol Libelt, who after his release from prison returned to Poznań and joined the Polish National Committee, noted from personal experience how uncomfortable the situation had become for Poles by mid-April: "It was not safe for Poles to be in Poznań. . . . Every person known to be a Polish patriot saw himself subjected to unpleasantness of every kind." Those arrested in the city found themselves exposed to "catcalls, insults, jabs, and punches by the Jewish and German population."[57]

Well before the elections took place, the situation in the grand duchy was reaching a crisis point. In the weeks leading up to Easter, both Catholics and Protestants were consumed by fears over the malicious intentions of the other party. Among Catholics, a chorus of worried voices speculated that Prussia and the Protestants were planning a full-scale assault on the Catholic Church. This notion was so widespread that General-Lieutenant Wedell, commander of the Fourth Division, felt compelled to counter it. He issued a bulletin urging Catholics "not to be fooled by the false testimonies of certain individuals that the military or the German population are intending to impinge upon the rights of the Polish nationality or the Catholic religion." [58] Ferdinand von Schleinitz, government president *(Regierungspräsident)* of Bromberg, noted that Catholics in his area were highly agitated over rumors that Protestants and Jews were poisoning their wells and food and plotting to murder Catholic priests. According to one story in circulation, two Catholic children fell ill after drinking water from a poisoned well. They were saved only after a portrait of the Virgin Mary was held over the well and prayers were said. In the town of Inowrocław (Inowrazlaw), rumors that the lives of two Catholic priests, Father Kantak and Father Turkowski, were endangered prompted hundreds of armed peasants to stand guard all night outside of their residence. Protestants were disturbed by fears of their own. According to Schleinitz, it was widely believed among Protestants that the Catholic clergy were hatching plans for a general uprising throughout the grand duchy. They would spread the word, it was thought, in the confessional booth during Easter week as Catholics participated in the sacrament of penance. [59]

On Easter itself, violent clashes were reported at various points in the province. County Councilor Illing noted that in the town of Strzelno, near Inowrocław, a Prussian soldier snatched the hat from the head of a Catholic priest and ripped off a small Polish cockade attached to the hat. The incident was magnified as the story was passed on. Before long, Catholics were telling one another that a monstrance had been trampled in the mud and that a church had been plundered of its pictures. Hundreds of outraged peasants, scythes and pitchforks in tow, poured into town. The outnumbered Prussian military unit stationed there had to call for reinforcements. The confrontation intensified into a battle, and by the end around fifty peasants had been killed and another fifty or so wounded. Just one soldier suffered injury. [60]

The dimming fortunes of the Polish movement put unbearable strains on the Polish National Committee and the broad coalition it sought to maintain. Wealthy Polish magnates were distressed by the presence of large bands of armed peasants, an uncomfortable reminder of the bloody Jacqueries that had occurred recently in Galicia (a region of the old Polish-Lithuanian Common-wealth under Austrian control) and other parts of Europe. Polish moderates, meanwhile, recognized the hopelessness of armed insurrection. But within the Polish military camps, enthusiasm for battle was running high. On April 25, after a heated debate, the committee voted to disband the camps. Mierosławski and his fellow commanders, however, refused to cooperate. Within days, the committee voted to dissolve itself. Military confrontation seemed inevitable.[61]

Colomb quietly had amassed around thirty thousand troops in the grand duchy and could count on additional support from the German and Jewish paramilitaries. In Poznań his troops distributed thirty-six hundred weapons to German and Jewish citizens in the event of trouble.[62] On April 29 he set in motion a plan for subduing the Polish military threat. He first concentrated his efforts against the camp in Książ, sending around forty-five hundred troops against the roughly one thousand Polish insurgents stationed there. The Prussian forces achieved their goal with little trouble. Half of the Polish fighters were killed or wounded, and the town was burned to the ground.[63]

Rather than come to the aid of Książ, Mierosławski opted to concentrate his forces in Miłosław. The next day a contingent of some three thousand Prussian troops under the command of General Blumen moved against the town. Mierosławski's ranks were bolstered by the arrival of two different companies of armed peasants, giving the Poles a decisive numerical edge. Superior armaments notwithstanding, the Prussians could not take the town and were forced to retreat after losing two hundred soldiers to death or injury.[64]

Despite this victory, the situation looked increasingly grim for Mierosławski. On May 1 he headed his forces toward Września, where, on the following day, he encountered yet another Prussian column, this time led by General Hirschfeld. The two forces came to blows in a swampy lowland near the village of Sokołowo. Benefiting from the support of the local population, the Poles forced Hirschfeld to withdraw, but they suffered heavy casualties. With munitions running low and the Prussians closing in on every side, Mierosławski's force began to contract through defections.

Mierosławski next turned north, with Rogoźno (Rogasen) as his goal. But the Prussians were hemming him into a corner, and with hope all but lost he abruptly resigned on May 6, seeking permission from the Prussian general Wedell to emigrate to France. His successor, Commander Brzeżański, capitulated on May 9. With the main Polish forces liquidated, the military turned its attention to pacifying any remaining pockets of resistance. The task was handed to General Ernst von Pfuel. Pfuel imposed martial law and oversaw a broad, sometimes brutal, military action that achieved its aim.[65]

As the last of the major Polish paramilitary units were being hunted down, word reached Poznań that the city had been officially taken into the German Union. The news overjoyed the German and Jewish populations, and their leaders set about planning a massive celebration for May 11. On that day thousands gathered in the market square to witness a festive parade and to listen to leading members of the German National Committee reflect on recent events. The crowd then joined in a robust rendition of the popular nationalist hymn "Was ist des Deutschen Vaterland."[66]

While the events of April and early May had certainly been polarizing, it is important to acknowledge that numerous residents challenged the logic of the German and Polish nationalist movements and remained committed to alternative visions for themselves and the province. Many Polish peasants maintained a conservative orientation. They were joined by a fair number of the Polish nobility, who discreetly dreaded the anarchy and erosion of tradition that a liberal mass movement could generate, and longed for a successful counterrevolution. This point of view was embodied by Eugeniusz Breza (1802-ca. 1860), a literary dilettante and scion of a prominent noble family from the Poznań region. Although he had taken part in the November Uprising of 1830–31, Breza displayed little of the Polish nationalist fervor typical of his fellow comrades-in-arms when he resettled in Poznań in 1840 after a decade-long exile in France. Motty writes that Breza preferred speaking French over Polish and "came across as a Frenchman in every respect." His self-distancing from Polish culture and the Polish nationalist cause manifested itself quite clearly during the Springtime of Nations, when Breza agreed to serve as editor of *Przyjaciela Chłopów* (Friend of the peasantry), a government-sponsored periodical designed to foster loyalty to the Prussian king among the rural underclass.[67]

On the German side, a small minority still clung to the region's multiethnic heritage. One such person was the doctor Johann Metzig from the town of Lissa (Leszno), south of Poznań. Metzig tirelessly championed the cause of peaceful German-Polish cohabitation, and in May he organized a petition in support of this vision. He could barely muster fifty signers. Two weeks later German nationalists in Lissa responded with a petition of their own, condemning "the evil of mixing both nations." This petition attracted more than a thousand signatures.[68]

Likewise, one can find instances where religious affiliation did not stimulate nationalist sentiments in the patterns presented above. Jan Wilhelm Cassius, the Protestant pastor and Polish patriot (see chapter 4), remained allied with Polish nationalist leaders until his death in 1848. Before his death he accompanied the Polish delegation that traveled to Berlin in March of 1848 to present their demands to the king, and he subsequently championed the Polish cause in Frankfurt.[69] Cut of the same cloth was Leon Chlebowski (1802–1887). Known by his Polish friends as the "Calvinist pope," Chlebowski was a devout member of the Reformed Peter's Congregation in Poznań. Yet he was also a Polish patriot and an active supporter of Polish aspirations in 1848. Despite all of the rancor that alienated Protestant Germans from Catholic Poles at this time, Chlebowski managed the rare feat of belonging in part to both camps.[70]

With the eclipse of their military efforts, Polish nationalists turned to their last remaining hope, the newly created mechanisms of representative government. But here their chances of success were little better. Polish independence no longer commanded much support in Germany, whereas the idea of dividing the province into Polish and German sectors now did. The only open question seemed to be where exactly the line of demarcation would be drawn. The latest proposal came from General Pfuel, who on June 4 recommended a line that would leave just one-third of the grand duchy available for political reorganization.[71]

Elections for delegates to the Prussian State Assembly were held on May 2. Of the thirty representatives chosen from the grand duchy, sixteen were Poles. Elections for the German National Assembly in Frankfurt took place in the middle of May. Voting in this instance was limited to those predominantly German counties that had previously been accepted into the German Union. Polish leaders opposed having any part of the grand duchy participate, for such would suggest that those regions belonged to Germany. They also realized that with only German areas voting, they stood little chance of fielding successful candidates. Only one Pole, Father Jan Janiszewski, managed to get elected. With his victory he became the sole official representative of the Polish national movement in Frankfurt.

In the end, the elections brought little benefit to the Polish movement. Neither legislative body contained a critical mass of delegates willing to support Polish independence, and the efforts of the small Polish factions repeatedly met with frustration. The German National Assembly eventually debated the Prussian plan to divide the grand duchy, and on July 27 the body affirmed it by a comfortable margin. Father Janiszewski resigned in protest. He was succeeded by Karol Libelt, who soon resigned in protest as well. Thereafter, Polish leaders abandoned all hope in the institution.

Interestingly, the two assemblies met with roughly the same fate as the Polish independence movement. They came into being on a wave of public enthusiasm for political change and instantly acquired a great deal of moral authority, trumping even that of official structures of power. What they did not achieve, however, was any real military power. The disciplined Prussian military remained firmly behind the conservative Prussian establishment, and when the latter regained its footing, it had little trouble asserting its will over the defenseless advocates of political reform. All that liberals could do was protest.

Detailing the complex course of the counterrevolution in Prussia lies outside the goals of this book. Suffice it to note that what began with a small clique of conservative advisers seeking to bolster the confidence of the rattled king eventually matured into a powerful movement. In mid-November the king's government, now under the leadership of his archconservative uncle, Count Brandenburg, suspended the Prussian State Assembly. Not long thereafter, on December 5, the king announced the imposition of a new constitution for Prussia. The State Assembly, whose very purpose was to develop a constitution, was not consulted, and it was rendered obsolete by the king's announcement. The new constitution itself was a stroke of diplomatic mastery. Its very creation satisfied the demands of moderate liberals, which assured its popularity across Prussia. At the same time it preserved the principles dearest to conservatives, including the assertion that the king ruled by the grace of God rather than the will of the people.[72] The document also preserved the Grand Duchy of Poznań in its entirety as an integral part of the Prussian state, referring to it now as the Poznań Province.

Despite the striking successes of the counterrevolution in both Prussia and Austria, the German National Assembly in Frankfurt continued to deliberate in its labored quest to create a unified Germany. A resurgent Austria had no interest in belonging to such a state, for it would by necessity entail a divorce from Austria's extensive non-German holdings in East-Central Europe and the Balkans. As a result, the National Assembly was denied the option that carried the greatest symbolic weight among nationalists: Großdeutschland (Great Germany), an entity encompassing almost all of the German-speaking peoples of Central Europe. In March of 1849 the National Assembly finally settled on the less appealing but much more practical option of Kleindeutschland (Little Germany), an entity centered on Prussia and excluding Austria. It offered the crown of this proposed empire to the Prussian king. Ensconced once again at the helm of a stable Prussian state, Friedrich Wilhelm IV refused to accept a crown forged in "the gutter." His resistance effectively killed the proposal. The National Assembly followed it to the grave shortly thereafter.

The revolutionary period of 1848 and 1849 has become enshrined in the collective memories of many societies and in the reflections of even more historians as the culmination of a long campaign to remake Europe according to liberal principles. This campaign, whose roots are routinely traced to the era of the French Revolution, combined the rhetoric of nationalism with calls for greater political enfranchisement and the guarantee of basic civil rights. As its intellectual leaders articulated the matter, Europe was a patchwork of nationalities, and it was the God-given right of the nations to determine their own political affairs. Such autonomy was necessary for the nations to fulfill their own destiny and for individual members to experience genuine freedom.

The word "freedom" was a common shorthand for the demands voiced by supporters of revolution across the continent. It represented the antithesis to a complex of oppressive institutions that long had obstructed the natural progress of the nations. This complex included empires like Russia and Austria that held captive an array of different nationalities within their boundaries. It included regimes large and small that silenced free speech and the rights of ordinary citizens to organize. It included traditional social hierarchies and governmental forms that restricted the political process to a privileged few. And sometimes it included the churches, on account of the legitimacy they lent in alliances between throne and altar.

But as the preceding analysis of the 1848 uprising in the Poznań region makes clear, the throne was not the altar's only suitor. Another potential ally was the barricade. In many respects the events in Poznań in 1848 can be seen as a classic expression of the values, aspirations, and temporary achievements associated with the Springtime of Nations. Leaders of the uprising characterized their endeavors as a fight for freedom, a concept heavily freighted with metaphysical assumptions about the will of God, the course of history, and the destiny of nations. And for a time these revolutionaries enjoyed remarkable success, driving the mechanisms of state to the margins, only to see their gains erode when faced with actual military power. From start to finish, religious concerns and institutions were central to the ideas that were expressed and the events that transpired.

Polish nationalists provided the primary impetus behind the revolt against Prussia, and they relied heavily on the resources of the Catholic Church. The National Council they founded to lead the uprising included in its ranks a number of priests, and it depended on the parish network to distribute its messages throughout the province. More remarkable still was the active engagement of Archbishop Przyłuski in transmitting the council's demands to Berlin and rallying the Catholic population behind the cause of independence. In addition to institutional resources, Polish revolutionaries skillfully interwove their aspirations with venerable Catholic symbols and perspectives. They drew correspondences between the liturgical calendar and the timing of the revolt, thus drawing God and destiny into the process. They tarred their enemies with charges of sacrilege against the holy symbols of the faith.

German-speaking leaders were no less adept in employing religion to promote resistance to the revolution. On account of the religious diversity within their ranks, an overt and extensive alliance with the Protestant churches was not an attractive option. Instead, the counterrevolutionaries played upon the religious fears of their target audience. They let it be known that the revolutionary call for freedom was but a brittle veneer masking the real intentions of a fanatical movement determined to promote Catholicism and suppress religious minorities. True freedom, they argued, could be found in a union with Germany to the west. This message galvanized Protestants and Jews in the region, but it tended to alienate German Catholics.

The conjunction of liberal nationalist aspiration and traditional religious affiliation is hardly surprising in light of historical developments in the decades leading up to 1848. When Prussia first began to rule the region in the 1790s, it could rely upon a measure of support from Catholic officials such as Archbishop Raczyński, who much preferred its traditional political model and ideology over the revolutionary currents recently manifested in France. That reservoir of goodwill gradually evaporated as Prussia systematically curtailed the Catholic Church's wealth and authority and enhanced the profile of the Protestant churches. Over the decades that followed, the state stripped it of its landholdings, sharply limited the jurisdiction of its courts, closed all but one of its cloisters, and requisitioned those church buildings deemed superfluous. So reduced, the Catholic Church no longer exercised its sway as advocate, judge, employer, or patron. Although it continued to manage the education of many Poznanians, the church now had to compete with the ambitious cultural role the state had staked out for itself, as well as the endeavors of the lay population.

Despite this, Catholicism maintained a substantial degree of suasion over the large majority of those raised under its aegis. Deprived of many of the powers it once had used to coerce its members into religious observance, the church still had a theology and ritual life that provided answers to core existential questions and an orientation for living. If anything, there was something of a religious revival in this period, particularly among nationalist-minded Poles. As they engaged in a punishing battle for an independent Poland, many among them came to appreciate what the church could contribute to the cause. At a time when the institutions and traditions of the Polish state were retreating in favor of Prussian models, Catholicism offered a living connection with the preceding era. Its churches were veritable museums, bearing witness to the leading personages and common practices of the old commonwealth. What is more, Catholicism was a heritage that nearly all Poles, from the wealthiest magnates to the most humble of peasants, could call their own. It provided an important foundation for building a comprehensive national identity that could span the deep divisions of caste long endemic to Polish society.

By 1848, despite financial difficulties and a reduced number of priests, monks, and nuns, the Catholic Church enjoyed broad, enthusiastic support from among its members. The church-state turmoil of the 1830s had burnished its image as an effective opponent to Prussia's designs for the Poznań region. Unified by a common cause, church officials and nationalist leaders coordinated their efforts as never before. Meanwhile, nationalist intellectuals, be they historians, philosophers, or poets, were increasingly inclined to incorporate Catholicism squarely into their musings on the Polish national character. Illustrative of this fusion of Catholic and Polish national identity was the tendency for Catholic churches to serve as sites of nationalist expression. The Golden Chapel, with its intricate weave of Polish and Catholic symbols, offered the most visually striking example of this trend. In turn, points of nationalist reference were often embellished by traditional Catholic practices. The place where Babiński was executed, for instance, was sacralized by means of an elaborate ritual based on Catholic models.

Prussia's Germanization policy and the overt convergence of Polishness and Catholicism were disquieting for the city's German Catholics. The state's campaign to bind them to the German-speaking world came at a time when local Catholic officials were displaying their solidarity with the Polish national cause. Both factors contributed to a major upheaval within the German Catholic community and their growing alienation from their Polish coreligionists. But any impulse they may have felt to align themselves with the larger Protestant German community and the nascent German nationalism being fostered there was undermined by the heightened Protestant-Catholic tensions of the 1840s.

While its policies eroded the measure of support it initially enjoyed among Catholic leaders, Prussia was much more successful at winning the allegiance of Poznań's Protestant community. Prior to the onset of Prussian rule in 1793, religion had provided the city's Protestant minority a locus around which they maintained a relatively prosperous, inward-turned community life within a larger Catholic environment. Religious leaders served as an informal tribunal with wide-ranging powers, quietly resolving disputes and regulating relations within the community. Congregational life provided members a forum in which they cemented their primary personal and professional relationships. The Prussian state granted Protestants full religious equality with their Catholic neighbors. Protestants also enjoyed the state's generous patronage and preferential access to positions of influence within the local and provincial governments. Ironically, in some respects these benefits weakened the religious faith they were intended to support. The pronounced insularity and solidarity that once characterized their religious life were no longer necessary. Protestant congregations could no longer command the same degree of commitment from their members.

Nevertheless, religious faith remained a matter of central importance to most Protestants, and in some ways it was enhanced by the changes affecting the Poznań region. Protestants steadily were being incorporated into the dynamic environment of Protestant northern Germany, with its world-class theologians and lively network of religious publications and societies. Their coreligionists here tended to be confident in their faith and eager to "complete the work of Luther," reaching out to Catholics, Jews, and non-Christians abroad. This expansionist spirit and sense of mission stood in marked contrast to the effacement long practiced by Protestants in Great Poland, and it proved highly attractive. They rapidly adapted to the religious institutions and perspectives common to Protestant regions in Prussia.

By 1848 the tenor of Protestant life in Poznań was far removed from that of the late eighteenth century. Gone was the identification many Protestants once had felt with the multiconfessional, multiethnic Polish-Lithuanian Commonwealth and the affection they had had for the reform-minded Stanisław August. Looking back on those days fifty years hence, they tended to share the dismal evaluations of Poland commonly espoused by the Prussian establishment. By contrast, Protestant Germany was viewed very favorably—enlightened rather than superstitious, stable rather than anarchic—and they readily identified with it. In a marked departure from earlier practice, Protestants now asserted themselves in public life, promoting their views with non-Protestants and challenging Catholicism's old hegemony over the city. When this assertiveness stimulated an angry Catholic response, Protestants did not shy from conflict, as illustrated most notably by their active promotion of Deutschkatholizismus. Their religious commitments played a critical role in the growing alienation German Protestants felt toward their Polish-Catholic neighbors and, in turn, their increasingly strong identification with Prussia and Protestant Germany.

Like every city, Poznań has always been a collection of communities. The medieval walls that once protected it from the outside world contained within themselves subtler boundaries, dividing the space Poznanians shared in common into distinct and often conflicting spheres of interest and identity. The rise of Polish and German nationalisms in the city thus should not be seen as a fall from an earlier harmonious cohabitation. The new nationalisms were built in large part on the foundations of older patterns of identity, especially identities grounded in religion. Much of the power of the nationalist movements in this period can be traced to their ability to tap into the religious symbols and associations deeply etched into the mentalities of Poznań's residents. While drawing from this wellspring, Polish and German nationalisms never exhausted or eclipsed it. Rather than serving as replacements for religion among their disenchanted devotees, Poznań's early nationalist movements coexisted with still vibrant Christian churches, forming partnerships that were mutually transformative.

Notes

Bibliography

Index

Notes

Abbreviations

AAP	Archiwum Archidiecezjalne w Poznaniu (Archive of the Archdiocese of Poznań)
APP	Archiwum Państwowe w Poznaniu (National Archive in Poznań)
Abt.	Abteilung (division)
Adh.	Significance unknown
Fasz.	Faszikel (file)
GESK	Gmina Ewangelicka św. Krzyża w Poznaniu (Protestant Cross Congregation in Poznań)
GSPK	Geheimes Staatsarchiv Preußischer Kulturbesitz (Confidential State Archive of Prussian Cultural Heritage)
HA	Hauptabteilung (main division)
KEP	Konsystorz Ewangelicky w Poznaniu (Protestant Consistory in Poznań)
NPP	Naczelne Prezydium w Poznaniu (Provincial Presidium in Poznań)
Rep.	Report (report)
Sekt.	Sektion (section)
Tit.	Titel (title)

Introduction

1. Mark Juergensmeyer, *The New Cold War? Religious Nationalism Confronts the Secular State* (Berkeley: Univ. of California Press, 1993), 11.

2. Anthony D. Smith, *Nationalism and Modernism: A Critical Survey of Recent Theories of Nations and Nationalism* (London: Routledge, 1998), 1.

3. Anthony D. Smith, *Nationalism: A Trend Report and Bibliography* (The Hague: Mouton, 1973), 93.

4. Benedict Anderson, *Imagined Communities: Reflections on the Origin and Spread of Nationalism*, rev. ed. (London: Verso, 1991), 11.

5. Carlton J. H. Hayes, *Nationalism: A Religion* (New York: Macmillan, 1960), 164.

6. Eric J. Hobsbawm, *Nations and Nationalism since 1780: Programme, Myth, Reality*, 2d. ed. (Cambridge: Cambridge Univ. Press, 1992), 32–40.

7. Ibid., 121.

8. Brian Porter, *When Nationalism Began to Hate: Imagining Modern Politics in Nineteenth-Century Poland* (Oxford: Oxford Univ. Press, 2000).

9. Many of the historians who have written about the Catholic Church in this period (Fąka, Kumor, Noryśkiewicz, et al.) have been priests, and not surprisingly they have portrayed the church in a favorable light. The degree of their partisanship occasionally has been matched by the church's detractors, such as Bogislav Freiherr von Selchow.

10. Arthur Rhode's *Geschichte der evangelischen Kirche im Posener Lande* (Würzburg: Holzner, 1956) offers a survey of Protestant history in the region, but he treats the first half of the nineteenth century in just twenty-seven pages. While a serious history, the book suffers from the author's pronounced pro-German affections. Other authors who have written on the subject (e.g., Angermann and Henschel) have tended to be uncritical if not hagiographic in their treatments.

11. Jacob Katz, "The Forerunners of Zionism," in *Essential Papers on Zionism,* ed. Jehuda Reinharz and Anita Shapira (New York: New York Univ. Press, 1996), 40–41.

12. Thomas Nipperdey, *Germany from Napoleon to Bismarck, 1800–1866,* trans. Daniel Nolan (Princeton, N.J.: Princeton Univ. Press, 1996), 263.

13. George W. White, *Nationalism and Territory: Constructing Group Identity in Southeastern Europe* (Lanham, Md.: Rowman and Littlefield, 2000), 15.

14. Anderson, 44–45.

15. Karl Deutsch, *Nationalism and Social Communication: An Inquiry into the Foundations of Nationality,* 2d. ed. (Cambridge, Mass.: Massachusetts Institute of Technology Press, 1966), 97.

1. On the Threshold of a New Era

1. In his *Historisch-statistisch, topographische Beschreibung von Südpreußen und Neuostpreußen oder der koeniglich Preußischen Besitznehmungen von Polen in den Jahren 1793 und 1795 entworfen* (Leipzig, 1798), Sadebeck offers an early version of this view. He depicts a terminally ill Polish-Lithuanian Commonwealth riven with conflict that threatened to disrupt order in neighboring states. He writes: "Even without the French Revolution Poland would have exited from the ranks of nations. Its political order could not endure the pressing superiority of its neighbors. Its violent efforts to equal them and its foolish aping of France only accelerated its collapse" (28). (Note: English translations of quotations from this and all subsequent German and Polish sources are the author's own.)

2. Wacław Zawadzki, ed., *Polska stanisławowska w oczach cudzoziemców* (Warsaw: Państwowy Instytut Wydawniczy, 1963), 2:376.

3. Karl Friedrich von Voss, "Reisebericht des Ministers von Voss an den König...," 31 May 1793, in *Das Jahr 1793: Urkunden und Aktenstücke zur Geschichte der Organization Südpreußens,* ed. Rogero Prümers (Poznań: Eigenthum der Gesellschaft, 1895), 88.

4. Zawadzki, 2:195.

5. Ibid., 2:197.

6. The historian Jósef Łukaszewicz estimates that in 1567 the city's population stood at around thirty thousand. *Obraz historyczno-statystyczny miasta Poznania w dawniejszych czasach*

(Poznań: Czcionkami C. A. Pompjusza, 1838), 1:2. The judgment about Poznań's beauty was made by Kromer in his 1577 tome *Polonia*, 49.

7. The Good Order Commission, created by the national government to tackle a wide range of ills besetting the country, addressed the many neglected plots and buildings in the city that tarnished Poznań's image and squandered valuable space. It also issued regulations to combat the threat of fire, established a building police, and supplied the local government with seven thousand złoty annually to support building projects. See Zofia Ostrowska-Kębłowska, *Architektura i budownictwo w Poznaniu w latach 1780–1880* (Warsaw: Państwowe Wydawnictwo Naukowe, 1982), 39; and Łukaszewicz, *Obraz historyczno-statystyczny*, 1:41, 46.

8. Zawadzki, 2:198.

9. Ibid., 2:199.

10. Krystyna Kuklińska, "Gospodarka," in *Dzieje Poznania*, vol. 1, ed. Jerzy Topolski (Poznań: Państwowe Wydawnictwo Naukowe, 1988), 659.

11. Łukaszewicz, *Obraz historyczno-statystyczny*, 1:64–66. No reliable population records exist, making it impossible to determine with certainty the city's population at this time.

12. In the late eighteenth century the city owned Rataje, Żegrze, Luboń, Jeżyce, Górczyn, Winiary, Wilda, Dębiec, Bonin, and Szeląg.

13. When the Prussian government stripped the cloister of Baggerowo in 1798, the Franciscans fiercely protested, noting that it was their primary source of sustenance. 31 Mar. 1798, Hauptabteilung (HA) II, Südpreussen 10, no. 210, Geheimes Staatsarchiv Preußischer Kulturbesitz, Berlin (GSPK).

14. Łukaszewicz, *Obraz historyczno-statystyczny*, 1:309–19.

15. Sophia Kemlein, *Die Posener Juden, 1815–1848: Entwicklungsprozesse einer polnischen Judenheit unter preußischer Herrschaft* (Hamburg: Dölling und Galitz, 1997), 28; Drozdowski and Kuklińska, "Gospodarka w dobie odbudowy i wzrostu," in Topolski, 868.

16. Drozdowski and Kuklińska, 864–68.

17. Ibid., 844.

18. Ibid., 855–58.

19. Wojciechowski concludes that by 1780 roughly one-quarter of Poznań's adult population belonged to this burgeoning underclass. Cited in Stefan Abt, "Ludność w drugiej połowie XVIII wieku," in Topolski, 840.

20. 27 May 1793, HA II, Südpreussen 6, no. 2199, GSPK.

21. Heinz Schilling, *Die Stadt in der frühen Neuzeit* (Munich: Oldenbourg, 1993), 38–46.

22. Witold Maisel, "Zniszczenia wojenne. Rozwój przestrzenny," in Topolski, 628.

23. 11 July 1797, HA II, Südpreussen 6, no. 2269, GSPK.

24. Maisel, 627.

25. Jósef Łukaszewicz, *Krótki opis historyczny kościołów parochialnych, kościółków, kaplic, klasztorów, szkółek parochialnych, szpitali i innych zakładów dobroczynnych w dawnej dyecezji poznańskiej* (Poznań: Księg. J. K. Żupańskiego, 1858), 1:123.

26. Kemlein, 32–33.

27. Josef Perles, *Geschichte der Juden in Posen* (Breslau: Verlag der Schletter'schen Buchhandlung, 1865), 21.

28. Perles provides a grim catalogue of persecution against Jews in *Geschichte der Juden in Posen*.

29. Kuklińska, 673.

30. Quoted in Łukaszewicz, *Obraz historyczno-statystyczny,* 1:235.

31. For a lucid account in English of the state of the Polish-Lithuanian Commonwealth in the eighteenth century and the struggle for reform, see Jerzy Lukowski, *Liberty's Folly: The Polish-Lithuanian Commonwealth in the Eighteenth Century* (London: Routledge, 1991).

32. Quoted in Aleksander Gieysztor et al., eds., *History of Poland,* trans. Krystyna Cękalska (Warsaw: Państwowe Wydawnictwo Naukowe, 1979), 320.

33. The formal toleration of Protestant religious practice was granted in the Warsaw Tractate of 1768. During periods of persecution, Poznań's Jewish community often agreed to pay financial penalties for alleged crimes as a means of avoiding worse forms of retribution. These penalties snowballed into a massive debt load (947,546.19 złoty). In 1773–74 the Good Order Commission investigated the matter and eliminated the more spurious financial claims against the community.

34. Ostrowska-Kębłowska, *Architektura i budownictwo,* 90–93.

35. Deutsch, 88.

36. While acknowledging the personal nature of remembered experience ("autobiographical memory"), Halbwachs argues that much of our memory is socially conditioned ("collective memory"). We preserve memories by periodically reproducing them, and in the process they become connected to ideas in circulation within our social milieu. Likewise our social milieu encourages us to embrace its foundational memories as our own. Memory is important because in it "a sense of our identity is perpetuated" (47). See Maurice Halbwachs, *On Collective Memory,* ed. and trans. Lewis A. Coser (Chicago: Univ. of Chicago Press, 1992).

37. See introduction and part 1 of Teresa Dohnalowa, *Rozwój transportu w Wielkopolsce w latach 1815–1914* (Poznań: Państwowe Wydawnictwo Naukowe, 1976).

38. Jerzy Jedlicki, *A Suburb of Europe: Nineteenth-Century Polish Approaches to Western Civilization* (Budapest: Central European Univ. Press, 1999), 6.

39. Altgeld illustrates the parochial quality of German consciousness with the example of Friedrich Nicoli. A successful publisher in Berlin, Nicoli traveled to southern Germany and Switzerland in 1781. Intrigued by the exotic qualities of this very different part of Germany, he went on to publish fourteen volumes documenting the curious customs of its inhabitants, much as an early ethnologist might report on a distant country. Wolfgang Altgeld, *Katholizismus, Protestantismus, Judentum: Über religiös begründete Gegensätze und nationalreligiöse Ideen in der Geschichte des deutschen Nationalismus* (Mainz: M.-Grünewald-Verlag, 1992), 118–24.

40. Heinrich Heine, "Über Polen," in *Reisebriefe und Reisebilder* (Berlin: Rütten und Loening, 1981), 86–87.

41. Janusz Tazbir, *Kultura szlachecka w Polsce: Rozkwit, Upadek, Relikty* (Warsaw: Wiedza Powszechna, 1978), 86ff.

42. See Shmuel Almog, "People and Land in Modern Jewish Nationalism," in Reinharz and Shapira, 50–51.

43. Ferdinand Braudel, *Capitalism and Material Life, 1400–1800,* trans. Miriam Kochan (London: Weidenfeld and Nicolson, 1973), 399.

44. Kuklińska, 678.

45. Janusz Tazbir, *Historia Kościoła katolickiego w Polsce* (Warsaw: Wiedza Powszechna, 1966), 95.

46. Wojciech Kriegseisen, *Ewangelicy polscy i litewscy w epoce saskiej* (Warsaw: Semper, 1996), 189–206.

47. The commonwealth enacted a series of legal changes designed to weaken the Polish hierarchy's dependence on Rome and to increase the state's power over the church. The state also claimed some properties belonging to church institutions and leaders. These changes were similar in spirit to reform programs in Austria and Prussia, only much milder in scope. Tazbir, *Historia Kościoła,* 182–85.

48. Bishops Kossakowski, Massalski, Skarszewski, and Sierakowski allied themselves with the Targowice Confederation.

49. Zawadzki, 1:200.

50. Kriegseisen, 225.

51. See "Allgemeine Stolgebühren Verordnung. . . ," 13 June 1801, HA I, Rep. 7C, no. 25, Fasz. 17, GSPK.

52. The miller's guild, for instance, honored St. Joseph, the baker's guild St. Anne, and the brewer's guild St. Stanisław. Czesław Łuczak, *Przemysł spożywczy miasta Poznania w XVIII wieku* (Poznań: Nakł. Poznańskiego Tow. Przyjaciół Nauk., 1953), 63, and n. 73.

53. In *Krótki opis historyczny,* Łukaszewicz's exhaustive catalogue of Catholic institutions in the Poznań area, St. Mary Magdalene's is the only elementary school he mentions.

54. See report from Kriegs- und Domänenrath von Knobloch, 26 July 1793, and report from the Südpreussische Kammer, 28 Dec. 1793, in Prümers, 695–708, 723–28.

55. Łukaszewicz, *Krótki opis historyczny,* 1:91.

56. Perles, 7.

57. Friedrich Just, *Kreuzkirche: Bilder aus Geschichte und Leben der evangelischen Kirche des Posener Landes* (Berlin: Ernst Röttger's Verlagsbuchhandlung, 1922), 130.

58. The pope's 1775 breve limited official Catholic holidays to the following: all Sundays; Christmas (December 25); St. Stephen's (December 26); Christ's Circumcision (January 1); Epiphany (January 6); the Presentation (February 2); the Annunciation (March 25); Easter Sunday and Monday; Pentecost Sunday and Monday; Christ's Ascension; Corpus Christi; Sts. Peter and Paul (June 29); the Assumption (August 15); Mary's Birthday (September 8); All Saints (November 1); the Immaculate Conception (December 8); and the feast day of local patron saints.

59. Kuklińska, 679.

60. In 1790 a Catholic nobleman, Phillipus Dembrowski, ordered the baptism of a Jewish boy under the charge of one of his subjects. Polish law allowed such conversions after age seven, and Dembrowski rigorously defended his action during a legal process raised by the boy's parents. In his successful defense Dembrowski noted, "In that [the boy] has already been accepted into the Christian community through the sacrament of baptism, his return—or rather forced reentry—into the Jewish religion would annul this sacrament in contradiction to Catholic principles. I would be indirectly responsible, and my conscience burdened." 25 Sept. 1793, HA I, Rep. 7C, no. 32, Fasz. 8, GSPK.

61. Albert Werner, *Geschichte der evangelischen Parochieen in der Provinz Posen* (Poznań, 1898), 271ff.

62. In the seventeenth century Catholics in Denmark, Sweden, and Great Britain and Protestants in France and Austria suffered greater limitations than did Protestants in the Polish-Lithuanian Commonwealth.

63. Initially they traveled more than thirty miles south to Śmigiel (Schmiegel). They began worshiping in Swarzędz (Schwersenz), around seven miles east of Poznań, after the noble Zygmunt Grudziński, who owned the city, allowed resident Lutherans to build a church there.

64. In 1717 the National Assembly deprived non-Catholic nobility of the right to hold state office and titles. It also suggested that all non-Catholic church buildings erected after 1628 were illegitimate. In 1733 and 1736 the National Assembly further undermined the position of Protestant nobility, denying them the right to participate in national politics, to function in Polish and Lithuanian tribunals and treasuries, and to enjoy official dignities and titles. Kriegseisen, 44–45.

65. Tazbir, *Historia Kościoła,* 155.

66. Hugo Sommer, "Die Posener Unitätsgemeinde seit der Zeit der Religionsfreiheit in Polen," *Deutsche Wissenschaftliche Zeitschrift für Polen* 30 (1936): 74.

67. The Bohemian Brethren were closer theologically to Calvinism than to Lutheranism, and in 1627 the remaining members of the region's persecuted Brethren community united with the Calvinist confession at a synod in Scharfenort. See Sommer, "Die Posener Unitätsgemeinde," 73–74.

68. Journal entry, 20 Oct. 1790, Gmina ewangelicka św. Krzyża w Poznaniu (GESK), no. 39, Archiwum Państwowe w Poznaniu (APP).

69. Financial report, 1789, GESK, no. 119, APP.

70. Report from General-Senior Klose, 14 June 1793, in Prümers, 694–95.

71. Kriegseisen, 262ff.

72. Journal entry, 16 Apr. 1789, GESK, no. 39, APP.

73. Christian Meyer, ed., *Aus der letzten Zeit der Republik Polen: Gedenkblätter eines Posener Bürgers, 1760–1793* (Munich: n.p., 1908), 21–22.

74. Edward Hauptmann, *Z przeszłości polskiego zboru ewangelicko-augsburskiego w Poznaniu* (Poznań: Nakładem Polskiego Towarzystwa Ewangelickiego w Poznaniu, 1924), 27.

75. Hugo Sommer, "Die lutherische Kirche in der Stadt Posen seit 1768," *Deutsche Wissenschaftliche Zeitschrift für Polen* 29 (1935): 355.

76. Journal entry, 1783, GESK, no. 39, APP.

77. Ibid., 12 Feb. 1795.

78. Ibid., 18 Feb. 1786.

79. GESK, no. 51, APP.

80. Meyer, *Aus der letzten Zeit,* 21.

81. Ibid., 36–37.

82. At this time Prussia sought to weaken the Polish-Lithuanian Commonwealth in a variety of ways, including the printing of huge sums of counterfeit currency. Its policies hurt the commonwealth's entire population. Meyer, *Aus der letzten Zeit,* 58.

83. Ibid., 8.

84. Journal entry, 20 Oct. 1787, GESK, no. 39, APP.

85. These included the following feasts: Three Kings/Epiphany (January 6); the Presentation (February 2); the Annunciation (March 25); St. Stanisław (April 11); the Ascension; Sts. Peter and Paul (June 29); the Visitation (July 2); Mary's birth (September 8); All Saints (November 1); the Assumption (December 8); and St. Michael (September 29).

2. A Half Century of Change

1. 11 Feb. 1793, in Prümers, 3.

2. For an overview of the influence of the Enlightenment on Prussian political culture in the eighteenth century, see Matthew Levinger, *Enlightened Nationalism: The Transformation of Prussian Political Culture, 1806–1848* (Oxford: Oxford Univ. Press, 2000), 19–39.

3. Royal proclamation, 25 Mar. 1793, Prümers, 42–43.

4. As Sadebeck explains, the Polish king Bolesław III (d. 1138) divided his realm among his three sons, and the oldest son, Władisław, served as regent. Władisław was driven out of Poland by his brothers, but his lineage endured until the seventeenth century. Friedrich Wilhelm II was related to Władisław's progeny. Sadebeck, 34–35.

5. For more on Polish and German stereotypes of one another, see Stanisław Salmonowicz, *Polacy i Niemcy wobec siebie: Postawy—opinie—stereotypy (1697–1815): Próba zarysu* (Olsztyn: Ośrodek Badań Naukowych im. W. Kętrzyńskiego, 1993).

6. Numerous examples of such requests can be found in Prümers.

7. For a brief overview of the emancipation question, see Andrzej Walicki, *Philosophy and Romantic Nationalism: The Case of Poland* (Notre Dame, Ind.: Univ. of Notre Dame Press, 1994), 42–45.

8. Prümers, 15–16.

9. Biester noted this in his published letters from Poland. See Zawadzki, 2:187.

10. An excellent example of Prussian attitudes toward Poland around this time can be found in Johann Friedrich Baumann, *Darstellungen nach dem Leben: Aus einer Skizze der Sitten und des Nationalcharakters der ehemaligen Pohlen* (Königsberg, 1803).

11. J. F. Streuensee, *Blikke auf Südpreussen von und nach dem Jahre 1793* (Poznań, 1802), 52.

12. Ibid., 48.

13. Klewitz to Altenstein, 27 Feb. 1826, HA I, Rep. 76 IV, Sekt. 4, Abt. 4, no. 2, vol. 1, GSPK.

14. 22 Feb. 1807, HA II, Südpreussen 1, no. 670, GSPK.

15. Andrzej Wojtkowski, *Edward Raczyński i jego dzieło* (Poznań: Nakł. Bibljoteki Raczyńskich, 1929), 33–34.

16. Minister des Innere to Sposetti, 10 July 1822, Naczelne Prezydium w Poznaniu (NPP), no. 1330, APP.

17. Baumann to Berlin, 28 Dec. 1827, NPP, no. 1356, APP.

18. NPP, no. 1355, APP.

19. Around three hundred Poznań residents crossed the Prussian-Russian border to support the uprising, including roughly one hundred gymnasium students, ninety artisans, and a handful of bureaucrats and professionals. Lech Trzeciakowski, "Aktywność polityczna Poznaniaków," in *Dzieje Poznania,* vol. 2 (1793–1918), ed. Jerzy Topolski and Lech Trzeciakowski (Poznań: Państwowe Wydawnictwo Naukowe, 1994), 330–31.

20. Eduard Flottwell et al., *Denkschrift des Oberpresidenten Herrn Flottwell, ueber die Verwaltung des Gros-Herzogthum Posen* (Strasbourg, n.d.), 1.

21. Before, area nobility voted for councillors *(Räte)*. After 1833 councillors were appointed by the government. See Bolesław Grześ, Jerzy Kozłowski, and Aleksander Kramski, *Niemcy w Poznanskiem wobec polityki germanizacyjnej, 1815–1920* (Poznań: Instytut Zachodni, 1976), 33.

22. Wojtkowski, 63.

23. For more on the Polish Democratic Society, see Peter Brock, *Nationalism and Populism in Partitioned Poland* (London: Orbis, 1973), 57ff.

24. Heinrich Wuttke, *Polen und Deutsche* (Schkeuditz: W. v. Blomberg, 1846), 73.

25. Of the dozens of Poznanians who crossed over the border to fight on behalf of the November Uprising, many had German last names. See Grześ, Kozłowski, and Kramski, 49.

26. Schultz and Hofrichter to Brenn, 13 Apr. 1831, HA I, Rep. 77, Tit. 503, no. 5, GSPK.

27. One indication of this can be deduced from the provincial congresses of 1834 and 1837, in which German councillors repeatedly demonstrated their loyalty to the Crown and their opposition to Polish political and cultural efforts. See Grześ, Kozłowski, and Kramski, 55.

28. Flottwell et al., 33.

29. Quoted in Moritz Jaffe, *Die Stadt Posen unter preußischer Heerschaft: Ein Beitrag zur Geschichte des deutschen Ostens,* vol. 119, *Schriften des Vereins für Socialpolitik* (Leipzig: Duncker und Humblot, 1909), 186n.1.

30. Marceli Motty, *Przechadzki po mieście* (Warsaw: Państwowy Instytut Wydawniczy, 1957), 1:83–86.

31. Trzeciakowski, "Aktywność polityczna poznaniaków," 325.

32. Jaffe, 181.

33. Grześ, Kozłowski, and Kramski, 66–67.

34. Mieczysław Kędelski, "Stosunki ludnościowe w latach 1815–1918," in Topolski and Trzeciakowski, 226.

35. Their numbers grew from 2,414 in 1831 to 4,794 in 1846. Witold Szulz, "Procesy industrializacji Poznania. Kredyt. Ubezpieczenia. Organizacje gospodarcze," in Topolski and Trzeciakowski, 148.

36. Szulz, 139–43.

37. Motty, 1:157–58.

38. Ibid., 2:355–56.

39. Teresa Dohnalowa, "Handel, transport, komunikacja," in Topolski and Trzeciakowski, 187.

40. Nipperdey, 175.

41. Dohnalowa, "Handel, transport, komunikacja," 188.

42. Manfred Laubert, "Ein Volksauflauf in Posen 1845," *Historische Monatsblätter für die Provinz Posen* 9, no. 12 (1908): 195–97.

43. Dohnalowa, "Handel, transport, komunikacja," 188.

44. In 1832 4,632 workers, or roughly 15 percent of the city's population, were busy building the fortress. An additional 5 percent of the population were engaged in labor related to this project. Lech Trzeciakowski and Maria Trzeciakowski, *W dziewiętnastowiecznym Poznaniu: Życie codzienne miasta, 1815–1914* (Poznań: Wydawnictwo Poznańskie, 1982), 132–33.

45. The service class expanded from 2,070 in 1819 to 3,236 in 1840. Krzysztof Makowski, *Rodzina poznańska w I. połowie XIX. wieku* (Poznań, 1992), 39.

46. Nipperdey, 127.

47. Walerian Kalinka, *Jenerał Dezydery Chłapowski* (Poznań: J. Leitgeber, 1885), 62–75.

48. Trzeciakowski and Trzeciakowski, 114.

49. The investors included Edward Raczyński and Karol Marcinkowski. Trzeciakowski and Trzeciakowski, 118.

50. Levinger, 56.

51. Population figures from the 1830s and 1840s are from Kędelski, 230.

52. Nipperdey, 179.

53. Dohnalowa, "Handel, transport, komunikacja," 188.

54. Grześ, Kozłowski, and Kramski, 28.

55. Trzeciakowski and Trzeciakowski, 69.

56. Miroslav Hroch, *Social Preconditions of National Revival in Europe: A Comparative Analysis of the Social Composition of Patriotic Groups among the Smaller European Nations,* trans. Ben Fowkes (Cambridge: Cambridge Univ. Press, 1985), 185–90.

57. 11 Jan. 1831, NPP, no. 1454, APP.

58. Kemlein, 96–193.

59. Baumann to Altenstein, 2 Sept. 1826, HA I, Rep. 76 IV, Sekt. 4, Abt. 4, no. 2, vol. 1, GSPK.

60. In *Germans, Poles, and Jews: The Nationality Conflict in the Prussian East, 1772–1914* (Chicago: Univ. of Chicago Press, 1980), William Hagen refers to the state's policy toward Poles at this time as Prussification (61). He distinguishes it from the harsher, more nationalistic policies of the late nineteenth and early twentieth centuries, which he labels Germanization. I use the word Germanization to describe Prussian policy in the early nineteenth century because that is how Prussian officials themselves described it.

61. Jürgen-Peter Ravens, *Staat und katholische Kirche in Preußens polnischen Teilungsgebieten, 1772–1807* (Wiesbaden: A. Harrassowitz, 1963), 140–59.

62. Jan Wąsicki, "Poznań jako miasto tzw. Prus Południowych (1793–1806)," in Topolski and Trzeciakowski, 77.

63. The law required children to attend school from age six to around age fourteen. Trzeciakowski and Trzeciakowski, 288.

64. Of an estimated 3,897 school-aged children, 2,813 were receiving some kind of formal education. Witold Molik, "Szkolnictwo," in Topolski and Trzeciakowski, 430.

65. Ibid., 436.

66. Quoted in Edyta Połczyńska, *"Im Polnischen Wind": Beiträge zum deutschen Zeitungswesen, Theaterleben und zur deutschen Literatur im Grossherzogtum Posen, 1815–1918* (Poznań: Wydawnictwo Naukowe UAM, 1988), 13.

67. The oldest such newspaper, *Südpreußische Zeitung* (South Prussian newspaper), first appeared in 1794 and continued to be published, under different names *(Posener Zeitung* and *Zeitung des Großherzogtums)* throughout this period. Starting in 1816 the state sponsored two new bilingual papers, the *Intelligenzblatt* (Intelligence page) and the *Amtsblatt der Königlichen Regierung zu Posen* (Office page of the Royal Government in Poznań). See Połczyńska, *"Im Polnischen Wind,"* 58–104.

68. See Manfred Jacobs, "Die Entwicklung des deutschen Nationalgedankens von der Reformation bis zum deutschen Idealismus," in *Volk—Nation—Vaterland: Der deutsche Protestantismus und der Nationalismus,* ed. Horst Zilleßen (Gütersloh: Gütersloher Verlagshaus G. Mohn, 1970), 51–110.

69. For more on Herder's thought, see Robert Ergang, *Herder and the Foundations of German Nationalism* (New York: Columbia Univ. Press, 1931).

70. Anderson, 67.

71. Niemcewicz's *Śpiewy historyczne z krótkim dodatkiem zbioru historji polskiej* (1816) traces the defining features of Polish history in thirty-three songs.

72. Mickiewicz's theory belongs to a general category of thought known as messianism. First developed by Jósef Maria Hoene-Wroński (1776–1853) in the 1830s, messianism posited the salvific missions of particular nations. Hoene-Wroński believed that the Slavs, under the leadership of Russia, would inaugurate a new and ultimate era of human history. Mickiewicz expanded upon and popularized this notion. In works like *The Books of the Polish Nation and of the Polish Pilgrims* (1832), he argued that each nation has its own historical mission, and together they serve as the motor of history, advancing the progress of humankind. As the Christ among nations, Poland's suffering would lead to the redemption of the world, overthrowing the reign of pride, greed, and exploitation. Walicki, 116–21, 248–50.

73. Motty, 1:207.

74. Edward Raczyński, *Wspomnienia Wielkopolska,* 2 vols. (Poznań 1842–43).

75. Edward Raczyński, ed., *Obraz Polaków i Polski XVIII wieku,* 20 vols. (Poznań, 1840–45).

76. Motty, 1:122.

77. Oskar Kolberg, ed., *Pieśni ludu polskiego* (Poznań, 1842–45).

78. Motty, 2:178–79.

79. Dioniza Wawrzykowska-Wierciochowa, *Promienna: Opowieść biograficzna o Klaudynie z Działyńskich Potockiej (1801–1836)* (Poznań: Wydawnictwo Poznańskie, 1976), 114.

80. Heine, 113.

81. From this proposition the authors went on to argue that Flottwell's Germanization policies, in denying the cultural expression inherent to the Polish nation, were fundamentally opposed to God's design for the world. Flottwell et al., 34.

82. Wojtkowski, 222.

83. Ibid., 225.

84. Eichhorn, Flottwell, et al. to Berlin, 14 Apr. 1846, HA I, Rep. 77 (CB), Tit. 343A, no. 62, GSPK.

85. Provinzial-Schul-Collegium to Eichhorn, 8 Jan. 1847, ibid.

86. Jaffe, 154.

87. Heine, 115–16.

88. Motty, 2:168.

89. Edyta Połczyńska, "Życie kulturalne Niemców w Poznaniu w XIX i na początku XX wieku," in Topolski and Trzeciakowski, 621.

90. Motty, 1:491–94.

91. Połczyńska, "Życie kulturalne Niemców," 622–23.

92. Grześ, Kozłowski, and Kramski, 58.

93. Wuttke, *Polen und Deutsche,* 92.

94. Grześ, Kozłowski, and Kramski, 66–67.

3. Catholic Poznań

1. Ravens, 106.

2. Two historical precedents existed for seizing church property. When Prussia wrested most of Silesia from Austria in 1742, it allowed Catholic institutions and offices to retain their landholdings in exchange for 50 percent of the annual revenues from the same. When Prussia gained control of Warmia and West Prussia through the first partition of Poland in 1772, it opted for a more aggressive approach, claiming outright ownership of all church property while allowing 50 percent of the revenues to the institutions and offices to which the properties formerly belonged. After considerable vacillation, King Friedrich Wilhelm II finally opted for the latter approach.

3. The most controversial aspect of these changes involved divorce. The state claimed the right to adjudicate over divorce proceedings between Catholics when one or both parties sought to have their trial heard before a secular court. The state also asserted its authority over marriages between Catholics and Protestants.

4. Clerics who supported the Kościuszko Uprising found themselves at a particular disadvantage in obtaining promotions. The state also placed a high value on priests who could speak German, and it required this competency for important posts such as the pastorship of Poznań's central parish, St. Mary Magdalene's. See magistrate to the bishop of Poznań, 13 Dec. 1796, KA II 337, vol. 1, Archiwum Archidiecezjalne w Poznaniu (AAP).

5. 13 June 1801, HA I, Rep. 7C, no. 25, Fasz. 17, GSPK.

6. As the Prussian minister Alvensleben explained, "The many recourses to Rome [by the local Catholic hierarchy] encourage superstition and waste time and money." Alvensleben to Voss, Hoym, and Schrotter, 20 July 1800, HA I, Rep. 7C, no. 25, Fasz. 22, GSPK.

7. Previously novices regularly entered the cloisters in their early teens. The new regulations required candidates to apply relatively late in life, a decision fewer were willing to make.

8. See HA I, Rep. 7C, no. 14m, Fasz. 31, GSPK.

9. 14 Dec. 1800, HA II, Südpreussen 10, no. 212, GSPK.

10. Prümers, 656.

11. While slow to challenge secular authorities, Raczyński grew increasingly frustrated with Prussian policy. His early hopes for a mutually beneficial, conservative union between throne and altar gave way to the conviction that the church's influence and authority were being irreparably harmed, thereby weakening the structures that buttressed Catholic morality and, in turn, civil society. In a rare display of spleen, he bitterly denounced the government's decision to allow secular courts to rule on divorces between Catholics in some instances: "In my view evil consequences will be unavoidable. In this religion to which I minister, the secrets, sacraments, dogma, and the rest of the articles of faith demand unrestricted obedience and submission, and there is no room for freedom of conscience." See his 19 June 1801 letter to the king, HA I, Rep. 7C, no. 25a, Fasz. 9, GSPK.

12. 22 Feb. 1807, HA II, Südpreussen 1, no. 670, GSPK.

13. Quoted in Stanisław Cynar, *Ignacy Raczyński: Ostatni prymas Polski porozbiorowej i jego działalność duszpasterska w okresie Księstwa Warszawskiego* (London: Veritas, 1954), 96. Later Raczyński protested the duchy's divorce policy, which allowed Catholics to bring their cases before secular courts, and he lodged complaints against the predominance of godless men in the

teaching field. In 1811 Raczyński and all of the duchy's Catholic bishops composed a formal memorial to the government, in which they reiterated these and other complaints. The memorial had little or no effect. See Cynar, 101–25.

14. The duchy adopted the Prussian approach toward property once held by church institutions, claiming ownership for itself while guaranteeing former owners 50 percent of the revenues. The government, however, stopped making regular payments on its obligations, and in 1809 it ceased payments altogether.

15. Cynar, 35–39.

16. Marian Fąka, *Stan prawny Kościoła katolickiego w Wielkim Księstwia Poznańskim w latach 1815–1850 wświetle prawa pruskiego* (Warsaw: Akademia Teologii Katolickiej, 1975), secs. 4.2–4.4.

17. 7 July 1826, HA I, Rep. 76 IV, Sekt. 4, Abt. 4, no. 2, vol. 1, GSPK.

18. Eager to avoid controversy, the king instructed his ministers that cloisters "should only be secularized where surrounding conditions make such an action advisable. The rest should die out of their own accord." 7 July 1818, HA I, Rep 76 IV, Sekt. 4, Abt. 13, no. 1, GSPK.

19. See figures from 1830, HA I, Rep. 76 IV, Sekt. 4, Abt. 13, no. 4, GSPK.

20. 26 Dec. 1824, HA I, Rep. 76 IV, Sekt. 4, Abt. 12, no. 1, vol. 1, GSPK.

21. 15 Mar. 1820, HA I, Rep. 76 IV, Sekt. 4, Abt. 2, no. 4, GSPK.

22. 12 Feb. 1833, HA I, Rep. 76 IV, Sekt. 4, Abt. 12, no. 1, vol. 2, GSPK.

23. Motty, 1:193–94.

24. This plan first emerged in 1824. Its principal architects were Prince Joseph von Hohenzollern, bishop of Warmia, and Jan Heinrich Schmedding, a Prussian minister. See HA I, Rep. 76 IV, Sekt. 4, Abt. 2, no. 3, GSPK.

25. Prussian authorities assumed that Breslau's archbishops would persuade the Catholic hierarchy in the grand duchy to adopt German cultural and educational models. Berlin planned to implement this project during the next archepiscopal interregnum. Before all of the pieces were in place, however, Archbishop Gorzeński of Poznań-Gniezno died suddenly on 20 December 1825. Worse still, relations with the Vatican had soured, rendering Berlin's position much less tenable. Prussian authorities shelved the plan and began examining potential candidates for the highest Catholic office in the province.

26. Flottwell's report, 17 Mar. 1831, HA I, Rep. 77, Tit. 503, no. 5, GSPK.

27. Flottwell to Altenstein, 27 Dec. 1836, HA I, Rep. 76 IV, Sekt. 4, Abt. 7, no. 23, GSPK.

28. 3 Jan. 1830, HA I, Rep. 76 IV, Sekt. 4, Abt. 4, no. 3, vol. 1, GSPK.

29. 1 May 1837, ibid.

30. Kurt Nowak, *Geschichte des Christentums in Deutschland: Religion, Politik und Gesellschaft vom Ende der Aufklärung bis zur Mitte des 20. Jahrhunderts* (Munich: C. H. Beck, 1995), 76.

31. See the various reports from throughout the archdiocese in October and November 1839, NPP, no. 1276, APP.

32. Zygmunt Zieliński, *Kościół katolicki w Wielkim Księstwie Poznańskim w latach 1848–1865* (Lublin: Tow. Naukowe Katolickiego Uniwersytetu Lubelskiego, 1973), 26.

33. Beurmann to Dunin, 15 Aug. 1842, HA I, Rep. 76 IV, Sekt. 4, Abt. 7, no. 23, GSPK.

34. Mieczysław Żywczyński, "Der Posener Kirchenstreit in den Jahren 1837–40 und die 'Kölner Wirren': Ein Beitrag zu ihrer Geschichte und zur Geschichte der Politik Metternichs," *Acta Poloniae Historica* (1959) 2:40.

35. Motty, 1:563.

36. Ibid., 1:68–69.

37. Ibid., 1:469–90.

38. Ibid., 1:268.

39. Ibid., 1:524–26.

40. Zieliński, 42.

41. For more on Koźmian, see Przemysław Matusik, *Religia i naród: Życia i myśl Jana Koźmiana, 1814–1877* (Poznań: Wydawnictwo Poznańskie, 1998).

42. 21 May 1816, Konsystorz ewangelicky w Poznaniu (KEP), no. 2167, APP.

43. 7 June 1816, KEP, no. 2167, APP.

44. The holidays were October 18 (the Battle of Leipzig), March 31 (the Capture of Paris), and June 18 (the Battle of the Belle Alliance). 24 Sept. 1816, KEP, no. 2167, APP.

45. Flottwell to Altenstein, 22 May 1832, HA I, Rep. 76 IV, Sekt. 4, Abt. 13, no. 6, vol. 2, GSPK.

46. 30 Jan. 1834, NPP, no. 5980, APP.

47. Commander of the Fifth Brigade to Flottwell, 6 Nov. 1839, NPP, no. 1276, APP.

48. Makowski, 124–25.

49. Commander of the Fifth Brigade to Flottwell, 6 Nov. 1839, NPP, no. 1276, APP.

50. Mar. 1804, KA II 337, vol. 1, AAP.

51. Jaffe, 159.

52. Dunin to Berlin, 9 June 1833, HA I, Rep. 76 IV, Sekt. 4, Abt. 7, no. 23, GSPK.

53. Police report, 30 June 1843, NPP no. 6180, APP.

54. 13 Aug. 1844, NPP, no. 5993, APP.

55. 26 Oct. 1844, ibid.

56. Cynar, 16.

57. Baumann to Altenstein, 2 Sept. 1826, HA I, Rep. 76 IV, Sekt. 4, Abt. 4, no. 3, GSPK.

58. Jan. 1830., ibid.

59. He fought in vain to retain the title of prince for his office. He was more successful at defending the distinctness of both archdioceses in the face of government efforts to blend them into a unified structure.

60. Quoted in Zofia Ostrowska-Kębłowska, *Dzieje Kaplicy Królów Polskich czyli Złotej w katedrze poznańskiej* (Poznań: Wydawnictwo Poznańskiego Tow. Przyjaciół Nauk., 1997), 33.

61. 22 Feb. 1807, HA II, Südpreussen 1, no. 670, GSPK.

62. Flottwell et al., 8.

63. Wawrzykowska-Wierciochowa, 49–50.

64. Matusik, 35.

65. Walicki, 247–66.

66. Motty, 1:431.

67. Walicki, 228.

68. Flottwell's report, 1 Apr. 1831, HA I, Rep. 77, Tit. 503, no. 5, GSPK.

69. Motty, 1:15.

70. Kufal was arrested at the border. Prussian officials were alarmed by his story and investigated his conversion and religious training in order to determine whether he had been pressured or manipulated in any way. May 1831, NPP, no. 1454, APP.

71. Manfred Laubert, "Beiträge zur Geschichte des deutsch-katholischen Kirchensystems

der Stadt Posen und ihrer Kammereidörfer," *Zeitschrift der Historischen Gesellschaft für die Provinz Posen* 20 (1905): 10–11.

72. Nov. 1840, KA 12 488, AAP.

73. 28 Dec. 1840, ibid.

74. 26 Jan. 1841, ibid.

75. Archdiocesan authorities agreed that Pawelke's innovations went too far and urged him to abandon the song board and to restore the statuary and funerary monuments to their original places. His intransigence, as well as some financial improprieties, finally prompted them to transfer him to Schwerin, one of the poorest dioceses in the province. Pawelke to archbishop, 13 Mar. 1848, KA 862, AAP.

76. 4 Mar. 1841, KA 862, AAP.

77. 15 Nov. 1840, KA 12 488, AAP.

78. Aug. 1841, ibid. For a fuller treatment of this incident, see Robert E. Alvis, "A Clash of Catholic Cultures on the German-Polish Border: The Tale of a Controversial Priest in Poznań, 1839–1842," *Catholic Historical Review* 88, no. 3 (2002): 470–88.

79. Walicki, 155.

80. Kalinka, 169–70.

81. Beurmann to Eichhorn, 5 Dec. 1846, HA I, Rep. 77 CB, Tit. 343A, no. 62, GSPK.

82. Beurmann to Eichhorn, 4 June 1844, HA I, Rep. 76 IV, Sekt. 4, Abt. 4, no. 7, vol. 1, GSPK.

83. Wuttke, *Polen und Deutsche,* 21.

84. Most Prussian officials recognized the inevitability of another Pole occupying the office, but this did not prevent some from advocating a German candidate. Berlin also sought to win greater influence over the process. These challenges, along with divisions within the Polish camp and the active engagement of the Vatican, stretched out the contentious process. Dunin's seat remained vacant until 21 October 1844. For a full account of the election see Zieliński, 62–80.

85. HA I, Rep. 77 CB, Tit. 343A, no. 62, GSPK.

86. Police report, 30 Nov. 1844, HA I, Rep. 76 III, Sekt. 7, Abt. 17, no. 26, vol. 1, GSPK.

87. Goltz to Beurmann, 24 May 1845, ibid.

88. Gerhard Graf, *Gottesbild und Politik: Eine Studie zur Frömmigkeit in Preußen während der Befreiungskriege, 1813–1815* (Göttingen: Vandenhoeck und Ruprecht, 1993), 65.

89. [Mar. 1845], HA I, Rep. 76 III, Sekt. 7, Abt. 17, no. 26, vol. 1, GSPK.

90. In a 4 Jan. 1845 letter to Eichhorn, Vicar Gaierowicz expressed his acute disappointment that the state was tolerating not only Czerski's movement but also the publicity it was generating. He wrote, "In a state where nothing gets printed without official permission, I have to excuse orthodox Catholics when they say that government bureaucrats are supporting Czerski's religious errors in order to devastate the Catholic hierarchy." HA I, Rep. 76 III, Sekt. 7, Abt. 17, no. 26, vol. 1, GSPK.

91. Arnim-Boitzenburg to Eichhorn, 23 Jan. 1845, ibid.

92. Minutoli to Beurmann, 20 May 1845, ibid.

93. "Geschichtliche Mitteilung" (1845), GESK, no. 39, APP.

94. Motty, 1:268–69.

95. Makowski, 42.

96. NPP, no. 1242, APP.

97. Beurmann to Eichhorn, 8 July 1846, HA I, Rep. 76 IV, Sekt. 1, Abt. 1, no. 8, vol. 1, GSPK.

98. Minutoli to Minister Bodelschwingh, 17 Feb. 1847, ibid.

99. Ibid.

4. Protestant Poznań

1. According to Sadebeck, Poznań was home to 2,033 Protestants in 1794. Cited in Łukaszewicz, *Obraz historyczno-statystyczny,* 1:65–66. The 1846 figure is from Kędelski, 229.

2. Perhaps Friedrich II's greatest impact in this regard was his decision to shape the faculty at Halle University in a rationalist direction. His effort had widespread ramifications because Halle trained the majority of Prussia's Protestant ministers up until the late 1830s. One indication of the tenor of the age was the lessening of conflict between the Reformed and Lutheran confessions in the realm. Differences in liturgical practice and theological emphasis, once a source of bitter conflict, ceased to arouse the same level of animus.

3. Robert M. Bigler, *The Politics of German Protestantism: The Rise of the Protestant Church Elite in Prussia, 1815–1848* (Berkeley: Univ. of California Press, 1972), 7.

4. They included numerous Protestant leaders such as Friedrich Schleiermacher, one of the most distinguished theologians of the nineteenth century. Deeply opposed to Napoleon's military ambitions, Schleiermacher rallied popular resentment against the French invaders through many impassioned sermons. At the same time, inspired in part by the French example, he encouraged his listeners to imagine a more democratic Prussia free of rigid caste distinctions. See Friedrich Schleiermacher, "A Nation's Duty Is a War for Freedom," in *Selected Sermons of Schleiermacher,* trans. Mary F. Wilson (New York: Funk and Wagnalls, 1890), 67ff.

5. Bigler, 21–25.

6. Rhode, 131–32.

7. 7 Dec. 1794, HA I, Rep. 7C, no. 27, Fasz. 30, GSPK.

8. Voss to [Massow], 15 May 1799, and subsequent correspondence, ibid.

9. 1 Dec. 1801 and subsequent correspondence, HA II, Südpreussen 6, no. 2287, GSPK.

10. South Prussian Consistory to the king, 17 Oct. 1796, HA I, Rep. 7C, no. 25e, Fasz. 2, GSPK.

11. King to South Prussian Consistory, 30 Nov. 1796, ibid.

12. Rhode, 145.

13. Victims of this restructuring were the local synods that previously had afforded the Protestant laity of the region a degree of administrative autonomy over their communities.

14. Berlin to Protestant Consistory in Poznań, 25 Aug. 1818, KEP, no. 472, APP.

15. 12 Oct. 1846, HA I, Rep. 76 III, Sekt. 1, Abt. 21, no. 61, vol. 2, GSPK.

16. Berlin issued just such a warning in an 1826 letter to the Protestant Consistory. It had come to the central government's attention that not all pastors in the grand duchy were paying attention to official regulations and the new decrees published regularly in the *Amtsblatt der Königlichen Regierung zu Posen* (Office papers). Should they continue to fail in this regard, the letter added, their positions would be jeopardized. Ministry of Religious Affairs to Protestant Consistory in Poznań, 10 June 1826, KEP, no. 472, APP.

17. Rhode, 135.

18. Minister of the Interior to Sposetti, 24 Sept. 1816, KEP, no. 2167, APP.

19. 11 Dec. 1830, NPP, no. 5756, APP.

20. King to Protestant congregations of Prussia, 27 Sept. 1817, KEP, no. 2159, APP.

21. Walter Wendland, *Die Religiosität und die kirchen-politischen Grundsätze Friedrich Wilhelms III und ihre Bedeutung für die Geschichte der kirchlichen Restauration* (Giessen: A. Töpelmann, 1909), 80ff.

22. Wendland, 107ff.

23. 18 Jan. 1842, KEP, no. 5765, APP.

24. Ostrowska-Kębłowska, *Architektura i budownictwo*, 30.

25. Journal entry, 26 July 1795, GESK, no. 39, APP.

26. Ibid., 7 Aug. 1815.

27. The state consented to these demands in the church constitution it prepared for the Reformed community in 1797. Sommer, "Die Posener Unitätsgemeinde," 75.

28. 2 Dec. 1815, GESK, no. 39, APP.

29. Stechebahr functioned as pastor of the Cross Congregation from 1779 to 1816. He also served as county elder and provincial superintendent.

30. Adolf Henschel, *Evangelische Lebenszeugen des Posener Landes aus alter und neuer Zeit* (Poznań: Friedrich Ebbeckes Verlag, 1891), 220–32.

31. Henschel, 364–82.

32. 24 Oct. 1817, GESK, no. 39, APP.

33. In cases where congregations of different confessions did merge, union was generally more superficial than real. In a letter to Berlin, an official from the Protestant Consistory in Poznań described the ways in which supposedly unified Lutheran and Reformed congregations in the province were handling this sensitive issue: "It is common in some places where different Protestant congregations share the same church that the items that decorate the altar are immediately removed after the first congregation's service, for such an altar arrangement does not suit the practices of the following congregation." Such actions, in this official's eyes, undermined interconfessional harmony and encouraged "the retention of superficial differences." Ministry of Religious Affairs to Protestant Consistory, 23 May 1828, KEP, no. 472, APP.

34. Although these meetings took place beyond officially sanctioned institutions, initially they did not appear to threaten the state churches, and the consistory allowed them to continue. Protestant Consistory to Altenstein, 8 Mar. 1823, HA I, Rep. 76 III, Sekt. 7, Abt. 17, no. 24, vol. 1, GSPK.

35. 18 June 1834, ibid.

36. They included two popular preachers, Rector Ehrenström and Pastor Lasius. According to Wangemann, Ehrenström misspent his youth in worldly pursuits and was a heavy alcoholic, drinking his first schnapps of the day for breakfast. Hermann Wangemann, *Sieben Bücher Preußischer Kirchengeschichte* (Berlin: W. Schultze, 1859–1860), 2:104–5. But Ehrenström was also a powerful evangelizer and attracted a body of followers in the town of Meseritz. He was closely allied with Lasius, a pastor in the town of Prittisch. Lasius's charisma is suggested by a report to the provincial governor accusing him of impregnating ten women in his congregation. 21 Dec. 1835, NPP, no. 5763, APP. Both men ran afoul of the law by leading unauthorized devotional groups and by their opposition to the state's claim to authority over religious affairs. After being suspended from their offices, they joined the Old Lutheran movement. They were joined soon

thereafter by Johann Wermelskirch, a highly respected revivalist preacher and missionary to the Jews, who organized an Old Lutheran congregation in Poznań. Other congregations were formed in the towns of Bromberg, Rogoźno (Rogasen), Lissa (Leszno), Neutomischel (Nowy Tomyśl), and Nakel (Nakło).

37. Scheibel's hostility to the hierarchical nature of the state church led him to adopt some controversial ideas regarding the proper nature of church government. He promoted a decentralized view of Lutheranism, arguing that everything from the formulation of doctrine to the ownership of property should be the purview of local congregations. This model had democratic implications that Prussian liberals were quick to seize upon. Bigler, 110–12.

38. A fair number of Old Lutherans opted to emigrate to more tolerant countries such as Australia and the United States. Rhode, 151.

39. Wangemann, 2:420.

40. One of the movement's more charismatic leaders, Pastor Gustav Adolf Wislicenus, came to advocate an overtly political program. In 1845 he called for the creation of "free congregations" *(Freiegemeinde),* unbound by any confessions of faith or government control, that were to form the kernels of a new, democratic social order. Wislicenus's drive never amounted to much, but both it and the Friends of Light caused considerable consternation within government circles. Bigler argues that the movement helped awaken the political consciousness of many Germans. According to his reading, the Friends of Light created channels through which liberal leaders could connect with a mass audience and ordinary Germans could identify with one another as part of a common cause. Bigler, 198–230.

41. Rhode, 156.

42. *Beschreibung der feierlichen Grundsteinlegung der evangelischen Petri-Kirche zu Posen am 3. August 1838* (Poznań, 1838), 13–14.

43. 6 Sept. 1840, HA I, Rep. 76 III, Sekt. 1, Abt. 21, no. 61, vol. 2, GSPK.

44. For a nuanced discussion of these issues, see Altgeld.

45. Many commentators have attempted to account for why Protestant Germany proved more receptive to nationalist ideologies than its Catholic counterpart. Protestant nationalists themselves long have pointed to Luther. His struggle against the Roman Catholic Church, they argue, should be considered as an early salvo in an unfolding struggle against the cultural imperialism of Latin Europe. His movement was at once a restoration of true Christianity and a call for national liberation. While there are major problems with this argument, it is clear that Luther's revolution helped inaugurate the growing degree of ethnic solidarity within the German-speaking world. Luther's translation of the Bible into German rightly has been touted as a major step both for the codification of the German language and for its eventual eclipsing of Latin and French as the language of law, scholarship, and polite society—an essential prerequisite for the culturally based nationalist ideologies that eventually developed in Germany. See Jacobs, 51–110. It also has been argued that pietism helped promote the profound social changes required for nationalism to take root. One of the movement's hallmarks was its tendency to level caste distinctions between its members. In addition, pietists were in the forefront of the push for universal elementary education. Though he overstates his case, the best English-language work on this subject remains Koppel Pinson's *Pietism as a Factor in the Rise of German Nationalism* (New York: Octagon, 1968).

46. Pinson, 153–74.

47. Jacobs, 100.

48. Levinger, 44.

49. Gerhard Graf, 4.2.1.

50. Altgeld, 128–33.

51. Bigler, 26.

52. Gerhard Graf, 1.2.1.

53. Ibid., 124.

54. Grześ, Kozłowski, and Kramski, 39.

55. Wendland, 139–43.

56. King Friedrich Wilhelm III once quipped that Catholic priests "eagerly spread the notion that we [Protestants] believe in nothing, and our rationalists have indeed brought things to the point where that seems to be the case." Ibid., 166.

57. Rhode, 142.

58. 22 May 1833, KEP, no. 288, APP.

59. Wuttke, *Polen und Deutsche,* 22.

60. Motty, 2:166–70.

61. David Barclay, *Frederick William IV and the Prussian Monarchy, 1840–1861* (Oxford: Oxford Univ. Press, 1995), 29–33, 49–52.

62. 12 July 1843, KEP, no. 2167, APP.

63. Eichhorn to Protestant Consistory, 10 Jan. 1846, KEP, no. 473, APP.

64. Protestant Consistory to Eichhorn, 10 Feb. 1848, ibid. (emphasis in original).

65. See KEP, no. 2168, APP.

66. Altgeld, 171.

67. Journal entry, 1845, GESK, no. 39, APP.

68. The *Stolgebühren* were eliminated in South Prussia not long after the Prussian invasion. Other taxes paid to Catholic officials gradually were rescinded as well. See Ravens, 106ff.

69. Reformed community elders to king, 1 June 1799, HA II, Südpreussen 6, no. 2289, GSPK.

70. Journal entry, 5 and 12 Feb. 1795, GESK, no. 39, APP.

71. Ibid., 6 Sept. 1817. See also letters from the same period in KEP, no. 5764, APP.

72. Rhode, 131, 135, 141.

73. Sommer, "Die Posener Unitätsgemeinde," 84–85.

74. According to Werner (290), Poznań was home to 1,213 Reformed Christians in 1850.

75. In 1858 part of the Lutheran community was split off into a daughter congregation named St. Paul's.

76. The church in question was formerly the property of the Catherinian women's cloister. After the cloister's secularization, the church was put to other uses by the military. King to Eichhorn, 1 Feb. 1846, and Beurmann to Eichhorn et al., 30 July 1846, HA I, Rep. 76 IV, Sekt. 4, Abt. 13, no. 66, GSPK.

77. Rhode, 137.

78. 1822, KEP, no. 2523, APP.

79. The society sponsored special Protestant services for Jews that generally were poorly attended. More successful were the free schools it established for Jewish youth. As soon as a

teacher so much as uttered the name of Jesus, however, Jewish parents usually pulled their children out. According to an official account of its activities (1829), in the years 1826–28 the society managed to baptize just three adults and three children. Those Jews who did convert generally were shunned by their erstwhile coreligionists. This could have disastrous consequences, as it did in the case of a Jewish man named Jaretzki. By converting, Jaretzki was cut off from the social relations upon which his livelihood depended. The society felt obliged to offer him financial assistance. See KEP, no. 2523, APP.

80. Protestant Consistory to Altenstein, 18 June 1834, HA I, Rep. 76 III, Sekt. 7, Abt. 17, no. 24, vol. 1, GSPK.

81. Rhode, 144.

82. Barclay, 81–84.

83. Eichhorn circular, 11 Jan. 1843, and Protestant Consistory to Eichhorn, 18 May 1843, KEP, no. 2154, APP.

84. August Angermann, *Die evangelischen Kirchen des Posener Landes seit 1772* (Poznań: Kommissionsverlag der Evangel. Vereinsbuchhandlung, 1912), 36.

85. 5 Dec. 1824, NPP, no. 6169, APP.

86. 13 May 1829, KEP, no. 2523, APP. The aggressive techniques employed by the society's missionaries eventually prompted the government to threaten them with expulsion from the province were they to continue plying their persuasions on fellow Christians. Protestant Consistory announcement, 31 Mar. 1833, ibid.

87. See NPP, no. 5750 and 5781, APP. The new rules did little to ease pressures along the Protestant-Catholic divide. On the contrary, the number of conversions shot up dramatically in the late 1830s and early 1840s, in large measure as a response to the mixed-marriage controversy. At this time, many priests required the non-Catholic partner in such unions to convert to Catholicism before the marriage could take place. Sometimes this pressure had its intended effect. At other times it was the Catholic partner who chose to convert.

88. Provincial government announcement, 31 Mar. 1842, KEP, no. 2143, APP.

89. Protestant Consistory to Protestant superintendents, 18 Oct. 1842, ibid.

90. 19 Jan. 1843, HA I, Rep. 76 IV, Sekt. 4, Abt. 4, no. 7, vol. 1, GSPK.

91. Ibid., 6 Jan. 1843.

5. A Revolutionary Spring

1. Antoni Gąsiorowski, "Nazwy poznańskich ulic," in Topolski and Trzeciakowski, 45–46.

2. Launched in 1828, the project was only completed in the 1870s. By that time it was already outmoded on account of dramatic improvements in artillery technology.

3. Quoted in Adolf Warschauer, "Ein hundert Jahre altes humoristisches Gedicht über Posen," *Historische Monatsblätter für die Provinz Posen* 5, no. 4 (1904): 24–29.

4. Quoted in Trzeciakowski and Trzeciakowski, 32.

5. Quoted in Wuttke, *Polen und Deutsche,* 27.

6. Trzeciakowski and Trzeciakowski, 30.

7. Quoted in Manfred Laubert, "Eine gescheiterte Denkmalserrichtung in Posen," *Historische Monatsblätter für die Provinz Posen* 6, no. 12 (1905): 214.

8. Quoted in Laubert, "Eine gescheiterte Denkmalserrichtung," 215.

9. See Hayden White, *Metahistory: The Historical Imagination in Nineteenth-Century Europe* (Baltimore: Johns Hopkins Univ. Press, 1987), 135–43.

10. Flottwell et al., 27.

11. Ostrowska-Kębłowska, *Dzieje Kaplicy Królów Polskich,* 94–95.

12. See Wuttke, *Polen und Deutsche.*

13. Ibid., 18.

14. In 1797 four neighboring towns on Poznań's western bank were incorporated into the city. Several years later four neighboring towns on the eastern bank experienced a similar fate.

15. Kemlein, 96–109.

16. Wolfgang Schivelbusch, *The Railway Journey: The Industrialization of Time and Space in the Nineteenth Century* (Berkeley: Univ. of California Press, 1986).

17. The total expense of this project was sixty-three thousand thaler. Jaffe, 71.

18. For a comprehensive account of developments in transportation in the Poznań region, see Dohnalowa, *Rozwój transportu.*

19. Barclay, 154.

20. Robert Hepke, *Die polnische Erhebung und die deutsche Gegenbewegung in Posen im Frühjahr 1848* (Berlin: Mittler, 1848), 4.

21. Motty, 1:54.

22. Stanisław Nawrocki, "Die revolutionären Ereignisse im Großherzogtum Posen und Westpreußen in den Jahren 1848–1849," in *Deutsche und Polen in der Revolution 1848–1849,* ed. Hans Booms and Marian Wojciechowski (Boppard am Rhein: H. Boldt, 1991), 27.

23. Polish National Committee to Prussia, 20, 21, 22 Mar. 1848, in Hepke, 34.

24. Heinz Boberach, "Die Posener Frage in der deutschen und der preußischen Politik 1848–1849," in Booms and Wojciechowski, 17–18.

25. Junker to Beurmann, 21 Mar. 1848, and "Co słychać naświecie?" in Booms and Wojciechowski, eds., 182–88.

26. Ibid., 184.

27. Wolfgang Kohte, *Deutsche Bewegung und preussische Politik im Posener Lande 1848–1849,* in *Deutsche Wissenschaftliche Zeitschrift für Polen* 21 (1931): 85–86.

28. German National Committee to grand duchy residents, in Hepke, 37.

29. Hepke, 8.

30. Nawrocki, 29.

31. Polish National Committee to the Polish people, in Hepke, 46–47.

32. Kohte, 28–29.

33. Quoted in Hepke, 14.

34. Ibid., 40.

35. 29 Mar. 1848, ibid., 42–43.

36. Ibid., 46.

37. Nawrocki, 32.

38. Kohte, 37.

39. Hepke, 15.

40. For a lucid account of Friedrich Wilhelm IV's actions and attitudes during the revolution, see Barclay, 138–83.

41. Kohte, 47–48.

42. Boberach, 19.

43. Willisen to grand duchy residents, 6 Apr. 1848, in Hepke, 55.

44. 11 Apr. 1848, in ibid., 69.

45. Ibid., 24.

46. Colomb requested reinforcements already on March 23, and additional troops began pouring into the grand duchy from other provinces over subsequent weeks. Kohte, 46.

47. Quoted in Gordon Craig, *Theodor Fontane: Literature and History in the Bismarck Reich* (Oxford: Oxford Univ. Press, 1999), 7.

48. In Hepke, 60.

49. Quoted in Kohte, 57.

50. For a fuller account of France's position on the Polish question, see ibid., 55–56.

51. Nawrocki, 34.

52. Quoted in Karol Libelt, *Stan rzeczy w Wielkiem Księstwie Poznańskiem* (Poznań, 1848), 160.

53. Kohte, 79–80.

54. Hepke, 76.

55. Kohte, 83.

56. Quoted in ibid., 86–87.

57. Libelt, 155.

58. 17 Apr. 1848, in Hepke, 68.

59. Schleinitz to Beurmann, 14 Apr. 1848, in Booms and Wojciechowski, 275–77.

60. Illing to Beurmann, 23 Apr. 1848, in Booms and Wojciechowski, 293.

61. Nawrocki, 35.

62. Heinrich Wuttke, *Städtebuch des Landes Posen* (Leipzig: Auf Kosten des Verfassers: In Commission bei Hermann Fries, 1864), 254.

63. Nawrocki, 36.

64. Ibid.

65. Prussian military units committed a number of abuses against the Polish population that resulted in the transfer of General Colomb and Chief of Staff Olberg out of the province. The central government took this action in order to facilitate reconciliation in the grand duchy. Kohte, 111.

66. Ibid., 106.

67. Motty, 2:103–4, and n. 22.

68. Kohte, 122.

69. Motty, 2:526–27.

70. Ibid., 1:165–68.

71. Pfuel's declaration, 12 May 1848, in Booms and Wojciechowski, 336–37.

72. Barclay, 180ff.

Bibliography

Archival Material

Archiwum Państwowe w Poznaniu (APP)

Naczelne Prezydium w Poznaniu (NPP)

1235: Gesinnung der katholischen Pfarrgeistlichen im Großherzogtum Posen [1831]

1242: Theilnahme mehrerer Kleriker an dem Attentat von 3. März 1846

1276: Von Seite der katholischen Geistlichkeit eingefuhrten (1) Kirchen-Trauer, (2) Verbreitung verbotener Schriften [1839]

1282: Ruckkehr des Erzbischofs v. Dunin nach Posen [1840–42]

1330: Schriftstücke bet. Polizeisachen, besonders polnische Umtreibe [1815–24]

1355: Beabsichtigte Versammlung des polnischen Adels [1827]

1356: Gesinnungen, das Thun und Treiben des polnischen Adels [1827–30]

1387: Zustand der Dinge im Königreich Polen und deren Einfluß [1826–36]

1454: Öffentliche Ruhe und Sicherheit in der Stadt und dem Kreise Posen [1830–36]

3123: Denkmal zum Andenken des Divisions-Generals v. Dąbrowski [1842]

3124: Thaers Denkmal [1843]

5750: Von der katholischen zu evangelischen Kirche und umgekehrt übergetretenen Personen [1830–41]

5756: Protestantische Kirchenwesen [1831–51]

5763: Kirchliche Separatismus [1833–36]

5765: Abwanderung der Separatisten [1836–47]

5781: Von der katholischen zur evangelischen und umgekehrt übergetretenen Personen [1842–51]

5887: Beschwerden des Herrn Bischofs zu Posen [1819–27]

5979: Feststellung des katholischen Festkalendars [1816–33]

5980: Feststellung des katholischen Festkalendars [1834–1902]

5982: Einsendung der jährlichen Kirchenkalendar [1817–53]

5993: Anmassungen der katholischen Geistlichen gegen andere Glaubensverwandte; feindselige Stimmung der christlichen Bevölkerung gegen die jüdische [1817–44]

6168: Entheiligung der Feiertage [1823–45]

6169: Beschwerden wider die katholische Geistlichkeit u. Schullehrer [1817–44]

6180: Beschwerden wider die katholische Geistlichkeit [1842–47]

8986: Beschwerden über verschiedene Anmassungen und Beeintrachtigungen christlicher Gerechtsamer von Seiten der Juden [1816–26]

Konsystorz Ewangelicky w Poznaniu (KEP)

288: Bischöfliche Sendschreiben an die evangelische Geistlichkeit [1788–1833]

472: Evangelische Kirchenwesen im Allgemein [1816–45]

473: Evangelische Kirchenwesen im Allgemein [1846–52]

2143: Kirchliche Feier der Sonn- und Festtage [1823–]

2154: Feier verschiedener Kirchenfeste [1816–1943]

2159: Kirchliche Feier des Reformationsfestes [1817–1926]

2167: Kirchliche Feier vaterländischer (politischer) Feste [1815–1922]

2168: Feier des 3. Mai und 11. November [1815–1931]

2172: Kirchliche Feier des Geburtstages Seiner Majestät des Königs [1845–1916]

2419: Verhütung der Teilnahme an politische revolutionären Umtreiben in den Gemeinden [1830–1907]

2523: Vereine zur Beförderung des Christentums unter den Israeliten [1822–44]

2976: Verhältnis der evangelischen Christlichen zum Judenthum [1821–1938]

2978: Austritt aus der Kirchengemeinschaft in Allgemein [1850–1923]

2990: Übertritt von Judentum zum Christentum [1817–1941]

3001: Katholische Dissidenten oder Deutsch respektive Christkatholiken [1845–73]

3002: Protestantische Freunde oder Lichtfreunde [1845–78]

5764: Evangelische-Lutherische Kirche in Posen [1816–31]

5765: Evangelische-Lutherische Kirche in Posen [1832–62]

5894: Überlassung der St. Martinskirche an die St. Petri Gemeinde [1835–37]

Gmina Ewangelicka św. Krzyża w Poznaniu (GESK)

39: Protokolarz [1760–1855]

48: Kronika gminy ewangelickiej św. Krzyża [1767–93]

51: Ode im Namen der Bekenner—do króla Stanisław

119: Einnahme und Ausgabe [1759–1815]

Archiwum Archidiecezjalne w Poznaniu (AAP)

KA 10 233: Gminy katolicko-niemieckiego w Poznaniu [1844–65]
KA 12 488: Kościół pofranciszkańskie generalia [1829–43]
KA 862: Personalia: Franz Pawelke [1831–67]
KA II 337, vols. 1–7: Ś. Maria Magdalena Generalia [1585–1827]
PA 324/69: Klasztor św. Anny—wydzierzawienia i sprzedaż [1820–28]

Geheimes Staatsarchiv Preußischer Kulturbesitz, Berlin (GSPK)

Hauptabteilung I, Rep. 7C

14m, Fasz. 24: Sachen der protestantischen Prediger Heise, Bothe, Rottwitt, Koch, und Hancke wegen Beförderung und Begünstigung der Insurrektion
14m, Fasz. 31: Untersuchung gegen Dominikanerkonvent zu Brzesc [1795]
18g, Fasz. 4: Verdacht, daß der Printz Anton Radziwill mit den polnischen Intriganten in bedeutender Verbindung stehe
25, Fasz. 5: Verminderung der Verwendungen nach Rom
25, Fasz. 17: Das katholische Kirchen- und Schul-Wesen in Südpreussen
25, Fasz. 22: Verwendung der catholischen Geistlichkeit nach Rom
25a, Fasz. 9: Geistliche Gerichtbarkeit in Südpreussen, Schlesien und Neuostpreussen
25e, Fasz. 2: Von den Protestanten in Südpreussen gefeyerten Feyertage der Catholiken
27, Fasz. 30: Verfassung und Einrichtung des evangelisch-lutherischen Kirchen- und Schulen-Wesens im Posenschen Departement [1793–1801]
27, Fasz. 32: Gesuch der evangelischen Geistliche um Befreiung von der Abgabe des zehnten Groschens ihrer baaren Einkunfte [1794–95]
28, Fasz. 3: Bittschrift der reformirten Gemeinde [1793]
32, Fasz. 8: Ergreifung eines jüdischen Kindes durch den Dembrowski [1793]

Hauptabteilung I, Rep. 76 III

Sekt. 1, Abt. 14, 4a: Verbesserung der evangelischen Liturgie und Agenda [1798–1812]
Sekt. 1, Abt. 21, 61, vols. 1–2: Militair-Kirchen-Angelegenheiten in dem Provinz Posen
Sekt. 7, Abt. 11, 12: Gustav-Adolphs-Verein in der Provinz Posen
Sekt. 7, Abt. 17, 7: Missionswesen
Sekt. 7, Abt. 17, 12: Von Geistlichen und Kirchengemeinden in der Provinz Posen gegen den Gebrauch der Kirchen-Agenda erhobenen Widersprüche [1847–50]

Sekt. 7, Abt. 17, 24, vols. 1–2: Secten- und Conventikel-Wesen im Ober-Präsidial und Consistorial-Bezirk Posen [1822–35]

Sekt. 7, Abt. 17, 26, vols. 1, 3: Errichtung einer deutsch katholischen Gemeine [1844–1906]

Hauptabteilung I, Rep. 76 IV

Sekt. 1, Abt. 1, 8, vol. 1: Im Großherzogtum Posen entstandenen revolutionairen Bewegungen, insbesondere die zu Abwehr derselben zu ergreifenden Maaßregeln [1846–61]

Sekt. 1a, Abt. 1, 78: Religiöse Bewegungen unter den Katholiken im Allgemein [1846]

Sekt. 4, Abt. 2, 2: Vereinigung des Erzbisthums Gnesen mit dem Bisthum Posen [1820–23]

Sekt. 4, Abt. 2, 3: Bei Erledigung des erzbischoflichen Stuhls von Gnesen und Posen beabsichtigte Verlegung dieses Erzbistums auf den bischöflichen Stuhl zu Breslau [1824–26]

Sekt. 4, Abt. 2, 4: Differenzien mit dem Bischof von Posen, über angebliche Eingriff in siene Gerechtsame [1820–21]

Sekt. 4, Abt. 2, 8: Bei dem Dienstantritt des Ober-Präsidenten der Provinz Posen Flottwell, zwischen diesem und dem Erzbischof von Dunin entstandenen Misshelligkeiten [1830–52]

Sekt. 4, Abt. 4, 1: Besetzung des Erzbisthums Gnesen und Posen durch den bisherigen Bischof von Posen Grafen von Gorczenski [1818–22]

Sekt. 4, Abt. 4, 2, vols. 1–3: Erzbischoflischen Stuhl von Gnesen und Posen und die Wiederbesetzung desselben durch den Dom-Probst v. Wolicki [1825–31]

Sekt. 4, Abt. 4, 3, vol. 1: Wiederbesetzung des erzbischoflichen Stuhls von Gnesen und Posen durch den bisherigen Prälaten und Weihbischof Martin v. Dunin [1829–31]

Sekt. 4, Abt. 4, 7, vol. 1: Wiederbesetzung des Erzbischoflichen Stuhls durch den seitherigen Dompropst Leo v. Przyluski zu Gnesen [1842–44]

Sekt. 4, Abt. 4, 9: Benehmen des Erzbischofs von Gnesen-Posen bei der Insurrektion in den polnischen Theilen des Großherzogtum Posens im Jahre 1848 [1848–1863]

Sekt. 4, Abt. 7, 21, vols. 1–2: Katholische Kirchen und Pfarrwesen der deutschredenden katholischen Gemeinde in der Stadt Posen [1829–90]

Sekt. 4, Abt. 7, 23: Katholische Kirchen und Pfarrwesen der Parochial Collegiat Kirche ad St. Mariam Magdalenam in der Stadt Posen [1833–1910]

Sekt. 4, Abt. 12, 1, vols. 1–3: Seminarium zur Bildung der katholischen Geistlichkeit in Posen [1816–38]

Sekt. 4, Abt. 12, 3: Katholische Marien-Gymnasium zu Posen und die darin herrschende Neigung zu politischen Umtrieben [1840]

Sekt. 4, Abt. 13, 1: Anfertigung und Einsendung der Personen- und Vermögungs-Verzeichnisse der Klöster im Ober-Präsidial-Bezirk von Posen [1819–32]

Sekt. 4, Abt. 13, 2: Anfertigung und Einreichung der Personen und Vermögens Verzeichnisse der Klöster im Regierungs-Bezirke von Posen [1832–55]

Sekt. 4, Abt. 13, 4: Angelegenheiten der Klöster im Großherzogthum Posen [1821–34]

Sekt. 4, Abt. 13, 6, vols. 1–2: Aufhebung sämmtlichen Klöster in der Provinz Posen, so wie die Verwendung des vorgefundenen Vermögungs [1828–36]

Sekt. 4, Abt. 13, 17: Franziskaner Kloster in Posen, die Aufhebung desselben und Bestimmung über das vorhandene Vermögen [1817–81]

Sekt. 4, Abt. 13, 66: Vormalige St. Catharinen Kloster Kirche und die Gebäude sowohl dieser, als des der Stadt Commune zu Posen zugehorigen Dominikaner Klosters [1843–82]

Sekt. 4, Abt. 14, 4: Angebliche Wunder-Erscheinung an dem Mutter Gottesbilde zu Jarocin; von den Bewohnern des Dorfes Jerzyce, angeblich zum Abhaltung der Cholera, veranstaltete Prozession [1831]

Hauptabteilung I, Rep. 77 (Ministerium des Innern)

Titel 343A, 66: Panslavistische Bestrebungen, 1846

Titel 503, 5: Benehmen der katholischen Geistlichkeit und der öffentlichen Beamten im Großherzogtum Posen, in Beziehung auf die Polnische Insurrektion [1831–35]

Titel 503, 22, Adh. 21: Petitionen aus dem Kreise und der Stadt Posen, Regierungs-Bezirk Posen um Ausschließung von der polnisch-nationalen Organisation des Großherzogthums Posen um Einverleibung in den deutschen Bund [1848]

Hauptabteilung I, Rep. 77 (CB)

Titel 343A, 58, Adh. 1: Hoch- und landesverraetherischen Unternehmungen der Polen

Titel 343A, 62: Kirchen- und Schulwesen in dem Großherzogtum Posen zu ergreifenden Maaßregeln [1846–47]

Hauptabteilung II, Südpreußen 1

431: Verhalten der diesseitigen Unterthanen gegen Frankreich, und die Maaßregeln gegen die feindlichen Absichten dieses Reichs [1793–95]

439: Verhältniss der dießeitigen Unterthanen gegen Frankreich und die Maaßregeln gegen die feindl. Absichten dieses Reichs [1801–5]

670: In Südpreussen, im Herbst 1806 ausgebrochen Insurrektion
671: Von der Cammern infolge der Insurrektion eingesandte Hauptsequestrations-
   extrakte und die Absendung der Sequestrationskommissarien [1795–99]

Hauptabteilung II, Südpreußen 6

2197: Besetzung der Altaristen Stellen bei der Marien-Magdalenen Kirche zu Posen;
   sowie die Angelegenheiten der Probstey überhaupt [1793–1805]
2199: Armen-Wesen und dahin gehorend Anstalten zu Posen [1793–1806]
2229: Besetzung des Posenschen Dohm-Decanats
2230: Angelegenheiten der Dominicaner zu Posen
2231: Angelegenheiten des Dohm-Capitals zu Posen [1800–6]
2269: Angelegenheiten der Juden zu Posen
2287: Acta wegen der Lutherischen Kirche und Gemeinde in Posen
2289: Angelegenheiten der Reformirten Kirchen Gemeinde zu Posen
2294: Franziskaner Mönchs-Kloster zu Posen [1799–1802]
2295: Carmeliter-Josephiner Mönchs-Kloster zu Posen [1802–6]
2296: Carmeliter Mönchs Kloster ad Corpus Christi auf der Wiese in Posen [1802–6]
2297: Benedictiner Nonnen Kloster zu Posen [1797–1806]
2298: Verlegung der Kathariner-Nonnen zu Posen [1806]
2299: St. Claren-Bernhardiner-Nonnen-Kloster zu Posen [1801–6]
2300: Dominikaner Nonnen-Kloster [1795–1805]
2301: Karmeliter Nonnen-Kloster [1796–99]
2302: Katharinen Nonnen-Kloster [1801–5]
2304: Theresien Nonnen-Kloster [1802–5]

Hauptabteilung II, Südpreußen 10

203: Güter, Grund Stücke und Nutzungen der Philippiner Congregation oder St.
   Margaretha Parochial Kirche zu Posen [1797]
204: Dominikaner Nonnen-Kloster (Catharinnen) [1797]
205: Beschuhten Carmeliter Manns-Kloster [1797–98]
206: Benedictiner Nonnen-Kloster zu Posen [1797]
207: Dominikaner Manns-Kloster [1797]
208: Dominikaner Nonnen-Kloster zu Posen (Catharinnen) [1797, 1800]
209: Carmeliter beschuhten Manns-Kloster zu Posen [1797, 1800]
210: Franciscaner Manns-Kloster zu Posen [1797, 1801]
211: Philippiner Congregation oder St. Margaretha-Parochial-Kirche zu Posen [1797]
212: Theresien-Carmeliter Nonnen-Kloster zu Posen [1797, 1801]
214: Benedictiner Nonnen-Kloster zu Posen [1797–1805]
215: Dominikaner Manns-Kloster zu Posen [1797–1805]

Hauptabteilung II, Südpreußen 14

57: Nachrichten aus dem ehemaligen Südpreussen enthaltend
58: Verschiedene geheime Nachrichten und Notizen enthaltend [1810]

Printed Primary Source Material

Baumann, Johann Friedrich. *Darstellungen nach dem Leben: Aus einer Skizze der Sitten und des Nationalcharakters der ehemaligen Pohlen.* Königsberg: n.p., 1803.

Beschreibung der feierlichen Grundsteinlegung der evangelischen Petri-Kirche zu Posen am 3. August 1838. Poznań: n.p., [1838?].

Booms, Hans, and Marian Wojciechowski, eds. *Deutsche und Polen in der Revolution 1848–49: Dokumente aus deutschen und polnischen Archiven.* Boppard am Rhein: H. Boldt, 1991.

Flottwell, Eduard, et al. *Denkschrift des Oberpresidenten Herrn Flottwell, ueber die Verwaltung des Gros-Herzogthum Posen, von Dezember 1830 zum Beginn des Jahres 1841. Nebst dem demselben seitens mehrerer Einwohner des Gros-Herzogthum Posen ertheilten Antwortschreiben.* Strasbourg: n.p., n.d.

Heine, Heinrich. "Über Polen." In *Reisebriefe und Reisebilder.* Berlin: Rütten und Loening, 1981.

Hepke, Robert. *Die polnische Erhebung und die deutsche Gegenbewegung in Posen im Frühjahr 1848.* Berlin: Mittler, 1848.

Kromer, Marcin. *Polonia sive de situ, populis, moribus, magistratibus et Republica regni Polonici libri duo.* Cologne: n.p., 1577.

Libelt, Karol. *Stan rzeczy w Wielkiem Księstwie Poznańskiem.* Poznań, 1848.

Łukaszewicz, Jósef. *Krótki opis historyczny kościołów parochialnych, kościółków, kaplic, klasztorów, szkołek parochialnych, szpitali i innych zakładów dobroczynnych w dawnej dyecezji poznańskiej.* Vol. 1. Poznań: Księg. J. K. Żupańskiego, 1858.

———. *Obraz historyczno-statystyczny miasta Poznania w dawniejszych czasach.* 2 vols. Poznań: Czcionkami C. A. Pompjusza, 1838.

Meyer, Christian, ed. *Aus der letzten Zeit der Republik Polen: Gedenkblätter eines Posener Bürgers, 1760–1793.* Munich, 1908.

Motty, Marceli. *Przechadzki po mieście.* 2 vols. Warsaw: Państwowy Instytut Wydawniczy, 1957.

Nachrichten über die Gründung der evangelischen Kreuz-Kirche zu Posen und der damit verbundenen Schul- und Armen-Anstalt. Poznań: n.p., 1836.

Prümers, Rogero, ed. *Das Jahr 1793: Urkunden und Aktenstücke zur Geschichte der Organization Südpreußens.* Poznań: Eigenthum der Gesellschaft, 1895.

Sadebeck [K. J. Hübner]. *Historisch-statistisch, topographische Beschreibung von Südpreußen und Neuostpreußen oder der koeniglich Preußischen Besitznehmungen von Polen in den Jahren 1793 und 1795 entworfen.* Leipzig: n.p., 1798.

Schleiermacher, Friedrich. *Selected Sermons of Schleiermacher.* Translated by Mary F. Wilson. New York: Funk and Wagnalls, 1890.

Streuensee, J. F. *Blikke auf Südpreussen vor und nach dem Jahre 1793.* Poznań: n.p., 1802.

Wuttke, Heinrich. *Polen und Deutsche.* Schkeuditz: W. v. Blomberg, 1846.

―――. *Städtebuch des Landes Posen.* Leipzig: Auf Kosten des Verfassers: In Commission bei Hermann Fries, 1864.

Zawadzki, Wacław, ed. *Polska stanisławowska w oczach cudzoziemców.* 2 vols. Warsaw: Państwowy Instytut Wydawniczy, 1963.

Secondary Literature

Abt, Stefan. "Ludność w drugiej połowie XVIII wieku." In Topolski, *Dzieje Poznania.*

Almog, Shmuel. "People and Land in Modern Jewish Nationalism." In Reinharz and Shapira, *Essential Papers on Zionism.*

Altgeld, Wolfgang. *Katholizismus, Protestantismus, Judentum: Über religiös begründete Gegensätze und nationalreligiöse Ideen in der Geschichte des deutschen Nationalismus.* Mainz: M.-Grünewald-Verlag, 1992.

Alvis, Robert E. "A Clash of Catholic Cultures on the German-Polish Border: The Tale of a Controversial Priest in Poznań, 1839–1842." *Catholic Historical Review* 88, no. 3 (2002): 470–88.

Anderson, Benedict. *Imagined Communities: Reflections on the Origin and Spread of Nationalism.* Rev. ed. London: Verso, 1991.

Angermann, August. *Die evangelischen Kirchen des Posener Landes seit 1772.* Poznań: Kommissionsverlag der Evangel. Vereinsbuchhandlung, 1912.

Barclay, David. *Frederick William IV and the Prussian Monarchy, 1840–1861.* Oxford: Oxford Univ. Press, 1995.

Bär, Max. *Die "Bamberger" bei Posen, zugleich ein Beitrag zur Geschichte der Polenisierungsbestrebungen in der Provinz Posen.* Poznań, 1882.

Baron, Salo W. *Modern Nationalism and Religion.* New York: Meridian, 1947.

Benedikt, Heinrich. *Das Zeitalter der Emanzipationen, 1815–1848.* Vienna: Böhlau, 1977.

Bigler, Robert M. *The Politics of German Protestantism: The Rise of the Protestant Church Elite in Prussia, 1815–1848.* Berkeley: Univ. of California Press, 1972.

Birke, Ernst, and Eugen Lemberg, eds. *Geschichtsbewußtsein in Ostmitteleuropa: Ergebnisse einer wissenschaftlichen Tagung des J. G. Herder-Forschungsrates über die geistige Lage der ostmitteleuropäischen Völker.* Marburg/Lahn: N. G. Elwert, 1961.

Boberach, Heinz. "Die Posener Frage in der deutschen und der preußischen Politik 1848–1849." In Booms and Wojciechowski, *Deutsche und Polen.*

Braudel, Ferdinand. *Capitalism and Material Life, 1400–1800.* Translated by Miriam Kochan. London: Weidenfeld and Nicolson, 1973.

Brederlow, Jörn. *"Lichtfreunde" und "Freie Gemeinden": Religiöser Protest und Freiheitsbewegungen im Vormärz und in der Revolution von 1848/49.* Munich: Oldenbourg, 1976.

Breuilly, John. *Nationalism and the State.* Manchester: Manchester Univ. Press, 1982.

Brock, Peter. *Nationalism and Populism in Partitioned Poland.* London: Orbis, 1973.

Conze, Werner. "Zum Verhältnis des Luthertums zu den mitteleuropäischen Nationalbewegungen im 19. Jahrhundert." In *Luther in der Neuzeit: Wissenschaftliches Symposium des Vereins für Reformationsgeschichte,* edited by Bernd Moeller, 178–93. Gütersloh: G. Mohn, 1983.

Craig, Gordon. *Theodor Fontane: Literature and History in the Bismarck Reich.* Oxford: Oxford Univ. Press, 1999.

Cynar, Stanisław. *Ignacy Raczyński: Ostatni prymas Polski porozbiorowej i jego działalność duszpasterska w okresie Księstwa Warszawskiego.* London: Veritas, 1954.

Davies, Norman. *God's Playground: A History of Poland.* 2 vols. New York: Columbia Univ. Press, 1982.

Deutsch, Karl W. *Nationalism and Social Communication: An Inquiry into the Foundations of Nationality.* 2d ed. Cambridge, Mass.: Massachusetts Institute of Technology Press, 1966.

Dohnalowa, Teresa. "Handel, transport, komunikacja," in Topolski and Trzeciakowski, *Dzieje Poznania.*

———. *Rozwój transportu w Wielkopolsce w latach, 1815–1914.* Poznań: Państwowe Wydawnictwo Naukowe, 1976.

Drozdowski, Marian, and Krystyna Kuklińska. "Gospodarka w dobie odbudowy i wrzostu." In Topolski, *Dzieje Poznania.*

Durkheim, Émile. *The Elementary Forms of Religious Life: A Study in Religious Sociology.* Translated by Joseph Ward Swain. London: G. Allen and Unwin, 1915.

Ergang, Robert. *Herder and the Foundations of German Nationalism.* New York: Columbia Univ. Press, 1931.

Fąka, Marian. *Stan prawny Kościoła katolickiego w Wielkim Księstwia Poznańskim w latach 1815–1850 wświetle prawa pruskiego.* Warsaw: Akademia Teologii Katolickiej, 1975.

Gąsiorowski, Antoni. "Nazwy poznańskich ulic." In Tolpolski and Trzeciakowski, *Dzieje Poznania.*

Gellner, Ernest. *Nations and Nationalism.* Ithaca, N.Y.: Cornell Univ. Press, 1983.

Giddens, Anthony. *The Nation-State and Violence.* Berkeley: Univ. of California Press, 1985.

Gieysztor, Aleksander, et al., eds. *History of Poland.* Translated by Krystyna Cękalska et al. Warsaw: Państwowe Wydawn. Naukowe, 1979.

Graf, Friedrich Wilhelm. *Die Politisierung des religiösen Bewußtseins: Die bürgerlichen Religionspartien im deutschen Vormärz: Das Beispiel des Deutschkatholizismus.* Stuttgart-Bad Cannstatt: Frommann-Holzboog, 1978.

Graf, Gerhard. *Gottesbild und Politik: Eine Studie zur Frömmigkeit in Preußen während der Be-*

freiungskriege, 1813–1815. Vol. 42, *Forschungen zur Kirchen—und Dogmengeschichte.* Göttingen: Vandenhoeck and Ruprecht, 1993.

Greenfeld, Liah. *Nationalism: Five Roads to Modernity.* Cambridge, Mass.: Harvard Univ. Press, 1992.

Grochowski, Lech. "Kryzyz i reorganizacja archidiecezji gnieźnieńskiej w latach 1793–1833." *Nasza Preszłość* 24 (1966): 203–41.

Grześ, Bolesław, Jerzy Kozłowski, and Aleksander Kramski. *Niemcy w Poznańskiem wobec polityki germanizacyjnej, 1815–1920.* Poznań: Instytut Zachodni, 1976.

Hagen, William. *Germans, Poles, and Jews: The Nationality Conflict in the Prussian East, 1772–1914.* Chicago: Univ. of Chicago Press, 1980.

Halbwachs, Maurice. *On Collective Memory.* Edited and translated by Lewis A. Coser. Chicago: Univ. of Chicago Press, 1992.

Hastings, Adrian. *The Construction of Nationhood: Ethnicity, Religion and Nationalism.* Cambridge: Cambridge Univ. Press, 1997.

Hauptmann, Edward. *Z przeszłości polskiego zboru ewangelicko-augsburskiego w Poznaniu.* Poznań: Nakładem Polskiego Towarzystwa Ewangelickiego w Poznaniu, 1924.

Hayes, Carlton J. H. *Nationalism: A Religion.* New York: Macmillan, 1960.

Hechter, Michael. *Internal Colonialism: The Celtic Fringe in British National Development, 1536–1966.* Berkeley: Univ. of California Press, 1975.

Henschel, Adolf. *Evangelische Lebenszeugen des Posener Landes aus alter und neuer Zeit.* Poznań: Friedrich Ebbeckes Verlag, 1891.

Hobsbawm, Eric J. *Nations and Nationalism since 1780: Programme, Myth, Reality.* 2d ed. Cambridge: Cambridge Univ. Press, 1992.

Hohenberg, Paul M., and Lynn H. Lees. *The Making of Urban Europe, 1000–1994.* Cambridge, Mass.: Harvard Univ. Press, 1995.

Howard, Thomas A. *Religion and the Rise of Historicism: W. M. L. de Wette, Jacob Burckhardt, and the Theological Origins of Nineteenth-Century Historical Consciousness.* Cambridge: Cambridge Univ. Press, 2000.

Hroch, Miroslav. *Social Preconditions of National Revival in Europe: A Comparative Analysis of the Social Composition of Patriotic Groups among the Smaller European Nations.* Translated by Ben Fowkes. Cambridge: Cambridge Univ. Press, 1985.

Iggers, George. *The German Conception of History: The National Tradition of Historical Thought from Herder to the Present.* Rev. ed. Middletown, Conn.: Wesleyan Univ. Press, 1983.

Jacobs, Manfred. "Die Entwicklung des deutschen Nationalgedankens von der Reformation bis zum deutschen Idealismus." In *Volk Nation Vaterland: Der deutsche Protestantismus und der Nationalismus,* edited by Horst Zilleßen. Gütersloh: Gütersloher Verlagshaus G. Mohn, 1970.

Jaffe, Moritz. *Die Stadt Posen unter preußischer Herrschaft: Ein Beitrag zur Geschichte des deutschen Ostens.* Vol. 119, *Schriften des Vereins für Socialpolitik.* Leipzig: Duncker und Humblot, 1909.

Jakóbczyk, Witold. *Karol Marcinkowski, 1800–1846.* Warsaw: Państwowe Wydawnictwo Naukowe, 1981.

Jedlicki, Jerzy. *A Suburb of Europe: Nineteenth-Century Polish Approaches to Western Civilization.* Budapest: Central European Univ. Press, 1999.

Juergensmeyer, Mark. *The New Cold War? Religious Nationalism Confronts the Secular State.* Berkeley: Univ. of California Press, 1993.

Just, Friedrich. *Kreuzkirche: Bilder aus Geschichte und Leben der evangelischen Kirche des Posener Landes.* Berlin: Ernst Röttger's Verlagsbuchhandlung, 1922.

Kalinka, Walerian. *Jenerał Dezydery Chłapowski.* Poznań: J. Leitgeber, 1881.

Katz, Jacob. "The Forerunners of Zionism." In Reinharz and Shapira, *Essential Papers on Zionism,* 33–45.

Kędelski, Mieczysław. "Stosunki ludnościowe w latach 1815–1918." In Topolski and Trzeciakowski, *Dzieje Poznania.*

Kemlein, Sophia. *Die Posener Juden, 1815–1848: Entwicklungsprozesse einer polnischen Judenheit unter preußischer Herrschaft.* Hamburg: Dölling und Galitz, 1997.

Kohte, Wolfgang. *Deutsche Bewegung und preussische Politik im Posener Lande, 1848–1849.* Special edition of *Deutsche Wissenschaftliche Zeitschrift für Polen* 21 (1931).

Kriegseisen, Wojciech. *Ewangelicy polscy i litewscy w epoce saskiej.* Warsaw: Semper, 1996.

Kuklińska, Krystyna. "Gospodarka." In Topolski, *Dzieje Poznania.*

Kumor, Bolesław, and Zdzisław Obertyński, eds. *Historia Kościoła w Polsce.* Vol. 2, pt. 1 (1764–1918). Poznań: Pallottinum, 1979.

Langer, Albrecht, ed. *Katholizismus, nationaler Gedanke und Europa seit 1800.* Paderborn: Schöningh, 1985.

Laubert, Manfred. "Beiträge zur Geschichte des deutsch-katholischen Kirchensystems der Stadt Posen und ihrer Kammereidörfer." *Zeitschrift der Historischen Gesellschaft für die Provinz Posen* 20 (1905): 1–26.

————. "Eine gescheiterte Denkmalerrichtung in Posen." *Historische Monatsblätter für die Provinz Posen* 6, no. 12 (1905): 211–16.

————. "Ein Volksauflauf in Posen, 1845." *Historische Monatsblätter für die Provinz Posen* 9, no. 12 (1908): 195–97.

Lefebvre, Henri. *The Production of Space.* Cambridge, Mass.: Blackwell, 1991.

Levinger, Matthew. *Enlightened Nationalism: The Transformation of Prussian Political Culture, 1806–1848.* Oxford: Oxford Univ. Press, 2000.

Llobera, Josep. *The God of Modernity: The Development of Nationalism in Western Europe.* Oxford: Berg, 1994.

Łuczak, Czesław. *Przemysł spożywczy miasta Poznania w XVIII wieku.* Poznań: Nakł. Poznańskiego Tow. Przyjaciół Nauk., 1953.

Lukowski, Jerzy. *Liberty's Folly: The Polish-Lithuanian Commonwealth in the Eighteenth Century.* London: Routledge, 1991.

Maisel, Witold. "Zniszczenia wojenne. Rozwój przestrzenny." In Topolski, *Dzieje Poznania.*

Makowski, Krzysztof. *Rodzina poznańska w I polowie XIX wieku.* Poznań: Uniwersytet im. Adama Mickiewicza w Poznaniu, 1992.

Marx, Anthony. *Faith in Nation: Exclusionary Origins of Nationalism.* Oxford: Oxford Univ. Press, 2003.

Matusik, Przemysław. *Religia i naród. Życia i myśl Jana Koźmiana, 1814–1877.* Poznań: Wydawn. Poznańskie, 1998.

Meyer, Christian. *Die Deutschen der Provinz Posen gegenüber dem polnischen Aufstand im Jahre 1848.* Munich, 1904.

———. "Die deutsche katholische Gemeinde zu Posen." *Zeitschrift für Geschichte und Landeskunde der Provinz Posen* 3 (1884): 164–79.

Molik, Witold. "Szkolnictwo." In Topolski and Trzeciakowski, *Dzieje Poznania.*

Nairn, Tom. *The Break-Up of Britain: Crisis and Neo-nationalism.* London: NLB, 1977.

Nawrocki, Stanisław. "Die revolutionären Ereignisse im Großherzogtum Posen und Westpreußen in den Jahren 1848–1849." In Booms and Wojciechowski, *Deutsche und Polen.*

Nipperdey, Thomas. *Germany from Napoleon to Bismarck, 1800–1866.* Translated by Daniel Nolan. Princeton, N.J.: Princeton Univ. Press, 1996.

Noryśkiewicz, Jan Kanty. "Sekularyzacja klasztorów w Wielkopolsce przez rząd pruski." *Przegląd Teologiczny* 3 (1925): 249–82.

Nowacki, Jósef. *Archidiecezja poznańska w jej granicach i jej ustroj.* 2 vols. Poznań: Księg. Św. Wojciecha, 1964.

Nowak, Kurt. *Geschichte des Christentums in Deutschland: Religion, Politik und Gesellschaft vom Ende der Aufklärung bis zur Mitte des 20. Jahrhunderts.* Munich: C. H. Beck, 1995.

Ostrowska-Kębłowska, Zofia. *Architektura i budownictwo w Poznaniu w latach 1780–1880.* Warsaw: Państwowe Wydawnictwo Naukowe, 1982.

———. *Dzieje Kaplicy Królów Polskich czyli Złotej w katedrze poznańskiej.* Poznań: Wydawn. Poznańskiego Tow. Przyjaciół Nauk., 1997.

Perles, Josef. *Geschichte der Juden in Posen.* Breslau: Verlag der Schletter'schen Buchhandlung, 1865.

Pinson, Koppel. *Pietism as a Factor in the Rise of German Nationalism.* New York: Octagon, 1968.

Połczyńska, Edyta. *"Im polnischen Wind": Beiträge zum deutschen Zeitungswesen, Theaterleben und zur deutschen Literatur im Grossherzogtum Posen, 1815–1918.* Poznań: Wydawn. Naukowe UAM, 1988.

———. "Życie kulturalne Niemców w Poznaniu w XIX i na pozątku XX wieku." In Topolski and Trzeciakowski, *Dzieje Poznania.*

Porter, Brian. *When Nationalism Began to Hate: Imagining Modern Politics in Nineteenth-Century Poland.* Oxford: Oxford Univ. Press, 2000.

Ravens, Jürgen-Peter. *Staat und katholische Kirche in Preußens polnischen Teilungsgebieten, 1772–1807.* Wiesbaden: A. Harrassowitz, 1963.

Reinharz, Jehuda, and Anita Shapira, eds. *Essential Papers on Zionism.* New York: New York Univ. Press, 1996.

Rhode, Arthur. *Geschichte der evangelischen Kirche im Posener Lande.* Vol. 4, *Marburger Ost-forschungen.* Würzburg: Holzner, 1956.

Salmonowicz, Stanisław. *Polacy i Niemcy wobec siebie: Postawy opinie stereotypy (1697–1815): Próba zarysu.* Olsztyn: Ośrodek Badań Naukowych im. W. Kętrzyńskiego, 1993.

Schilling, Heinz. *Enzyklopädie deutscher Geschichte.* Vol. 24, *Die Stadt in der frühen Neuzeit.* Munich: Oldenbourg, 1993.

Schivelbusch, Wolfgang. *The Railway Journey: The Industrialization of Time and Space in the Nineteenth Century.* Berkeley: Univ. of California Press, 1986.

Schoeps, Hans-Joachim. *Preußen: Geschichte eines Staates: Bilder und Zeugnisse.* Berlin: Propylaen, 1995.

Selchow, Bogislaw Freiherr von. *Der Kampf um das Posener Erzbistum, 1865: Graf Ledo-chowski und Öberpräsident von Horn: Ein Vorspiel zum Kulturkampf.* Marburg/Lahn: N. G. Elwert (G. Braun), 1923.

Siwicka, Dorota. *Romantyzm, 1822–1863.* Warsaw: Wydawn. Nauk. PWN, 1995.

Smith, Anthony D. *The Ethnic Origins of Nations.* Oxford: Blackwell, 1986.

———. *Nationalism and Modernism: A Critical Survey of Recent Theories of Nations and Nationalism.* London: Routledge, 1998.

———. *Nationalism: A Trend Report and Bibliography.* The Hague: Mouton, 1975.

Smith, John E. *Quasi-religions: Humanism, Marxism, and Nationalism.* New York: St. Martin's Press, 1994.

Sommer, Hugo. "Die lutherische Kirche in der Stadt Posen seit 1768." *Deutsche Wissenschaftliche Zeitschrift für Polen* 29 (1935): 353–69.

———. "Die Posener Unitätsgemeinde seit der Zeit der Religionsfreiheit in Polen." *Deutsche Wissenschaftliche Zeitschrift für Polen* 30 (1936): 73–86.

Szulz, Witold. "Procesy industrializacji Poznania. Kredyt. Ubezpieczenia. Organizacje gospodarcze." In Topolski and Trzeciakowski, *Dzieje Poznania.*

Tazbir, Janusz. *Historia Kościoła katolickiego w Polsce, 1460–1795.* Warsaw: Wiedza Powszechna, 1966.

———. *Kultura szlachecka w Polsce.* Warsaw: Wiedza Powszechna, 1978.

Topolski, Jerzy, ed. *Dzieje Poznania.* Vol. 1, pt. 1—2 (to 1793). Poznań: Państwowe Wydawnictwo Naukowe, 1988.

Topolski, Jerzy, and Lech Trzeciakowski, eds. *Dzieje Poznania.* Vol. 2, pt. 1 (1793–1918). Poznań: Państwowe Wydawnictwo Naukowe, 1994.

Truchim, Stefan. *Historia szkolnictwa i oswiaty w Wielkim Księstwie Poznańskim, 1815–1915.* 2 vols. Łódz: Zakład Narodowy im. Ossolińskich, 1967.

Trzeciakowski, Lech. "Aktywność polityczna Poznaniaków." In Topolski and Trzeciakowski, *Dzieje Poznania.*

Trzeciakowski, Lech, and Maria Trzeciakowski. *W dziewiętnastowiecznym Poznaniu: Życie codzienne miasta, 1815–1914.* Poznań: Wydawn. Poznańskie, 1982.

Walicki, Andrzej. *Philosophy and Romantic Nationalism: The Case of Poland.* Notre Dame, Ind.: Univ. of Notre Dame Press, 1994.

Walser-Smith, Helmut. *German Nationalism and Religious Conflict.* Princeton, N.J.: Princeton Univ. Press, 1995.

Wangemann, Hermann. *Sieben Bücher preußischer Kirchengeschichte. Eine aktenmäßige Darstellung des Kampfes um die evangelisch-lutherische Kirche im XIX. Jahrhundert.* 3 vols. Berlin: W. Schultze, 1859–1860.

Warschauer, Adolf. "Ein hundert Jahre altes humoristisches Gedicht über Posen." *Historische Monatsblätter für die Provinz Posen* 5, no. 4 (1904): 24–29.

Wawrzykowska-Wierciochowa, Dioniza. *Promienna: Opowieść biograficzna o Klaudynie z Działyńskich Potockiej (1801–1836).* Poznań: Wydawn. Poznańskie, 1976.

Wąsicki, Jan. *Powstanie kościuszkowskie w Wielkopolsce.* Poznań: Wydawn. Poznańskie, 1957.

———. "Poznań jako miasto tzw. Prus Południowych (1793–1806)." In Topolski and Trzeciakowski, *Dzieje Poznania.*

Wendland, Walter. *Die Religiosität und die kirchen-politischen Grundsätze Friedrich Wilhelms III und ihre Bedeutung für die Geschichte der kirchlichen Restauration.* Giessen: A. Töpelmann, 1909.

Werner, Albert. *Geschichte der evangelischen Parochieen in der Provinz Posen.* Poznań, 1898.

White, George W. *Nationalism and Territory: Constructing Group Identity in Southeastern Europe.* Lanham, Md.: Rowman and Littlefield, 2000.

White, Hayden. *Metahistory: The Historical Imagination in Nineteenth-Century Europe.* Baltimore: Johns Hopkins Univ. Press, 1987.

Wojtkowski, Andrzej. *Edward Raczyński i jego dzieło.* Poznań: Nakl. Bibljoteki Raczyńskich, 1929.

Zieliński, Zygmunt. *Kościół katolicki w Wielkim Księstwie Poznańskim w latach 1848–1865.* Lublin: Tow. Naukowe Katolickiego Uniwersytetu Lubelskiego, 1973.

Zilleßen, Horst, ed. *Volk Nation Vaterland: Der deutsche Protestantismus und der Nationalismus.* Gütersloh: Gütersloher Verlagshaus G. Mohn, 1970.

Żywczyński, Mieczysław. "Der Posener Kirchenstreit in den Jahren 1837–40 und die 'Kölner Wirren': Ein Beitrag zu ihrer Geschichte und zur Geschichte der Politik Metternichs," *Acta Poloniae* (1961), 2:17–41.

Index

WITHDRAWN